GLOBAL CORPORATE ALLIANCES AND THE COMPETITIVE EDGE

GLOBAL CORPORATE ALLIANCES AND THE COMPETITIVE EDGE

Strategies and Tactics for Management

MARTIN K. STARR

Q

QUORUM BOOKS
New York • Westport, Connecticut • London

Library of Congress Cataloging-in-Publication Data

Starr, Martin Kenneth
    Global corporate alliances and the competitive edge : strategies
and tactics for management / Martin K. Starr.
       p. cm.
    Includes bibliographical references and index.
    ISBN 0–89930–586–5 (alk. paper)
    1. Technological innovations—Management.   2. Organizational
change—Management.   3. Joint ventures—Management.
    4. Corporations, Foreign—United States—Management.
    5. Competition, International.   I. Title
    HD45.S753   1991
    658'.049—dc20   91–8725

British Library Cataloguing in Publication Data is available.

Library of Congress Catalog Card Number: 91–8725
ISBN: 0–89930–586–5

First published in 1991

Quorum Books, 88 Post Road West, Westport, CT 06881
An imprint of Greenwood Publishing Group, Inc.

Printed in the United States of America

The paper used in this book complies with the
Permanent Paper Standard issued by the National
Information Standards Organization (Z39.48–1984).

10 9 8 7 6 5 4 3 2 1

Copyright Acknowledgment

The author and publisher gratefully acknowledge permission to use the following copyrighted
materials:

Excerpts from David Kennedy, "Flexible Manufacturing, Inflexible Manufacturing," July 1985,
and Jay W. Forrester, "Changing Economic Patterns," August-September 1978, both reprinted
with permission from *Technology Review*, copyright 1985 and 1978.

Contents

Figures and Tables

FIGURES

TABLES

Preface

Many of the ideas found in this book originated with research studies conducted over a ten-year period. They came from surveys of foreign-affiliated firms operating in the United States. Comparisons were made with U.S. firms having no foreign affiliations, and with foreign firms operating in their own countries. There were differences in practices; therefore, it was logical to sort out and categorize those differences. It was also desirable to ascertain which practices helped companies to become globally successful in a changing world.

The picture could not be drawn in proper perspective without examining the causes responsible for the changing situation. What could explain the difficulties experienced by established companies that formerly commanded the field? What made it possible for firms from abroad to capture growing market shares in what had previously been the secure territory of large U.S. companies? What happened to the comfortably stable markets of the 1950s and 1960s?

Once the fundamental causes of change had been identified, it was relatively straightforward to identify the factors that accounted for the success of firms in the global arenas. None of the factors were mysterious nor were they counterintuitive. Some might say that the new factors were extensions of present practices. Others might disagree, because certain well-accepted practices are not followed by the newly successful contenders for global markets.

Following a rational set of premises, it is possible to set down the causes of economic turmoil and the effects of such turmoil on the basics of manufacturing and management systems. With this foundation, it is then feasible to suggest some effective means of breaking out of the system of constraints that debilitates the previously invulnerable established Fortune 1000 companies. And that, in a nutshell, is the basis of this book.

My intent is to confront the reader with a combination of challenging ideas. How do companies survive the long-wave economic forces unleashed by major technological changes? Which concepts of organizational design and affiliation enable firms to achieve global success? Many management principles from the 1950s don't work because technological change has rendered them archaic. The global corporation is a relatively new invention. Different forms of global corporate alliances are being used effectively for doing business in new settings. I have drawn on various sources to bring together in a comprehensive framework what is known about such issues, and I wish to thank the many individuals whose work contributed toward this end.

The basics of the framework are:

1. Technological change is driven by forces that are too great to be controlled by the normal powers exercised by people or companies in pursuit of their daily bread. The short (one to two years) and medium-length (three to five years) rhythms of economic cycles are not driven by the technological cycle of invention, capitalization, and replacement of technology.

Many economists agree (no matter what they call the phenomena) that the longer cycles are reflections of technological change. It is not clear whether government agencies, such as the Japanese Ministry of International Trade and Industry (known as MITI), have (or could have) altered the natural rhythm of economic change. MITI certainly has supported the use of new technology by Japanese firms involved with international markets. The MITI initiative has been so successful that many other countries have considered using a similar industrial policy to their own advantage.

However, an industrial policy may exist even if it is not explicit. Many say that the United States has an industrial policy that is inconsistent because it is unformulated. This school of thought holds that every country has an industrial policy, including those countries that say they have none. That is, when a nation does not have an explicit industrial policy, it is still perceived by the global community as having a policy, albeit haphazard and created by the effects of uncoordinated pressure groups. Global forces unleash new effects. This realization carries a message for those nations that adhere to "free-market" conditions without recognition of the larger system within which that free market operates.

2. Technological change feeds on itself. New product and process developments outmode the older ones. As the pace of change increases, the usual levels of economic turbulence are exceeded. When the rate of change of the long wave nears its peak, many unusual things begin to happen. We call this condition *special economic turmoil*. Surfers are said to wait for the ninth wave, which is credited with being the largest and most perfectly shaped wave. Risk-taking managers and entrepreneurs, like these surfers, are waiting for their "windows" to exploit opportunities generated by conditions of extreme turmoil. Correct timing for start-ups is essential.

3. Mature organizations have difficulty adapting to major changes in technology that outmode their production systems and their established product lines. Bureaucracy hampers change and protects the status quo. Therefore, methods for relaxing the bureaucratic grip are being utilized by firms that are striving to become global competitors.

Corporate alliances have become increasingly popular as a means of maneuvering outside the bounds of bureaucratic constraints as well as the limitations imposed by forces for protectionism. Organizational inventions will determine the forms that these alliances might take in the future. For example, a Japanese scholar, Ken'ichi Imae, has suggested that keiretsu (examined in Chapter 6) could be opened to foreign participants as the keiretsu system evolves into global corporate networks. While this may be hard to believe, all conventional wisdoms will be sorely tested in the future. New methods are being employed increasingly by a great number of companies. Two approaches, in particular, are being used with some signs of success.

The first approach changes production and engineering methods with the expectation that they will engender organizational changes. Quality achievement is used as a catalyst. Fast response and proper timing are the primary missions. They are expected to maximize value-added for the firm, and to create the conditions for successful innovations.

The second approach reconstructs the organization to free it of bureaucratic constraints. This is done with the belief that the new entity can move quickly to update the equipment and change the management and engineering methods. Joint ventures are a favored means. The small organizational size of these business partnerships allows a multifunctional systems approach to planning and decision-making. They foster organizational innovation.

If this book is successful, it will be read by those who are in a position to help U.S. firms in the quest of becoming global. It will shed real light on what is happening and what is responsible for the conditions of extreme economic turmoil in which business finds itself during the 1990s. The text lays out the causes of turmoil and the effects of those causes on the business environment of the 1990s. Then come the steps (unique to each company) that can be taken to gain advantage from the situation. These two approaches provide the major initiatives for companies that are intent upon becoming global. The starting point is to recognize that what is occurring is a worldwide phenomenon, not limited to a particular industry or company. Then it is possible to put that perspective to work.

Comprehending that external economic forces driven by technological change are bringing about major economic turmoil provides great opportunities for those who perceive the situation correctly. The business climate is irreversibly altered by these waves of technological change. The principal advantage goes to those who recognize that the production component is crucially involved with the start-up of new products and processes. There are tactical production concepts and strategic concepts that must be understood for the production function to prosper. Everything is accelerated by computers, telecommunications, and fast delivery systems. Research and development (R&D), marketing, production, and finance decisions cannot wait for phases or stages. The network of participants is formidable as it works together with a systems sense of what each is doing to support the other.

Because of total global changes, strategic alliances and joint ventures make it feasible for companies to survive and prosper during the turbulence of technological wearout and replacement. To take advantage of these opportunities that come once every 50 or 60 years, it is essential to fully understand the long-term patterns of technological change.

I express my appreciation for the years of survey work and research that were done at the Columbia Business School. Such work continues there. The learning does not stop because the worldwide competitive situation evolves at what seems like an ever-faster rate. I also want to thank Nancy Bloom, Patrice Hall, and especially Zhuang Yang for their ideas and research work that led to the appendixes of this book. This research also influenced many of the ideas that I have expressed in this book. The fine graphics were contributed by Polly Starr. I thank her for that help, but I thank her far more for her ingenious insights about the underlying causal systems that make things work the way they do, while being almost entirely hidden from view.

PART I _____

CAUSES

Part I consists of Chapters 1 and 2, which examine the causes of "extreme" economic uncertainty that characterizes the present economic climate on a global scale. By "extreme" we mean out of the ordinary, or an extraordinary level of economic turmoil. In Chapter 2, this situation is referred to as "special economic turmoil." By "special" we mean to convey the fact that individuals, groups, companies, industries, and governments are not accustomed to experiencing such uncertainty and volatility. In a statistical sense, these conditions are likely to reflect an unstable economic system.

The existence of special economic circumstances is an important fact because it provides perspective for interpreting the causes of managerial failures, as well as successes. The knowledge that special external circumstances exist helps to deal with the question: Who is to blame for decreasing profits, contracting market shares, and inability to compete? That knowledge also helps managers to clarify what must now be done to improve company performance.

Chapter 1 is intended to provide a perspective for seeing the book as a whole. Chapter 2 deals at some length with the long-wave concept of Nikolai Kondratieff, whose theory was based on the consequences of major technological change.

CHAPTER 1 _____

Perspectives on Winning the Business Olympiad

"Vision is the art of seeing things invisible."

Jonathan Swift
Thoughts on Various Subjects (1711)

Some people never start to read a new book at the beginning. Others cannot resist turning to the end shortly after beginning. Still others habitually shuffle forward and backward as they steer a course through their book. What is needed for such people is a bird's-eye view. For them, and for those who like a summary, this chapter on perspectives presents an overview that can be used as a guiding system.

Although this overview summarizes the course of the book, it does so, as much as possible, without duplication. It is designed to look briefly, and in a different way, at the material it synopsizes; but the basic theme prevails. Business is increasingly taking place on a global scale. There will be reversals of one sort or another from time to time. International trade talks will falter, then spurt ahead. In the longer course of events, business will become yet another activity in the worldwide olympics.

Countries will be judged by the quality of their participation. The winners will be those whose continual adaptations to new technologies permeate the fabric of their organizations. Rather than let organizations dictate strategic responses, these winning organizations will change and adapt according to the circumstances of global markets and planetary levels of technology. Winners will always be working at being faster and better in the stimulus-response mode. Competitiveness will be achieved by those organizations that blend the conscious efforts of individuals to adapt their organizations, with the inertial characteristics of group dynamics, evolving cultural factors, and technological change.

THE PART STRUCTURE OF THE BOOK

Part I sets the stage for understanding the causes of major changes in the global economic environment. These changes, which have been accelerating for more than a decade, are redefining the boundaries of nations and the political alignments between them. New kinds of institutions are being forged that substantially alter the character of global competitiveness. Transformations of such great magnitude have created an environment of economic and political turmoil. Extraordinary events that once seemed improbable or impossible, such as the swing to capitalism in Eastern Europe, the accomplishments and tribulations of the European Economic Community, the dissolution of the Soviet super-power, and the United Nations response to national aggression in the Middle East, have become thoroughly accepted as commonplace shortly after they occur.

Destabilization of long-existing arrangements and agreements increases regional and global uncertainty. That is the background in the 1990s for redefining economic as well as political competitiveness. Companies on every continent, attempting to do business as usual, are caught up in these new cross-currents and vortices of what had formerly been placid waters. Organizations, using methods and arrangements that had worked so well for many years, begin to lose their way. As their managers struggle to regain control, they look for information about what is happening. Without understanding causes and effects, directions taken tend to be random. Success in achieving objectives becomes elusive.

Part II discusses the effects of special economic turmoil on the competitiveness of existing technologies, and on the adaptability of traditional management systems. Especially important, in this regard, are the effects of rapid and intense technological change on the competitive status of manufacturing processes (Chapter 3) and on the methods and strategies for the management of organizations (Chapter 4).

Part III examines adaptation strategies that require reorganizing the company, to some degree. The ability to change—to do business in a new way—is essential if the old way is not succeeding. However, before managers can employ organizational redesign to improve a system, they must understand what is happening to that system and what is going wrong. Before they will decide to change the system, the force of dissatisfaction must overcome the costs (including nonmonetary costs) of giving up the status quo.[1]

Part III continues by delineating the kinds of changes, on a worldwide basis, that improve adaptation to the effects of special economic turmoil. There are a variety of competing and cooperative strategies fashioned to fit unique situations. Chapter 5 explores the different competitive eras and the changing character of business competition, over time. Chapter 5 goes on to explore the means of becoming more competitive, including the use of continuous improvement of quality, speeding new products to market, downsizing, increasing value-added, and expanding vision by systemwide management. Intrapreneuring and the use of cooperative alliances between unions and management are discussed. Then, Chapter 6 examines the employment of a number of different cooperative organizational arrangements (such as tactical and strategic alliances, mergers and acquisitions, and joint ventures) to take advantage of organizational synergies and symbiosis.

Part IV introduces Chapter 7, which focuses on time-based strategies. Time and change, taken together, are the Achilles heel of bureaucracies. Bringing to light the temporal quality of strategy-making can help to correct the problems associated with bureaucracies. Chapter 7 analyzes the advantages gained by fast response organizations. It does this, first for the tactical operations of firms that use the just-in-time (JIT) method. Then it does this for the use of new methods of project management that speed up the company's ability to respond to changing market conditions, and to create them as well. Chapter 7 concludes with a discussion concerning management's sense of timing and its ability to orchestrate the multiple functions of the business. This total system orchestration includes being in step with the marketplace, and with the appropriate stages of the economic cycle.

Two appendixes conclude the book. Appendix A summarizes the characteristics of Japanese firms operating in the United States. Five companies, each in different industries, with quite diverse alliance arrangements, responded to a written survey. Then they were visited for on-site completion of this study. The appendix presents a very concise synopsis of the full report.

Appendix B provides a synopsis and rewrite of a recently completed survey of foreign-affiliated firms in America. About two-thirds of these firms are subsidiaries or branches of at least one foreign organization. The other one-third are U.S. firms, many of which have joint ventures, licensing agreements, and other forms of strategic alliances. The survey was designed to analyze how these alliance-oriented firms were responding to increased competition.

Twenty years ago, much of this book would have seemed like science fiction. Many of the relevant factors we will be discussing made their first appearance as conjectures about ten years ago. In the early 1990s, what is new is the way the warp and the woof of the fabric (specifically, all of the parts of this book) come together. With this perspective in mind, let us consider the elements and issues of Part I—Causes.

CAUSES OF SPECIAL ECONOMIC TURMOIL

The logic is simple: Because old technology has been wearing out and new technology is coming in, a major shift in economic conditions is occurring. Consequently, the decade of the 1990s will be witnessing the culmination of 20 years of global economic instability. As a result, many unexpected economic, political, and military situations have arisen and will continue to arise. For example, a partial list would include significant realization of the European Economic Community's 1992 goal, the end of the Cold War between the USSR and the United States, unification of East and West Germany, the Middle East imbroglio, which began in August 1990. Such unpredictable changes, happening so fast, provide great opportunity for those who wish to compete rather than coast along. Alternatively, those managements that do not want to rock the boat are unlikely to become new winners in the business olympiad.

The other side of the coin is that present-day firms are under great pressure to adapt to the evolving competitive situations. Although seasoned players, they have to redress the problems of growing old and slowing down in a speeded-up, dynamic world. It is widely acknowledged that understanding the existing management system and knowing how to change it is the most important challenge of the next decade.

Meanwhile, Chapter 2 examines the Kondratieff long-wave explanation of the cause of special economic turmoil. Nikolai Kondratieff was a Russian economist who was exiled to Siberia for his ideas about the economies of capitalist countries. He wrote that the performance of the capitalist economies cycled regularly, with a long wave occurring every 50 or 60 years. Why would anyone get sent to Siberia for that kind of thinking? The reason is that the communists contended that capitalism was untenable and doomed to progressive deterioration. Therefore, it could not cycle between good times and bad times, or even between changing times. Even while exiled in Siberia, his ideas were published in various languages and increasingly discussed by economists.

Kondratieff's thesis was based on his scholarly studies, which spanned several hundred years.[2] He provided a cyclical explanation for economic volatility that has been considered, by some, to be a "reasonable" interpretation of what is causing significant competitive instability.[3] While some economists are not sympathetic to Kondratieff's hypothesis concerning the long economic cycle (or long wave), there are few who reject the possibility of some form of long-wave phenomenon. In fact, there are other long-cycle theorists to choose among.[4] Even if the long cycle is not appealing as a recurring phenomenon, the notions of technological wearout and technological replacement are not to be dismissed.

Whichever theory you prefer, the underlying explanation is that major bundles of interdependent technologies (such as river and canal transportation, jet propulsion aircraft systems, petroleum-based energy systems, and telecommunication technologies) develop together. These interrelated bundles go through a development cycle of roughly 50–60 years. The cycle starts with the introduction of products that embody relatively new and unexplored scientific and engineering principles. Next comes a competitive race with increasing numbers of entries trying to capitalize on the emerging opportunities. Then, as profitabilities drop, the shake-out phase commences.

A small set of winners becomes associated in the mind of the customers with the (now) widely accepted form of the technology and its side shoots. Finally, when most of the ageing technology applications have been exhausted by competitive actions, there is great pressure for replacement by new technologies that still have to be converted from theory to practice. A new cycle begins. The old technologies have worn out, but there are always new ones to replace them.

Alternatively, this 50- to 60-year cycle can be said to start with overexpansion of capital investment in the old technologies. The lack of profitability fuels investments in new technologies. Another long-term cycle ensues. Research that delineates this long wave is typically unscientific, as are most contentions in the "dismal science" of economics.

Nevertheless, intelligent observation and logic provide a reasonably comfortable basis for tentatively accepting the theory. Since conjecture about the existence of a long wave is essentially speculative, the ultimate criterion must be empirical. In other words, the issue needs to be examined in terms of actual observations of the effects of technological wearout and replacement on an economic system.

THE EFFECTS OF SPECIAL ECONOMIC TURMOIL

Given the point of view that technological wearout creates extreme economic volatility, we want to examine the effect of major technological change on the economic well-being of industrialized countries. Specifically, which technologies may be said to have worn out, and which new technologies might be candidates to replace the ageing technologies. With this perspective in mind, let us consider the elements and issues of Part II—Effects. Chapters 3 and 4 expand on cause and effect by concentrating on two major effects: those on manufacturing processes, and those on management systems.

Evidence of Technological Wearout

The evidence begins with the many companies that in earlier times had successful products with commanding shares of their markets. The managers of these companies watched with a surprising degree of helplessness as their market shares eroded. Spending money on advertising, or a larger sales force, or on research, and so forth, didn't help. To illustrate, Detroit's executives spent billions of dollars on R&D, product changes, brand new plants with robots and automatic guidance vehicles. But after years of such remedial behaviors, the "big three" U.S. automakers continue to lose market share. Other industries also have had minimal success defending their markets against upstart companies from faraway places.

Many U.S. firms moved their production facilities offshore (as close as across the border in Mexico, and as far away as Thailand or Singapore). The ostensible reason for moving away from the United States was cheaper labor, but the ability to use new technology in a compatible environment should not be overlooked. Starting up a new facility permits the entire production process to be configured in completely new ways. Updating an existing facility creates serious problems of meshing the new with the old. It is very difficult to design replacement equipment that delivers new-tech potentials when surrounded by old-tech facilities and procedures.

The philosophies do not jibe. Unions and managers alike tend to view new technology as a way to decrease dependency on labor. While they see this situation in the same way, they have diametrically opposed attitudes about it. Workers trained to use the new tech operate on a different wavelength than the rest of the workers whose skills reflect a different era. The lack of technological homogeneity is a disruption that must be offset for a smooth-flowing plant. Part of the reason for this is that new technology generally is able to deliver tighter tolerances than older technology and thereby has the potential for higher quality products. The blue-collar content of new tech is lower; the white-collar (knowledge-based) content is higher. Similar comments apply to change-over procedures. They are software-driven, which means that wrenches and muscles are side-lined in favor of programming skills. In an unexpected way, C. P. Snow's conflict of two cultures[5] appears on the plant floor.

Even more pervasive than the offshore moves of companies is the use of offshore suppliers. Again, labor costs are often cited as a major reason. Another factor that has been given is that the quality and costs of the foreign supplier are not available at home. The overlooked common denominator is the homogeneity of new technology that is used by these suppliers, which provides them with an overwhelming competitive advantage as compared to companies in the United States that have been in the business for years, and that can, at best, point to a few new-tech machines that are not well-integrated with the rest of the company's production processes.

The average age of equipment of the companies losing market share is considerably greater than that of the companies that are gaining the lost shares. But the age of equipment is not a sure indicator of the degree of technological updating that is embodied in the new equipment. Primarily, this is because the new equipment can be dedicated to old management objectives related to high volumes of low variety outputs.

In the section entitled "Changes in Manufacturing Technology," which appears later, there is a description of an aerospace company that replaces old equipment with new equipment that exactly replicates the old equipment. The shareholders of that company are still wondering why, with all the capital expenditures that their company made, it consistently lost contracts and failed to recapture shares of markets that the company formerly dominated. Accordingly, it is necessary to assess the age of technology that is being used rather than the age of equipment. With this in mind, the prognosis for the future of many American companies remains one of hard times.

The life cycle age of the product line of cars is mature. For all the differences that consumers perceive, the basic design of automobiles has not changed significantly since the automatic starter replaced the hand crank in the 1930s. So the question arises: Are these long-cycle effects related only to mature products, and not applicable to products that only recently emerged from their start-up stage?

The answer to this question negates the concept of the age of the product as the key. We need only consider the still-developing silicon chip industry. Since the 1970s, memory size continues to quadruple about every four or five years. Chip making is not a mature industry, yet Silicon Valley firms are having a hard time. A similar story can be told about the television and related electronics industry. These businesses were developed and launched in the United States, and in a matter of 30 years these pioneering firms went from extensive domestic production facilities to the point where name-plating was their only value-added claim. It is evident that wherever the technological factors are important, there has been serious erosion of production facilities, related R&D, and profit margins.

Buying the product abroad is not limited to mature industries. The electronics business is almost completely under the control of the Pacific Basin countries. This would now be a middle-aged American industry had it lasted here. Even while that business was evaporating, U.S. companies showed next to no aggressive response and little willingness to invest in regaining the TV and stereo markets. Apparently, the economic turmoil is not related to the product being a new development. Rather, it seems to be related to the technological perturbation of the production processes that are used to make the products. This holds whether they are new ones or old ones, high-tech ones or low-tech ones.

Overall, this is a period in which "established firms" are consistently and continually losing out to "start-up firms." The U.S. industrial system, which was seemingly unassailable, is associated with playing catch-up across a variety of product classes. To view the extent of change that this signifies, recall that in the 1950s and 1960s, the United States gained world acclaim for its Marshall Plan, designed to restore the economies of Western Europe. In France, Jean-Jacques Servan-Schreiber warned that American managerial dominance was a serious threat, and all of Europe listened.[6] He coined the term "brain-drain" to describe the way in which the most able Europeans were being hired by American industry.

The Phoenix Phenomenon

While the fame of U.S. management practices reached a zenith, the countries where industry had been destroyed by bombing searched for means to rebuild. They could have just replaced what had existed before, but with U.S. managerial help they sought better solutions that could be combined with the latest technologies that had been developed. The U.S. management advisors had great perceptions of what could be done with a system that was starting up from scratch. First, basically new technology was available because the old technology was wearing out. Second, this new technology permitted inadequacies in management practice to be corrected.

Thus, at the conclusion of World War II in the Pacific theater, General Douglas MacArthur assembled a talented crew with the mission of rebuilding Japan. The key rebuilders were engineering and manufacturing personnel from Western Electric, which was AT&T's manufacturing unit from the 1920s until divestiture in the 1980s.[7] The story may have several interpretations about the MacArthur agenda,[8] but there is no disagreement that American manufacturing know-how propelled the impressive changeover of Japanese industry to its critical parameters for success.

Some 30 years later, the increasing extent of Japanese ownership of U.S.-based assets, and the excess of imports over exports, have led to serious calls for protection of American industries. The Japanese automakers continue to expand their shares worldwide. Japanese-made television sets, stereos, and other consumer electronic products are favorites of U.S. consumers. Most recently, the auto parts business has become increasingly vulnerable in spite of many steps taken by U.S. auto parts makers to fend off trouble.

Autos, consumer electronics products, tires, auto parts, among other products, are either made in Japan or by Japanese transplants in the United States. Although computer chip production started in the United States, as the memories expanded, the production requirements became increasingly complex, causing many U.S. companies to drop out. Who would have believed in the 1960s that Pacific Basin countries could be more profitable with high-tech design and production than advanced U.S. and European industries? Practically no one, because the importance of process design was missed by observers trained to evaluate market potentials for new products (not processes). The same can be said about financial analysis based on passé concepts of market responses to quality fundamentals and production contributions to bottom-line performance.

Similar questions can be raised about developments in Europe. How is it that the only commercial supersonic airplane is flown by British Airways and Air France? The obvious answer is that supersonics are not profitable, and U.S. companies are driven by short-term profit considerations. Unfortunately for short-termers, the future always becomes the present. What were once long-term goals ultimately become short-term opportunities. As present U.S. aerospace technology suffers wearout, experience with supersonic technology may give the Airbus Industries (a European consortium) substantial advantages for future aerospace products.

The European Economic Community (EEC) has focused the attention of the 12 member countries on the potentials for the largest common market in the global economy. The Japanese are distinctly interested, making major investments in the United Kingdom to provide entrance into the EEC. The U.S. dollar is one of the weakest currencies of the industrialized countries. Above all, the economic situation is so volatile that not a single industry is secure. National commissions to study competitiveness have been created by a succession of U.S. Presidents,[9] but the problems of restoring competitiveness remain rampant.

EFFECTS OF TECHNOLOGICAL CHANGE

The turnover and change in rank of Fortune 1000 firms has been rapid in recent years. Because of technological syzygy, this rate will get even faster in the next decade. Syzygy is an astronomical term used to describe the simultaneous conjunction of common forces. A powerful syzygy can produce very high tides. By analogy, technological syzygy is when bundles of economically important technologies are wearing out together. This is the long-wave phenomenon described by Kondratieff. It will continue to create economic turmoil and to buffet established firms for many years. The effects on the status of specific firms will be traceable to the kinds of technology that they use, and the extent to which such technology is wearing out and being replaced by new forms.

Chapters 3 and 4 deal with two major but substantially different forms of technology change that are relevant at this time. The first relates to the manufacturing process and the equipment that is used. The second relates to the management systems that are used to plan and control what is made; as well as when, where, and how it is made. Although the focus is on manufacturing, the processing of information in a service-oriented firm can be treated as being equivalent to manufacturing. In other words, work that is accomplished by machines (including computers) and the people that run them can range from traditional manufacture of products to the less-conventional production of services. Some examples of repetitive service systems include airlines, electric utilities, hotels, restaurants, hospitals, insurance policies, banks, and brokers.

Changes in Manufacturing Technology

Pictures of factories in the early 1900s show rows of machines driven by belts that are connected to drive shafts that often run the length of the building. For many New England factories, these master drive shafts were turned by water wheels driven by small man-made waterfalls located in adjacent rivers. Steam turbines were another major source of motive power. Later, when the drive shafts were connected to motors that used electricity, manufacturing technology was considered to have made a giant leap forward. Writers of the time extolled the "modern" factories.

One of the most pressing issues in early manufacturing was how to turn the drive shafts that powered the machines. The long wave of technological change was concerned with making machines move. Although this aspect of manufacturing has run its course, it may be due for another long-term development. There are important conjectures emerging about the use of superconductivity to reduce the size of motors and to increase their efficiency. This remains an area of technological development to track. For the present, a different issue characterizes the replacement of manufacturing technology for the factories of the future.

The immediate long wave in technological development for manufacturing is related to new capabilities of machines and the consequent change in the relationships of workers and their machines. In the past, the questions of importance about the relationships were: How much worker skill (such as coordination, precision, and memory) is required to use the equipment? How much weight must be lifted and moved? How repetitious is the job and how comfortable is the working environment? Old machines could not function, or be repaired, without skilled, blue-collar workers to guide them.

What about the new technologies? Starting before 1980, such equipment began to be replaced by new technologies that have computer drivers. Problem-solving for the new technologies requires software intelligence. The blue-collar designation is slowly disappearing as the need to lift, move, and position heavy parts is replaced by programmable equipment that supplies mechanical strengths, as well as coordination skills that supplant eyes and muscles.

The software that drives the newer equipment is created by smart programmers who are best classified as knowledge workers. Often, the people that tend these machines must also be smartly competent with computer systems. The computer systems are programmed to produce the products and also to change the settings from one product to another. The programming for changeover involves stopping the prior job, removing its tools, cleaning up, resetting controls, changing inventories, and starting up. The changeovers are accomplished by mixtures of computers and people working together. A similar description can be applied to white-collar office workers who need to be increasingly smarter to deal with computers processing information.

Many of these newer machines belong to the class of flexible manufacturing systems (FMS), and flexible office systems (FOS). All flexible systems lend themselves to more comprehensive meta-systems called "islands of automation," which aggregate the individual components of a typical FMS or FOS. As we reach higher and higher levels of integrated flexibility, we approach the ideal of real computer integrated manufacturing (CIM). Alternatively, this aspect of information integration is being called computer integrated management with the same CIM acronym being applicable.

We have to be careful to describe the degree of change in manufacturing machine technology. Significant change occurs when new machines accomplish at least one of the following:

1. Replace at least some important manual skills with computer software controls.
2. Make major improvements in the costs and times of changeover from one job to another.
3. Make major improvements in the productivity and quality of the production output.

Real change is unlikely to occur if none of the above three points is present. To illustrate, the production manager of an aerospace company, which allowed our college class a plant visit, showed the students some new equipment, recently received. It had been set up in the same large room with the old equipment. There were two parallel lines. One was the new line, and the other was 40 years older. They seemed identical except that one line was clean and shiny and the other was worn and old.

A student commented on the similar appearance of the two lines, and was told: "We were so satisfied with the old equipment that we didn't want to change it. The machine supplier copied it as exactly as possible, so the main difference between the old and the new is that the new is not aged and it's not worn out." In subsequent conversation we learned that computer controls could have been added to the design, but that would have delayed the replacement, destroyed the turnkey implementation, jeopardized federal funding approval, and required learning adaptation by workers. It seems fair to say that although the company acquired new equipment, it did not acquire new technology. It is doubtful that this "not really new" technology will add to the company's competitiveness, or that it represents a useful response to the forces responsible for special economic turmoil.

Concern for manufacturing adaptability has been on the agenda at the national level for many years. In 1985 the National Academy of Engineers published a widely distributed book entitled "Education for the Manufacturing World of the Future."[10] In 1986 the Manufacturing Studies Board published another extensively distributed report with the title "Toward a New Era in U.S. Manufacturing: The Need for a National Vision."[11] Meanwhile, the major magazines and newspapers that are publications for business professionals have featured thousands of stories on this subject.

Clearly, lack of awareness that there is a problem is not the problem. What is at the nub of the technological wearout and replacement problem is the question of what steps management should take to adapt and correct the situation. How can the firm regain the competitiveness that it has lost? What is the antidote for bureaucracy? Chapter 3 looks at the complex effects of technological change on manufacturing systems.

Changes in Management Systems Technology

Understanding the traditional lines of plant management is necessary to perceive what changes are occurring in management systems technology. The traditional approach was rooted in the Industrial Engineering (IE) concepts developed at the beginning of the 1900s by Frederick W. Taylor, Henry L. Gantt, Frank Gilbreth, and other famous founders of the production disciplines. At the same time, early organizational theorists such as Chester Barnard, Henri Fayol, and Lillian Gilbreth paralleled the operational considerations with notions about authority, responsibility, leadership, and span of control.

Division of work on the production line permitted specialization, which fostered accountability and allowed managerial control to reign supreme. Specialization was based on repetitive work and the application of IE studies to find the "right way to do the job." By extension, functional divisions became hard and fast. Everything was partitioned into domains of hierarchical responsibility that epitomized bureaucracies. Management technology centered around accounting systems with established standards. Variances signaled the need for management action. The communication system was slow, with the result that feedback corrections were delayed, which produced minimal penalties since the demands on the system were relatively stable. This kind of management approach became increasingly ineffective as the demands on the system became destabilized and turbulent economic forces prevailed.

An unusual aspect of 1990s technological changes is the degree to which management systems are affected. Because computers and new information systems technology are at the root of the 1990 changes, the impact on management is unique. This may be the first time (not excluding the printing press) that a machine-based technology so completely alters traditional management practice. The reference to the printing press is somewhat facetious, but the similar root of information reproducibility and its effect on knowledge dissemination is worth considering.[12] The boardroom and the golf course are invaded by telecommunication portals to computer systems that provide global network participation in planning, decision-making, and controlling.

The entire array of human resource policies, including hiring, training, promotions, and replacements, interact with a companywide data base. Functional organization falters because events occur too quickly to permit any one functional area to reach decisions in isolation. Systems considerations overpower the functionally partitioned approach to decision-making that is traditionally used by bureaucratic hierarchical organizations.

The new technology supports an information systems architecture that is companywide. Software development is continuous, requiring new methods of project management, which are discussed in Chapter 7. Software development costs are high. They constitute fixed rather than operating costs and share budget appropriations with product and process development. Software interconnects computer hardware with operating machines and the judgments of all levels of employees. As a result, the role of every worker (from chief executive officers [CEOs] to janitors) is altered. The expectation is that they are all raised to a new level which may be unrealistic for the CEOs. Not so for the janitors, which has demonstrable benefits for the company.

The machines are smarter, which means that workers must be smarter to program the machines. Smarter workers are needed to answer questions that were not anticipated in the programming. When these smarter machines stop or malfunction, someone must have the answers to set things right. When smart machines and smart workers function properly together, the result is a smart factory. The effect of technological wearout has led to the design of smart factories, which are getting increasingly smarter. The cumulative amount of smartness may be the best new measure of a firm's competitiveness.

The old management technology was based upon high volumes of production. The related economic principle is known as "economies of scale." These circumstances favored a management approach that was continuously looking for deviations from standards. When a problem would arise, management's assignment was to correct the deviant situation as quickly as possible. In this environment, quality improvement meant reducing deviations from the standard criterion—that is, assuring that the standard is met. An antonym for standard is "extraordinary." Thus, with the old technology, ever-better quality was not a conceivable objective.

With technological wearout, the replacement technology required changes in the management process to cope with the potentials of the new equipment. The new equipment emphasized flexibility that deemphasized high volumes of production. Greater variety of output involved management's ability to change over from one set of specifications to another. With each run, there was opportunity to improve qualities. Rather than concentrating on the elimination of deviations, management focused on doing better and better in product design, quality, and costs. In this environment, it became critical to motivate workers to do their best, rather than policing workers to insure conformance to standards. Overall, the management system was forced to change from the reduction of uncertainty to constant innovation.

ADAPTATION STRATEGIES

Once the effects of technological change have been examined, the main concern becomes adaptation to the situation—specifically, which adaptation strategies are available to established firms so that they can regain the competitive edge that they once held. Start-up companies are excluded because they do not have an established bureaucracy to impede adaptation and fast response. This gives us a clue to an adaptation principle: when properly managed, start-up firms are small enough to operate like a team. People know each other and have commonly held goals. Small size supports the vitality and enthusiasm to outplay the established firms.

Ecological studies are quite definitive: the size of an organism increases with its age. The same relationship applies to organizations of biological entities. Namely, the sizes of the organizations increase with age. At the same time, fervor and stamina of the organization decrease as it ages and grows larger. There should be a trade-off—namely, the older the organization, the greater the wisdom of its members. Similarly, the larger the organization, the greater the pool of talent and experience to draw upon. Observation of bureaucracies does not support this expectation.

Changing the Organization

Awareness of the need for change is not at issue. These days everyone in large bureaucratic firms agrees that change is required. How to change is another matter. In this regard, there is a big difference between what management says it is doing to restore competitiveness and what is actually taking place in their organizations. In many companies, what the CEO announces as the strategy to bring about change is neither real nor workable. Public relations departments, advertising agencies, and stockholder relations groups often preempt what might work with what sounds good. Announcements are not one of the means for achieving change, although it is necessary for everyone in the firm to understand which principles of change are about to be put into practice. In the final analysis, bureaucratic organizations are unable to change by dictum.

The mechanisms for change require alterations in the structure of existing organizations. Bureaucratic organizations have very poor adaptability because no matter what anyone says, they have too much inertia to shift patterns in any meaningful way. This, under the proper circumstances, is one of the strengths of bureaucracies. Such organizations prosper when their environment is stable. They develop routines for handling demands that reoccur repeatedly.

In the history of the natural sciences, it may take a succession of generations for a species of organisms to adapt to major changes in its environment. Some, like the dinosaurs, did not have the time to succeed. What could the dinosaurs have done to survive? Probably get smaller. But that is a different discussion that properly belongs in another medium. In an organization, who could draw up the plan to change to survive? In such an organization, given the mandate, who would undertake changing the organization? The problem does not lend itself to a seat-of-the-pants solution.

An understanding of the many-faceted theory of successful transformation and adjustments to the newly emerging global competitive situation is essential. It takes on many different forms, which are discussed in Chapters 5, 6, and 7. An adaptive approach that is relatively permanent comes from organizational redesign. Such alterations can be addressed to the changes in an organization that make it more competitive. Alternatively, they can be addressed to cooperative alliances as an appropriate organizational response.

Competitive Organizational Responses

Being a better competitor has meant different things over time. The geographic frame within which competition occurs has been continuously expanding, although it should be noted that, in their own way, the Phoenicians were no slouches when it came to global trade. The earliest years of trade were dominated by such items of concern as tea and spices from Cathay and the Indies. Henry Hudson, Ferdinand Magellan, Christopher Columbus, and other explorers were the entrepreneur-explorers of their day.

The legal and regulatory frame for competition has also changed markedly in keeping with the requirements of the period. At the turn of the twentieth century, American business was dominated by monopolistic leaders of basic industries. Although we now call them robber barons, they were much admired in their own times for their vision, ability to surmount physical and financial obstacles, and their willingness to take risks. Andrew Carnegie, John D. Rockefeller, Edward H. Harriman, and others were, at least in part, motivated by the ability to monopolize their industries of steel, oil, railroads, and such.

While the methods may be different now, the same need to justify capital investments is still in operation. Today, competitors all over the world attempt to stack the cards in their favor. This drive explains the need to lobby for governmental support. Hardly a new invention, lobbying has been going on since commerce connected the mandarins of China and the rajahs of India with the courts of King Louis XIV, who built Versailles.

Arguments abound with respect to competitive lobbying in the United States. A great deal of money has been spent by the big three automakers from Detroit in a continuing effort to reduce the legal requirements for allowable amounts of auto emissions and companywide average fuel efficiency in miles per gallon. It seems fair to query whether the same level of expenditure in the research laboratories might have been better used to reduce auto emissions and increase fuel efficiency. The Europeans and Pacific Basin nations employ lobbying in the United States, while in Europe the American multinational corporations have always been adept at this. Big arguments exist because Japanese markets have not been accessible to lobbying. European countries, until 1992, have been much tougher on the Japanese than the United States. It seems that this will be less true after 1992.

With open markets, competition has always meant reduced costs for consumers, better quality, and a faster stream of innovative designs. Thus, competitive strategies for changing the organization are based upon the achievement of better quality, lower costs, and thereby superior value for consumers.

A distinction needs to be drawn between obtaining efficiencies by doing the same things better, and changing the way things are done to be more effective. The objectives of management to change the organization should not be construed as a recommendation to ignore savings that can be gained by doing things better. However, the prescription is first to change what is done before refining the way it is done. In this sense, the competitive strategies for changing the organization include the following:

1. Downsizing by systematically and pervasively altering the systems and procedures for doing business. This should be compared to work force reduction, where fewer people are expected to work longer and harder to do the same amount of work. The key point is that there is an optimal size organization for competitive performance, but that size is predicated on a properly designed support system for a smoothly functioning continuous production system.

2. Improving value-added by adopting new work flows that keep the product moving. Stationary inventories for both work-in-process (WIP) and finished goods are eliminated. Parts that are expensive to make are out-sourced to superior suppliers. These kinds of issues are time-based tactical improvements based on systems changes rather than elimination of inefficiencies.

3. Speeding-up product innovations is one of the most promising areas for organizational redesign. Without fundamental changes in the organization, such speeding-up is likely to produce disasters. We are accustomed to callbacks for autos, safety problems with appliances, malfunctions with computers, and serious errors in new releases of software. These are most often associated with efforts to "rush" new products to market. Rushing occurs when unaltered systems are pushed beyond their capacity.

Cooperative Organizational Responses

Alliances are partnerships entered into for the mutual advantages that can be derived by all participants. Cooperative arrangements have many potential benefits. They must be planned and managed with great care to prevent onerous failures with complex repercussions. Depending upon the success of their design, alliances can be catalysts for good change or bad change. When effective, alliances can help break through the paralysis of bureaucratic organizations.

There are many categories of alliances. Among these are tactical ones, which bring partners together to do a better job with production processes, inventories, quality control, and shop floor management. Strategic alliances are tied to broader objectives, such as new product development, production, and marketing; new process development and its relationship to new product lines; pioneering the use of unique distribution channels; opening up new markets that allow A's product into B's marketplace and vice versa.

Mergers and acquisitions (M&A) are really two different perceptions of strategic alliances. Thus, to merge is "to unite so as to become one and lose individual identity"; to acquire is "to come into possession of." In fact, the M&A phrase generally has been construed to mean that a more powerful firm takes over a less powerful firm.

Joint ventures represent another form of strategic alliance where a new entity is created. Because of their special properties, many joint ventures are global alliances. In addition, they are often easy to enter into, and hard to get out of without proper planning. When joint-venture arrangements are flawed, there can be substantial penalties associated with ending the arrangement. What propels a lot of companies to use joint ventures is the fact that they expect to get a lot back from a relatively small investment. Also appealing is the fact that joint ventures require the assignment of only a small portion of a firm's resources. This leaves the rest of the organization unfettered and quite independent of the experimental joint venture.

Companies all over the world are entering into global alliances at an unprecedented rate. The mutual benefits that all alliance partners expect to derive are predicated on gaining access to that which otherwise they could not obtain. This includes marketing advantages or learning about technology, such as comes from sharing production and operations management techniques. Another common motive is to gain access to R&D results and lab know-how.

There is an even more important benefit that can be derived from new alliances. For a firm where change is stymied by inertia, alliances provide a means for mobilizing new forces. The rules are changed and established roles are altered. This brings into play modified planning and decision structures for every aspect of doing business. Domestic enterprises find this particularly appropriate when venturing into a globally competitive environment.

However, to be successful, alliance partners must need each other and know why they need each other. Otherwise, the stronger partner overpowers the weaker ones. Establishing mutual need is easier with transnationals because each partner realizes the others' cultural advantages in their home markets. The same reasoning applies to dealing with work forces and suppliers speaking different languages. There is less mystery and uncertainty to be dealt with in strictly domestic alliances. But the increased uncertainty of global alliances can also backfire by creating excessive expectations.

Significant features of successful alliances include the following: 1. Achieving optimal organizational sizes when blending two or more firms together. For example, who decides which managers should leave and which should remain after a merger. The same kind of question applies to production facilities. Following an acquisition, which plants should continue to operate and which ones should be closed down? With joint ventures there is an on-going question concerning in what way are they autonomous, and to what degree are they captives of the participating business units. Joint ventures require information systems that reflect the real systems of authority and responsibility. The successful joint venture balances the benefits of centralization and decentralization of different functions.

2. Integrating organizational functions so that production and operations management, marketing, distribution, R&D, finance, accounting, and human resource management simultaneously share responsibility for systems planning and implementation. This requires synthesis of the technological change issues as they are created by R&D, implemented by engineering, and backed up by policies for hiring, training, and paying all levels of workers.

3. Developing information systems to facilitate sharing of communications among integrated organizational functions. Most global alliances employ worldwide telecommunication networks to coordinate centralized functions such as technology transfers and purchasing. In the most highly developed information systems, interfunctional coordination is mapped by a computer integrated manufacturing model of the firm.

There are various global companies (such as Aerospatiale of France) that describe integrated organizational functions as computer integrated management. The intent is to apply the same concept of integrated information systems to a broader frame than manufacturing. The fact that the identical acronym, CIM, results is intentional. It is meant to elevate the companywide perception of CIM from an engineering orientation to that of overall management. Another label that some firms employ is computer integrated enterprise (CIE). Adherents claim that CIE emphasizes the accounting systems for measuring performance. However, the accepted meaning of CIM must include accounting information, so the choice of a name is more a matter of having a different name than a unique concept.

4. Establishing the strategic and tactical importance of production and operations management decisions for both manufacturing and service industries. The focus on production technology emphasizes flexibility of shop floor procedures to adapt to a stream of innovative product and process changes. Fast response organizations, which are discussed in Chapter 7, stress the important role of production to achieve optimal timing.

The point needs to be made that production and operations management decisions have been relegated to the shop floor for many years in the United States, and to a major extent in Europe as well. That is because production factors were not viewed as having the competitive leverage of marketing and financial issues. Production methods and engineering decisions were assumed to be identical in all firms, in accord with the production volume, as dictated by marketing plans for price and distribution. The fact that this may no longer be the case is important. Evidence that the role of production and operations has been reevaluated can be gathered from various observations of what companies are doing. In this regard, global alliances are being employed by many companies as a means of elevating the importance of production strategies in a bureaucratic system that would otherwise squelch major realignments of power.

Strategic alliances are changing the priorities with which competitive dimensions are viewed. The quality of production outputs is continually improving as new technology is employed. Consumer loyalty is highly elastic to perceived product quality. This perception is related to the degree of superiority of the product chosen over what else is available.[13] Consequently, to be competitive, production facilities must have access to sufficient capital to employ new technologies. Short-term competition takes place on perceived value (which emphasizes costs and prices, fast response capabilities, and warranties). Long-term competition focuses on the optimal timing of a succession of product improvements. While this is essential for industrial markets, it also applies to consumer products.

Global alliances are occurring all over the world for many of the reasons already mentioned. Most of these reasons also promote being able to overcome bureaucratic inertia, thereby supporting both short- and long-term competitive success. This is occurring, in spite of the fact that global alliances do not guarantee success and may lead to financial and organizational failures.

Breaking Bureaucratic Barriers

One of the most important forms of strategic alliances is the joint venture (JV). They are relatively autonomous, start-up organizations that are aimed at developing and supporting new competitive strategies. Even when the sponsoring firms are very large, joint ventures are always small to medium-sized organizations. Agility is related to size. How long does it take for communications to traverse the organization from top to bottom? Joint ventures gain their strength from their ability to take action quickly. Another way of viewing the advantage of lean-and-mean size is that fast communications enable the firm to have the superior strength of systems perspectives, the advantage of decisions based on negotiations, and the faster response capabilities derived from breaking through bureaucratic barriers.

Bureaucracies are among the most effective organizational designs for controlling and removing the causes of deviations from established standards. But bureaucracies are ineffective for achieving continuous improvement. They are reluctant to work at changing standards rather than meeting them. A saying that succinctly captures this idea is: "The cautious bureaucrat thinks twice before he says nothing" (attributed to Arthur Laffer).[14] Joint ventures break through bureaucratic barriers. The JVs can then develop unique manufacturing techniques using new process technologies and new management systems.

TIME-BASED STRATEGIES

A strong bias toward implementing time-based strategies has emerged from analyzing the characteristics of successful global competitors. Anecdotes and war stories abound that support the notion that quick thinking and decision-making without foot dragging are plentifully rewarded by the market. Suppliers that can deliver small quantities regularly and without delay are usually the highest quality, lowest price producers. Companies and suppliers working together in a coordinated system have a big advantage over passive participants who spend most of their time putting out fires.

The tactical and strategic characteristics of fast response organizations (FROs) are examined in Chapter 7. Then, in the same chapter, the benefits of management synchronicity and the means of achieving a well-orchestrated system are explored. In addition to the logical appeal of time-based, total systems management, there is ample research that indicates that fast response firms are adaptive to contingencies and competitively prosperous.

It may be useful to draw the analogy between these firms and ballet groups (in a three-dimensional choreographic sense). If done properly, every participant knows exactly where they are on the stage, at any moment of time, and where they are going to be the next minute. Another useful analogy is the symphony orchestra, which is led by the conductor who directs and coordinates the patterns of communication according to the musical score. Orchestration abilities are worthy of study and emulation.

Fast Response Organizations

The success of FROs is related to what they appear to be to customers and competitors alike. It is useful to refer to a production model to explain the difference between continuous output rates that appear to be consistently fast and batch output rates that appear to be lumpy and slow. This distinction, which is also known as the flow shop (continuous output) versus the job shop (batch output) configuration, is described in Chapter 5. The key to successful flow shops is synchronicity.

The advantages of FROs are derived from their ability to change course quickly. Yet fast response does not mean knee-jerk reaction. Perhaps a better caption would be "fast enough" to consider what can and should be done to avoid failures and penalties (on the negative side), and "fast enough" to capitalize on rewarding opportunities (on the positive side) as they appear on the horizon. Thus, the fast response capability includes being totally aware, capable of quick analysis and quick decision, and action-oriented. The fact that these characteristics work to enhance the competitiveness of FROs is based upon both logic and evidence.

The disadvantages of not being an FRO is the other side of the coin. With profound global changes related to the Kondratieff effect taking place, there is more reason than in calmer times to be fast on the uptake. Preparedness for adaptation to swiftly moving events is not characteristic of large, established bureaucracies. The penalty is further inroads on market shares by new and unexpected fast-moving competitors. They are able to find new ways of doing the job, including new product designs, different market niche strategies, and well-coordinated fast response transformations of operational (production and distribution) systems. This is explained by means of a systems model that *finds* new market opportunities, *designs* the appropriate product, *makes* the product, and *ships* the finished goods out the door without entering inventory—a continuous flow of output that maximizes the value-adding activities of the firm.

Are strategic alliances better suited to being FROs than other forms of organizations? They have the potentials associated with youth, small size, newly formulated goals, and orientation for learning. They have the problems of no experience, untested relationships between new partners, and, especially with respect to global alliances, the risks and uncertainties associated with international events. The performance of alliances could be inhibited by the rules and regulations of specific countries. In particular, the European Economic Community is still formulating policies, and trade protectionism against Japan. The same approach is developing extensive support in the United States.

Successful FROs are more complex than the traditional organization. They are structured as smart systems that are composed of smart machines and smart workers. Coordinating managers are learner-facilitators with a consultant's ability for recognizing underlying systems interactions.

1. FRO's employ total quality control and just-in-time methods to function successfully on the tactical side of operations management. Operations research and management science are helpful in achieving systemwide scheduling productivity.

2. Continuous on-going or nonstop project management is a major new development on the strategic side of successful FRO's. Quantitative analysis capabilities combine with matrix organization (each individual functions as a production worker and as a project team member) ideas to provide the new windows of opportunity.

Management Synchronicity

Timing is crucial in two ways. First, there is correct timing for entry into the market. It is possible to be too early, too late, or just-in-time. Second, there is the timing of steps that must be taken to support a new product launch. This requires coordination of product and process research, engineering development, design and implementation of the production line, determining the marketing strategies for prices, warranties, and methods of distribution.

Synchronicity refers to orchestration of all the functions needed to achieve successful entry. A great deal of insight and preparation are essential to do the job right. Planning, awareness of what is happening everywhere in the system, and communication to keep in phase are the elements that make appropriate timing possible.

Adequate planning requires informed opinion about the competitors' strategies. This includes competitors' timing as well as our own. If it doesn't matter whether a new computer product reaches the market in February, June, or October, then the system is not sensitive to timing. Years ago, delays of several months might hardly have mattered. There was ample time to adjust strategies. That is no longer the case in the 1990s. The game is played against the clock. All moves are synchronized so that delays do not cause penalties.

In an era that is characterized by economic turmoil created by pervasive technological wearout and replacement, timing takes on a new role. Being able to do the correct things quickly (as with FROs, described in Chapter 7) is a boon to proper timing. It is not, however, sufficient to carry the day. Further, as will be discussed in Chapter 7, what seems to be fast response may be the perception of a slower, but continuous output system. This involves the timing of support steps based on contingency plans that probably originated long before the actual need to do something different occurred. Under such circumstances there is ample time to adjust. If knee-jerk response systems are used, then management is so occupied putting out fires that there is no time to respond properly. The costs of not being coordinated are likely to be exorbitant. For this reason, in the 1990s, timing has become the overriding factor of importance.

NOTES

1. Change can be built into a company's structure. For example, the Boeing Company has been masterful in following one product improvement by another. In 1957 the company designed and released the 707, which became the first commercially viable jet. At the same time, the British aircraft industry designed Comet I. It was in commercial use but had serious flaws that Comet II was supposed to remedy but apparently did not. Boeing's 747 (1969) remains a unique success in the aircraft industry. But the company persevered with changes. The 757 and 767 jet aircraft appeared in 1982. These fuel-efficient planes are being followed by the 777, which represents a continuation of Boeing's ability to make technological change part of the company's fabric. The contrast with its competitors is marked. This can be used to signal the fact that there is a right way of doing things. Businesses are not "damned if they do, and damned if they don't."

2. The most basic essay entitled "Long Economic Cycles," was published in the journal *Voprosy Konyunktury* (Problems of Economic Conditions), 1, no. 1 (1925). On February 6, 1926, it was read as a paper at the Economics Institute of the Russian Association of Social Science Research Institutes.

3. See later references in Chapter 2 to Wesley C. Mitchell, director of the National Bureau of Economic Research at the turn of the century; Joseph Schumpeter,

Harvard economist and author of a major two-volume study of business cycles; Jay W. Forrester, Germeshausen Professor at MIT; and Bruce Merrifield, former assistant secretary of the U.S. Department of Commerce.

4. There are various books that describe different long-cycle schools of thought. For example, see Dick A. Stoken, *Cycles* (New York: McGraw-Hill, 1978).

5. C. P. Snow, *The Two Cultures and the Scientific Revolution* (The Rede Lecture, 1959) (New York: Cambridge University Press, 1961). Snow's argument is that scientists are accused by humanists of oversimplifying and, in turn, they accuse humanists of creating antiscience complexities.

6. J.-J. Servan-Schreiber, *The American Challenge* (New York: Atheneum, 1968).

7. Kenneth Hopper, a journalist who had studied the economic rebirth of Japan, presented a seminar at the Columbia Business School in the mid-1980s. He described the role of engineers from Western Electric (the production arm of AT&T) as being considerable in establishing new production methodologies for postwar Japan. The Japanese president of an American subsidiary of Sumitomo, who was present at the seminar, agreed with this assessment.

8. According to Hopper's account, the teams assembled by General MacArthur worked closely with the industrial leaders of prewar Japanese industry, especially the chairman of Sumitomo. On the other hand, Pat Choate, in his 1990 book, *Agents of Influence* (New York: Alfred A. Knopf), indicates that American banking and business interests with holdings in Japan prevailed against a MacArthur plan to break up "the family-owned super-conglomerates that dominated Japan's prewar economy. . . ."

9. For example, President Ronald Reagan authorized the Report of the President's Commission on Industrial Competitiveness, *Global Competition: The New Reality*, Vol. 1 (January 1985). John A. Young was the chairman of the commission.

10. This monograph was published in 1985 by the National Academy Press, 2101 Constitution Avenue, NW, Washington, D.C. 20418. It was produced by the National Academy of Engineering, which shares in the responsibility given the National Academy of Sciences under a congressional charter granted in 1863 to advise the federal government on questions of science and technology.

11. This is another report sponsored by the National Research Council and published in 1986 by the National Academy Press.

12. Johann Gutenberg, a German printer, was probably the first European to print from movable type (circa 1468).

13. Various marketing models relate demand to the measure of relative quality, which compares the quality of one firm's product to the quality range of other available products in the same class. For example, see the computer market models of the Hendry Corporation, Croton-on-Hudson, New York.

14. Since all bureaucrats are cautious, we assume that this tautology is meant to emphasize the obvious.

CHAPTER 2 ⎯⎯⎯⎯⎯⎯⎯⎯⎯⎯⎯⎯

The Causes of Special Economic Turmoil

> A prophet is one who, when everyone else despairs, hopes. And when everyone else hopes, he despairs. You'll ask why. It's because he has mastered the great secret: The Wheel Turns.
>
> Nikos Kazantzakis[1]

In a free market economy, some degree of economic turmoil is commonplace. As the number of interacting nations that participate in the global economy increases, the expected amount of turbulence increases. Also, over time, the volatility level waxes and wanes. Since variability is the expected norm, what is the basis for saying that—the present time is a period of "special" economic turmoil?[2]

SIGNS OF SPECIAL ECONOMIC VOLATILITY

Under normal circumstances, it is expected that companies will experience some fluctuation of profits and occasional losses. However, the present time is a period when so many companies have losses that the situation can be considered abnormal. The average amount of the losses is greater than normal. The number of periods of consecutive losses is out of line with expectations and is increasing. In the same sense, it is not unusual for firms to experience cash flow problems, market share losses, and other negative performances. What makes the circumstances special? When the occurrences are unusually frequent (many more firms are in the red than would be expected), the losses are persistent (repeated periods), and their severity is great (often threatening or causing bank-ruptcy), then it seems fair to say that conditions of special or unusual economic turmoil exist.

Perhaps the most telling aspect of special economic turmoil is that substantial market shifts occur with established companies losing share to relatively unknown (and often smaller) competitors. Many of these competitors appear to arise out of nowhere. How is it possible that the leading firms did not anticipate such competition?[3] Why didn't company intelligence know how to track these hidden competitors? The unexpected sources of competition usually are not listed on the major domestic stock markets, or in reference books of producers and suppliers. Rather, they are headquartered in faraway places and unpronounceable foreign sites. When a high number of such occur-rences becomes commonplace, it is reasonable to assume that some special form of economic turmoil exists.

Other signs of economic volatility include continuous currency fluc-tuations of substantial size; a scourge of junk bond buyouts, which jeopardize the investments of individual lenders as well as the pension funds of otherwise conservative organizations; bank failures (starting with the Continental Illinois Bank, and rapidly growing to include hundreds of savings and loan banks), which will cost taxpayers half a trillion dollars; bankruptcy (or near bankruptcy) of previously stable organizations such as Eastern Airlines, Southland Corporation (parent of the 7–Eleven convenience stores), Drexel Burnham, and Polly Peck of London. The list of bankruptcies goes on and on.

Governmental Interventions

In times of great volatility, one would expect government intercession and mediation. That is precisely what is occurring in this era of turbulence. There were few precedents for the government rescue of such major companies as Chrysler Corporation, Grumman Aerospace, Con-tinental Illinois Bank, and hundreds of savings and loan institutions (S&Ls). The bolstering steps taken by U.S. agencies fall well outside expectations in normal times. However, the interventions are not part of an overall plan that could be called an "industrial policy." They are not even part of an informal plan, such as has been recommended by the President's Commission on Industrial Competitiveness.[4] Instead, they are reactive rather than proactive actions.

It is not usual for members of Congress to get involved with trade protection threats against nations that have captured export-import advantages. Yet such threats are escalating. In the United States, it is not customary for state and federal governments to make efforts to limit foreign ownership. But in these times of economic turbulence, an increasing number of people want to curb foreign acquisitions of real estate. There has been significant negative reaction to the purchase of landmark buildings, famous hotels, golf courses, and farmland acreage. On the other hand, as states vie for manufacturing investments by foreign companies, they offer substantial tax breaks and other benefits.[5]

Trade issues dominate relations between nations. The evolving global community consists of spheres of common interest. The coming together of the 12 nations of the European Economic Community has riveted attention on a market potential of 325 million people. Other common markets that will be emerging include the United States, Canada, and Mexico (Canada and the United States have already moved toward the formation of a North American Common Market); the Pacific Basin countries; Eastern Europe and the USSR; Latin America and the Caribbean countries. Thus, as nations everywhere experience the effects of global economic turbulence because of the changeover of technology, new alliances abound.

Being caught on the horns of a dilemma whereby you are "damned if you do, and damned if you don't" is another symptom of volatility. In this case, groups face up to each other with contradictory objectives. Simultaneously, there are conflicting efforts by some groups (such as state governments) to bring in foreign investment money while other groups (for example, those that represent constituencies concerned with protecting jobs) are hostile to importing it. The sides that are hostile to foreign investment lobby governmental support. The foreign companies also spend money for lobbying. Ultimately, there are warnings of reprisals unless the foreign countries open their markets to U.S. products and investments.

When there is major economic volatility, business failures occur at a rapid rate; the number of start-ups decreases. In an effort to survive, many companies downsize severely and repeatedly. What is particularly noteworthy is the number of (long) established businesses that experience serious reversals. Fortune 1000 companies seem to be more susceptible to the ravages of competitors than relatively unknown midsized companies. There are buyouts and mergers as the weaker companies become vulnerable and their stocks fall below threshold values for acquisition.

Strategic Alliances

To deal with difficult times, strategic alliances, including joint ventures, have been entered into by thousands of American firms with foreign partners. Such means for becoming global competitors is discussed in Chapter 6. The use of business alliances is not a recent invention. We only need to consider the British Commonwealth, which stretched its alliances around the world from England to Canada, India, and Australia. What is unique is the degree to which strategic alliances are now being used. The extent to which they represent corporations rather than nations, and the range of different national roots, is also exceptional. Noteworthy is the fact that many of the partnerships have one or more firms whose home base is in nations that only a short time ago were classified as less developed or developing countries.

Even without reading the fine print, many new types of partnerships exist. This occurs because countries have different rules and regulations governing ownership, taxes, and methods for doing business. Also, the partners often have quite disparate reasons for entering into alliances. Joint ventures have become a favorite form of alliance, but the character of these new entities is far more varied than the label "joint ventures" implies. The simplest explanation of why the occurrence of alliances now numbers in the tens of thousands is that firms are trying to become global, and alliances help them overcome inertia. Alliances permit experimentation with new forms of organizations that can overcome inertia. That is the only way to survive and prosper in an era of extreme economic turmoil.

The Effects of Economic Turmoil on Communism

As another aspect of volatility, conditions of global economic turmoil set the stage for social-economic-political changes. In the 1980s and 1990s, major geopolitical shifts have taken place, such as the removal of the Berlin Wall—symbolic of the end of communist domination in Eastern Europe. While not as dramatic, the emergence of many small Pacific Basin countries as industrialized nations has changed the balance of economic power in the world. Observant communists could not help noticing how cities like Singapore and Hong Kong, and poor nations like Thailand and Indonesia, were outstripping the communist world. For many prior years, the geopolitical system was frozen by the balanced confrontation of the superpowers. Equilibrium had prevailed under military conditions with a nuclear standoff in a stable world economy.

Premier Gorbachev of the Soviet Union became the spokesman for the obvious. Military equilibrium siphoned off resources and empowered bureaucratic organizations to stifle adaptation by the Soviet system to extreme economic turmoil.

What had upset the equilibrium of the stable world economy? One factor was the ability of the Japanese to become one of the leading world powers through industrial might. This incredible fact was not overlooked by the beleaguered management of the communist countries. Japan had succeeded in doing what the USSR, and all of its satellite countries in Eastern Europe, could not do with troops, planes, nuclear arsenals, and government ownership of farms and factories. Looking behind the scenes, Japan had taken advantage of an economic phenomenon that was affecting all industrialized countries—namely, the final phase in the long-wave cycle of technological development. We will discuss this in a section entitled "The Phoenix Phenomenon."

What also upset the stability of the communist system was the fact that as its old manufacturing technology was wearing out, it was increasingly difficult to farm efficiently and to manufacture products within tolerances. The manufacturing technology in the USSR is among the oldest of the old technology that is currently being used by any industrialized country. Meanwhile, a peek at the world outside revealed an overabundance of farm produce, bright red Hyundai automobiles made in neighboring Korea, Sony Trinitron TVs made in Tokyo, and an array of VCRs made in Taiwan and Hong Kong that sold at prices too absurd to contemplate for those bureaucrats who managed the state-run stores. Less developed countries that embraced the new technologies were far surpassing the standard of living of Eastern Europe and the USSR. Because bureaucracy affected every aspect of life in the communist countries, there was no hope of escaping what Chinese managers in the People's Republic of China (PRC) call the iron teacup.

Communism reeled under the conditions of global economic turmoil, but so did the U.S. economy. Uncertainty, which grew in leaps and bounds as a result of economic volatility, always favors those who have liquidity. Established firms with large plants filled with old manufacturing equipment have at least one foot in the past. There is ample evidence that they cannot get up to speed as quickly as those who are starting up for the first time. As technology changes, the investments in old technologies represent sunk costs. Managers with large sunk costs are unable to turn their backs on the past and move into the future with the same energy and alacrity as managers without old capital commitments.

Some call the litany of economic ills a sign of national decline. Armchair historians have a tendency to reference the fall of Rome. What is seldom cited is the fact that the situation may be caused by exogenous factors that are not recognized as such. As a result, the focus is on the situation and not the causes. Thus, the newspapers are a daily reminder of many disturbing situations, such as a steep, nationwide downturn in real estate values; the constantly expanding list of banks having problems with billions of dollars of losses by savings and loans; the pervasive credit squeeze; legislative paralysis for reducing the federal budget deficit; halfway solutions to the budget deficit that do not inspire large investments in new technologies; breakdowns of ethics on Wall Street and in the Chicago commodity markets; bankruptcy and consolidation in the retail industry. Any pair or triad of such circumstances might be accepted as normal, but the litany is too long to be characterized as "business as usual."

During World War II the United States shifted from the Depression economy of the 1930s to one that supplied war materiel and related delivery systems to itself and its Allies. After the war ended, the United States was in an ideal position to became the sole major producer to the world's consumers. The factories of major manufacturers in Europe and Japan had been destroyed. In contrast, the U.S. manufacturing base was not only intact, it was large and growing. American firms quickly invested in the latest technology to meet the worldwide demand for new products. Engineering was admired and production systems prospered with the application of operations research and management science.[6] The 1950s were so growth-oriented that economists predicted that the "Soaring 60's" would best describe the continuation of the prosperity that marked the postwar years.

IS ECONOMIC TURMOIL REALLY DIFFERENT NOW?

It may not be common knowledge, but it is well-known to economists that business in the United States began to run into trouble more than 25 years ago. The mid-1960s ushered in the beginning of economic troubles. By the 1970s, students of the U.S. economy had begun to spot the signs of troubles. The important question was: Do the difficulties result from temporary, random effects, or are they signs of long-term pervasive changes in the economic system? Even years ago, it was possible to answer that the trends were caused by fundamental forces that were changing. They were not random aberrations.

Pervasive Deterioration in Productivity Improvement

During the 1980s, the U.S. economy was extremely volatile, and it will remain so during the 1990s. One example of this volatility has been the inability of established companies to remain profitable. Changes occur suddenly that formerly happened gradually. Market share shifts take months that previously took years. Technological changes seem to be implemented overnight. In the background there has been a continuous and ominous decline in the growth of manufacturing productivity that substantially impacts margins and reduces the reserves of a company. This curtails a firm's ability to change directions. It inhibits escaping from present dilemmas into new challenges and opportunities.

The decline of productivity growth translates into higher costs of doing business, lower profit margins, and loss of market shares. It is notable that these negative factors apply to a broad spectrum of industrial sectors that add up to the state of the economy as a whole. That is why the stock market's volatility reflects investors' concern about the overall economy, rather than a particular company or industry. In a single day, sudden precipitous declines have wiped out more than 10 percent of the perceived industrial value of the U.S. economy.[7] While such lemming-like conduct appears to be irrational, it reflects thresholds that trigger mass psychological behavior impacting on managerial decisions. The market selloff raises the cost of what can be borrowed. The drop in stock value—triggered by the chain of events that starts with lower productivity—has many negative impacts on the company. These can take months and years to repair—if, in fact, they can be repaired at all.

It should be noted that many large firms outside of the United States have suffered similar productivity setbacks in recent years. Some West European companies have experienced undesirable fluctuations in their productivity growth, as well as related measures of financial turbulence.[8] The U.S. economy is so interwoven with European and Asian economies that what happens to one country affects the rest of them. Thus world markets go up and down in a correlated fashion, revealing the interlinked uncertainty of investors worldwide.

Economic volatility results from the interactions of competitive strategies. This means that when Japanese companies adopt new technology to improve their productivity, then their competitors in the United States and Western Europe who continue to use old technology would be adversely affected. As their profits fall, the losing firms look for remedies such as tariffs, quotas, and other forms of protectionism. In one form or another, there is retaliation. Even if the tariffs are not enacted, the discussions heighten tensions, which increase economic volatility.

Interactions of this kind were always the case, but in the globally connected economies the effects are amplified. Using post-1980 telecommunications technology, competitive effects are transmitted almost instantly through markets. Meanwhile, the reaction rate of established companies to be more competitive is slow. Bureaucratic organizations, being risk-averse, tend to try things out in bits and pieces. They take far longer to incorporate new production technology than leaner start-up companies. The disparate time rates amplify volatility.

Productivity growth, which had been increasing for 30 years in the United States, began to slow down by 1963. The absolute measure of productivity still went up in value, but by an increasingly smaller amount. The pattern of decelerating growth in productivity was consistent. Year after year, productivity growth slowed down until (in the 1980s) it reached zero and even took on negative values, which meant that absolute productivity was falling. In the early 1990s, productivity growth is sporadic, but on average it is inching along, with relatively small percentage gains for the absolute measure. This is a far cry from the days when U.S. productivity improvements zoomed ahead of the rest of the world's performance.

Productivity can be (and is) measured in many ways, for many purposes. The two main purposes are to find out how labor productivity is faring, and how capital investment is contributing to an increase in the ratio of output over input.[9] No matter how productivity is measured, it should reflect the contribution that technology makes toward increasing output volume and decreasing input costs. For example, technology that reduces defective product increases output volume while decreasing the cost of goods sold. Therefore, when technology improves, it is reasonable to expect that productivity will increase. When technology wears out, productivity falters, as it has in the United States.

Partial Explanations for Productivity Problems

The decline in the growth of U.S. productivity has been the subject of continuous study for over 20 years. In the 1970s, economists tried to explain the 10 years of consistent decline as a hiccup or a burble that would be reversed in the longer view of things. In the 1980s, the anomaly was accepted as fact. (Productivity growth for the United States was expected to average more than 4 percent per year—but the actual growth was less than 1 percent per year.) However, the explanations for the difference between what was expected and what was happening were not accepted.

Researchers have looked for one or two factors that can explain it all. These included the consistent reduction in R&D spending by U.S. companies; the emphasis on military research, which has usurped the most creative scientific minds in the country; the high ratio of the value of the dollar to other major foreign currencies, which meant that doing research inside the United States was more expensive than doing it outside;[10] the shortage of capital for investment in new plant and equipment; and, finally, that the age of equipment in the United States was 10 to 15 years greater than in Japan and some parts of Europe. There is general agreement that such arguments, as cited above, partly explain the situation. There is also agreement that these arguments are not sufficient. What is missing is a unifying theory to explain the causes of pervasive productivity decline.

From 1970 on, the explanations of U.S. productivity decline ranged broadly and consumed many pages of learned journals. There was overall agreement. The continuous reduction in productivity growth could not be explained fully by any of the traditional interpretations of economic behavior. One factor, however, appealed to common sense (which is not always a good criterion)—the age of equipment. Logically, new equipment is more productive than old equipment. However, the age of equipment, by itself, does not provide a sufficient explanation. The next two paragraphs provide illustrations of this statement.

Toyota, Nissan, and Mazda have been able to achieve large gains in productivity with robots. American automakers, using the same robots, experienced small productivity gains at best. In fact, there were numerous examples of productivity decreasing when robots were employed. The best explanation is that new equipment must be used in new ways to be effective. For example, if a computer installation duplicates the existing office or manufacturing routines that involve cumbersome and repetitive paper shuffling, then, at best, only minor improvements can be expected. The computer software may be difficult to master. In many instances, hardware and software bugs can be encountered that take many hours to track and remove. Not unexpectedly, productivity drops.

NUMMI (New United Manufacturing Motors, Inc.) was established as a joint venture by Toyota and General Motors (GM). Each of the partners had different reasons for entering into this relationship. Various sources have attributed GM's participation to interest in observing Toyota's newest plant technology. However, Toyota eschewed the use of high-tech equipment. Without the use of new technology, NUMMI increased the productivity of GM's Fremont, California, plant in a dramatic fashion by using assembly training. The best explanation of these results is that new management methods can be used without new equipment to radically improve productivity. (The NUMMI example is further discussed in Chapters 3 and 6.)

If new equipment is employed in new ways, then an interaction occurs that produces maximum productivity improvement. Analysts expected that a discontinuity prevails between the productivity of "older" equipment and "newer" equipment. This is correct, but only when appropriate changes are made in the management systems that are employed with the new equipment. The age of equipment is only a partial surrogate for the kind of technology that is being employed. The kind of technology influenced the kind of management systems that often, but not always, were being utilized when the "newer" equipment was being employed.

In the same vein, when old equipment interacts with new computer information systems, a hybrid results. Such crossbreeding requires new management methods to blend and balance the capabilities of the combinations. The bureaucracies of established firms inhibit changes in management methods. Therein lies a good part of the mystery of what is causing productivity problems for American manufacturers. Thus, the mystery of how to account for the U.S. slump in productivity growth was hardly likely to stump a Sherlock Holmes. Most economists and business professors do not have sufficient backgrounds in production and operations to catch the clues cited above. Also needed is the Holmesian flair for deduction. As a result, although this should not be so, the same mystery concerning U.S. productivity problems prevails today, as it did 15 years ago.

The Phoenix Phenomenon

The phoenix phenomenon, according to ancient Egyptian mythology, is related to the ability of this regal bird to rise again, after it has been destroyed.[11] The analogy may be faulted, yet it is striking how countries that have been decimated by war can regroup their resources to become viable nations having fully functioning economies. Germany accomplished this after World War I. It became powerful, but not prosperous. Difficult economic conditions led to the rise of Hitler and the onset of World War II.

More recently, the manufacturing capability of industrial countries in Europe and Japan were destroyed during World War II. How does such destruction provide a fertile field for new seeds to germinate and rise again with greater strength? One phoenix (namely, West Germany) rebuilt its industrial plant with the same management systems principles—more or less—in place that had prevailed before the war. The equipment was new. To some extent, the technology was new; but the management style and methods were not new. When the Berlin Wall was torn down, the old equipment of East Germany was merged with the newer equipment of West Germany. The management techniques, cultures and styles of West Germany were inculcated into the combined Germany. The powerful alliance of East and West Germany created a major new global competitor for world markets. But it is also an alliance that demands a great deal of assimilation and adjustment. The assimilation process has been a lot more expensive, difficult, and time-consuming than many had projected when the two Germanys became one.

In contrast, the competitive business standards for the next generation were being set by the Japanese. At first, during their recovery from war devastation, Japanese industry experimented with various combinations of new and old management techniques, cultures, and styles. They adopted new technologies and production methodologies to amplify the effectiveness of those aspects of their management experiments that seemed to work well in the penetration of world markets. Gaining market share was not considered an end in itself.

The Japanese management phoenix homed in on new production techniques that delivered high quality at low costs. Production accomplishments worked hand in glove with marketing fundamentals of competitive success that were well-known, if not developed by, the U.S. marketing community. Namely, it costs more to gain a new customer than to hold on to existing customers. In line with this, bargain prices attract new customers. On the other hand, top quality and superior service are effective strategies for holding on to existing customers.

The United States with its Allies created the potential for the phoenix arisen. Destruction of an industrial system with support for its rebirth (the Marshall Plan in Europe and the MacArthur Commission in Japan[12]) allowed the new and the better to reemerge in the resurrected economy. But all phoenixes do not arise with the same capabilities. In this case, the conditions for innovation favored the growth of Japanese economic power. European rebuilding did not fare badly either.

Harking back to the days when U.S. automakers had full command of their domestic markets, the three major Detroit auto companies permitted their dealers to carry the fledgling Japanese brands of autos. They did so because they perceived no threat from that baby auto industry. What they did not anticipate was a major petroleum crisis. Even when it was at its worst, Detroit assumed that the fuel shortage was a transient affair. Over the course of the decade, it turns out that they were right for a while, and then wrong again. The Japanese cars were small, inexpensive, and fuel-efficient. U.S. sales of large automobiles had fallen. Detroit reasoned that the augmented product line would help their dealers weather the problems of an economic downturn.

If the Japanese automakers had not secured broad distribution in the United States so easily, they would have had a much tougher time penetrating the U.S. market. General Motors, Ford, and Chrysler did not foresee that the Japanese renewal had incorporated the ability to change rapidly as market conditions were altered. The Japanese shifted strategies in keeping with market conditions and always with an acute sense of the importance of maintaining and building customer loyalty.

These events underscore how times have changed. The secure, stable auto market disappeared. Later, after the horse was out of the barn, American auto companies fought for quotas on imports. The quotas carved out a 30 percent share of market for Japanese imports. As volatility increased, and sentiment for tariff protection grew, the Japanese auto companies undertook major investments by building factories in the United States. There was a great deal of complaint that domestic content was low for the new factories, so the Japanese invested in more U.S. plant to increase the domestic content.

One of the root causes of severe economic turmoil is that the technology of the post-Depression 1930s has worn out and the technology of the postwar 1950s is wearing out rapidly. In manufacturing companies all over the world, the model of manufacturing that began in the United States in the 1930s, and continued to develop in the 1950s and 1960s, is being replaced. First, the old equipment had no computer controls. Grandfather computers such as Whirlwind at MIT and Eniac, which preceded Univac, were large, slow, and awkward. It was not until the 1960s that CNC (computer numerical control) machines began to be operational.

Thus, in summary, Japan and Germany received aid for restoration from their status as defeated nations. In their own ways, they both have been revitalized, in keeping with the phoenix rebirth syndrome. In sport terms, they were reinvigorated, and able to play a better game. Meanwhile, the United States, which had long been accustomed to being the winner, failed to use accelerated depreciation to write off old equipment. The United States failed to replace old equipment with new equipment, old systems of management with new systems, and thereby overlooked the learning inspired by the new technologies. This allowed the potential phoenixes to become actual phoenixes.

The rising phoenix could act like a clone of the previous system. It would still have an advantage of youth over age, but it would lack the substitution of new methodology to go along with the new technology. Essentially, the German industrial system has done that. It has utilized the new technologies without revamping the old methodologies. On the other hand, the rising phoenix could reject imitation and copying of the management system that had been employed before—in favor of innovation and improvement of the old model. Essentially, that is what the Japanese industrial system has done. In either case, a phoenix has an advantage over the systems that destroyed it.

Is the Variation Statistically Significant?

Is the amount of volatility really unusually great? What do we mean by volatility and how do we measure it? One thing is certain; there has always been a lot of volatility. The continuous changes, over the decades, in the list of Fortune 500 companies provides ample evidence that "the more things change, the more they stay the same." This famous saying, attributed to Alphonse Karr in the 1800s, meant that change is a constant part of life.[13] In-depth research on how U.S. companies have changed their rankings at different points in the economic cycles that have been recorded over many decades would be illuminating. For example, in 1911 U.S. Steel was the largest company in America. In 1990 USX (the renamed company) announced its interest in divesting itself of the steel business in favor of the energy focus that it developed after acquiring Marathon Oil and other energy companies that account for most of its profits.

The specific aspects of industrial and commercial competition are always changing. Weather provides a useful model. During stable eras, the year-to-year variation is considerable. One January may be warmer than another; some Aprils may be wetter than others. A big blizzard can take place, exceeding all previous records for a March month in Boston. Yet these are expected variations for the time of year and the locale because a great deal of variation is entirely normal. Now, a new question has arisen about global warming attributable to the greenhouse effect. Scientists disagree about whether the weather is fundamentally altered.

Another point of view is that weather cycles through warmer and cooler periods and the same applies to precipitation, and other weather factors. A very long-cycle weather theory relates to the waxing and waning of ice ages, but there isn't much information about events that transpired 25,000 years ago. On an entirely different level, the warning about the greenhouse effect must be viewed as a noncyclical change. This has serious impact for those who get solace from thinking that "nothing has changed, and eventually everything will return to the way it once was." This status quo hypothesis brings comfort to farmers whose crops are dying in a drought; to sailors as becalmed as the Ancient Mariner; even to Detroit's automobile executives. Some of them have always hoped that a logical progression is taking place that will eventually return things to the way they were.

There are no simple measures of volatility, but common sense tells one when the normal vicissitudes of business give way to abnormal situations, and when extreme volatility takes over from business as usual. Change takes place when chaos occurs. Volatility is evident. Many observers agree that the winds of change are blowing. Some think that the recession is severe with gale force destruction. While there may be disagreement about how to classify the situation, there is no doubt about what competitors must do. They must adapt to the situation to be competitive.

Instability and volatility in the 1980s lead to many bankruptcies. Market shifts can be traced to purposeful disruptive behaviors as new businesses seem to change the rules. For example, the Japanese excel at developing improved systems of manufacturing. These new procedures, interacting with global market potentials, have irreversibly altered the previously existing standards. How do established firms react? One response is to form new alliances to precipitate change. These partnerships, which are of many kinds, including joint ventures, will be discussed in Chapter 6.

During unstable or volatile eras, competitive changes occur so fast that tracking is bewildering. The question is: Will things eventually return to the way they were? While the turmoil appears to be special, we do not know about any statistical analyses to support this contention. A rational numerical argument would not be hard to develop, however. For example, if the number of jobs lost in manufacturing from 1980 to 1990 was compared to such jobs lost in any other decade, the adjusted results would take us back to the 1930s. A similar comparison for financial service jobs might be without precedent. Also, there are a variety of indirect measures to cite. For example, a survey conducted after the market plunge of October 19, 1987, found that employees of companies (world-wide, but especially in the United States) contended that their situations had deteriorated markedly. [14] Almost exactly two years later, economists agreed that the United States had entered into a recession.

Recessions are not either–or, like lost or found. Instead, there are many shades of gray at work. Whether a recession exists, or does not exist, is simply a matter of definition. The signal that a recession has begun depends upon a convention determined by economists, who are in charge of such signals. Whatever we call it, the data support the fact that the United States has been experiencing a deteriorating economic situation for over 25 years. It would be nice to be able to show, with statistical significance, that the variation levels of volatility are abnormally high, but common sense will have to do. Yet, common sense cannot provide the historical perspective of decades concerning whether the pattern is part of a cycle that takes many years to run its course.

EXCUSES VERSUS CAUSES

Have we caused our own pervasive problems? Is this a failure of management, which some like to describe with the words of Pogo, who said: "We have met the enemy, and they is us."[15] Is this a failure of workers who some say are not competent, and others say are motivated only by paychecks? Is this a failure of national purpose, the educational system, or law enforcement? Is the competitive problem caused by a drug culture in the United States, unfair foreign subsidization (the playing field is not flat), dumping, adversarial union-management relations, or all of the above and more?

The answer we propose is that we have not caused our own problems. An external system of events has caused the problems, but this is not to say that we have reacted in the best possible way to the situation. The external system of causes includes the fact that technological wearout is an inevitable life cycle occurrence. Those competitors that enjoy a phoenix rebirth have the upper hand with respect to the competitive power of the replacement technology they will use.

Stockholders, investment bankers, workers and union leaders, government leaders and their economic advisors, and even managers (who should know better) ask, "What are we doing wrong?" The inability to steer the ship of business is as much a mystery as the subject of global warming. What causes it and what should be done about it? Is the poor performance the fault of top management? If so, why are the top executives of so many companies failing to run their companies in such great numbers?

The question "What are we doing wrong?" implies that you brought the situation on yourself. It is our contention that this is not so. External factors changed, and none of these managers could change them back.

If doing wrong means not correcting the environment, then management is not to blame. But if doing wrong means not adapting to environmental changes, then management deserves some blame.

Each manager thinks in terms of his or her own company's problems and thereby believes that it is his or her fault that "things" have gone awry. They also blame other managers in the company, the state of the economy, unfair competition, blundering governmental rules, unions, incompetent and unmotivated workers. Such obvious explanations that place blame elsewhere are preferred to a personal guilt trip. Consequently, it is not unusual to fault management in a class action while avoiding personal opprobrium.

Calling on the innovation literature, there is the pathology of successful companies; namely, the inability to follow new paths that require phasing out those strategies for product designs and processes that once were the key to success. To some it seems that only the arrogance borne of once having it all could account for such adamant resistance to change. Without invective, it is the power of status quo that is an organizational equivalent of mechanical inertia. Large, established, and once highly successful companies seem to be most prone to the inability to leave the sinking ship.

While all of these explanations are correct, in one sense or another, the best hypothesis of the cause of competitive failure is technological wearout. Whichever theory of cycles is preferred, and there are many of them, the idea that periodicity prevails in determining economic conditions has been broadly accepted by managers, economists, and government agencies. The major disputes revolve around the length of the cycles, how constant that length might be, how regular the phases of the cycles are, and what drives them.

KONDRATIEFF'S LONG-WAVE HYPOTHESIS

Some cycles are accepted as a fact of life. Natural cycles, such as the tides and the phases of the moon, are indisputable. Biological cycles are evident, although many of them, such as the impact of circadian rhythms, remain a matter of conjecture. Business cycles are even more speculative, partly because they are so difficult to define and measure. Even those who are true believers and adherents of cycle theories generally agree that economic cycles are of variable length, strength, and severity.

Various short business cycles have been experienced by industry. One of the shortest is related to annual seasonality. For example, farmers live by the planting-to-harvest cycles. In turn, food producers are tied into the timing of the harvest by the need to start canning or freezing their produce. Global sourcing of harvests (following summer, north and south around the globe) with refrigerated ships, planes, and trucks has altered the cycle-dependencies of food producers. This example shows how simple it is to demonstrate that technology can alter agricultural cycles. Another example would be hydroponic and greenhouse farming. Nevertheless, most farmers are still dependent on the seasons. And, just as salmon fishermen on the Colorado River must wait for the spawning run, the managers of industry know of no alternative but to wait for business cycles to run their course.

There are 3- to 4-year cycles, usually called Kitchin cycles. These are too short to reflect decisions about major changes in production processes that involve significant capital investments. The medium-wave, 10-year Juglar cycle is not as well-known as the Kuznets cycle, which spans 15 to 25 years. Neither of these cycles encompasses sufficient time to be identified with a complete capital improvement investment cycle. Major shifts in capital investment follow longer periods, which are related to the length of time it takes to bring about significant changes in the technology of production processes.

The 45- to 60-year long-wave Kondratieff cycle allows enough time. Roughly, it is divided as follows. The cycle begins with investment in plant and equipment based on new technology. Because this investment pays off, it is followed by more and more capital clamoring for the same type of investment. The investment stage takes 30 or 40 years to reach a peak. Eventually, these investments become excessive, and they start to lose money. Thus, after the peak, there is an investment plateau of about 10 years. This is followed by a recession or depression, which lasts another 10 years, and then the cycle begins again to climb to the next peak.

The names of these cycles are associated with the people who identified them. All are hypothetical and there is a fair degree of mistrust about them. Part of the reason for skepticism is that they do not occur with the precision and regularity of the seasons. The advantage of thinking in terms of cycles is that they remove the belief that economic situations are entirely unique. If it is to be of any use, history must live up to the saying that it repeats itself.

Without awareness of cycles and periodicity, forecasters tend to project a continuation of existing trends (up or down). This always extends the prevailing pattern, but trends do not go on forever. The most important information about how an economic system will behave in the future is related to its "turning points." These are the points at which something that has been going up starts to come down, and vice versa. The knowledge of what causes long waves is so valuable that it is worth speculating about. As another way of looking at what needs to be known, we can ask: What causes these widely spaced turning points? To have the wisdom to use long-wave cycles for predictions of what the future holds, you have to have vision that spans the turning points that marked the start of a new wave and the end of that wave (say, on average, a 50-year period). It helps to have lived long enough to have seen the beginning and the end of the last wave. Then the beginning of the next wave might be recognized for what it is.

Applied to business conditions, turning points call attention to the rhythm with which causes and effects are predisposed to wax and wane. Cycle theorists tend to look at the periodicities of recessions, inflation, trade imbalances, and so on. There is ample evidence that all such cycles are variable in their lengths, strengths, and periodicities. The driving forces behind these cycles are different and variously explained. The attributed causes range from the buildup and depletion of inventory levels as they shift from overstock to out-of-stock, real estate swings from a renter's market to a landlord's paradise and back, changes in the availability of investment funds, interest rate movements, unemployment cycles, and stock market oscillations.

To find the probable turning point for the beginning of the regrowth of the U.S. economy, we would add about 20 years. This would fix 1994 as the start of the new technological era. Figure 2.1 illustrates some important turning points (real and hypothetical) for the U.S. economy over a period of 250 years.

Having presented this figure does not mean that we accept Kondratieff's hypotheses. It also doesn't mean that we reject them. It seems imperative to clearly state the case as we see it. Specifically, it doesn't matter whether Kondratieff was entirely right, partially right, or basically wrong about the regularity of the long wave. The idea that this text supports is that technological wearout and replacement moves in cycles of irregular length and severity. All technology is going through life cycling. Technological developments are interrelated so that a kind of resonance is built up over time, whereby many small waves of associated technologies get in sync to create larger waves. Also, the idea that we are at present going through some major episodes of turbulence caused by intense technological change makes sense.

One of the most important adherents of long-wave cycles was the so-called father of cycle theory, Wesley C. Mitchell (1874–1948). Mitchell, who was the director of the National Bureau of Economic Research,

Figure 2.1
The Kondratieff Long Wave, 1780–2000
(Based on his Composite Measure of World Business Conditions to 1920)

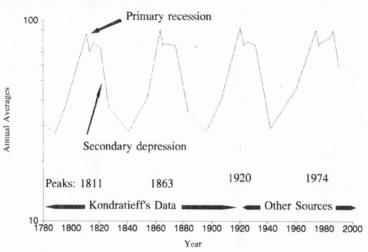

started developing a chronology of business cycles in the 1920s. He separated long-wave cycles into the two phases of expansion and contraction. Arthur F. Burns, who was a student of Mitchell's, continued his work through the 1940s. Geoffrey H. Moore, who is the director of the Columbia Business School Center for International Business Cycle Research, has been working on cycle theory since the 1940s. For over 50 years he has contributed to the chronology for cycle analysis, which exists on a monthly basis from December 1854.[16]

Joseph Schumpeter, the renowned Harvard economist, published his classic, two-volume study of cycles in 1939. Schumpeter noted that substantial investment occurred after the invention of the cotton gin (1793);[17] during the expansion of the railroads (1840–90), and starting with mass production of automobiles (Ford Motor Company, 1903). Each expansion produced a period of prosperity followed by economic depression. Thus Schumpeter inferred that long-wave cycles were caused by the beginning and end of changes in important technological characteristics of economic systems.

In any erudite discussion of cycles, there is a great deal of controversy about the long-wave cycle described by Kondratieff.[18] His studies, which were concentrated on capitalist economies, found the 45- to 60-year cycle, described above. Communist theorists held that capitalist economies were headed for extinction. Proof of cycles contradicted this hypothesis. They implied that the capitalistic system was capable of self-correction and rejuvenation. True, for every cycle at first things went from good to bad; but then they renewed themselves, going from bad to good again. Kondratieff was banished.

The Russian economists weren't the only ones who disapproved of Kondratieff's long-wave cycle. U.S. and European economists, basing their ideas on the work of John Maynard Keynes, believed that they had identified the factors that drive economic systems. Since these drivers were relatively short-term, long-wave cycles were anathema. Thus, as Julian Snyder wrote:

In both socialistic and capitalistic countries, the idea began to grow that an all-powerful central economic authority with capacities for (1) unlimited creation of money, (2) wage and price controls, (3) credit allocation, (4) targeted planning, such as the Soviet five-year plans, and (5) development of "fine tuning" techniques . . ., could complete man's mastery over economic affairs. . . .[19]

Long-wave notions did not enhance the concept of a powerful central economic authority.

The outright rejection of all aspects of long-wave economic cycles seems to be purposeless. There is no reason to believe that means for controlling the performance of economic systems cannot affect, and be affected by, the periodicity and severity of cycles. Gradually, the rejection of long waves has ameliorated over time. Acceptance of long-wave cycles might further accelerate now, since the revision of Soviet economics to many capitalistic ideas. In turn, dogmatism in cycle theory is not reasonable. It is essential that cycle theorists embody flexibilities of many kinds in their views of cycle regularities.

Kondratieff's studies were limited by the earliest periods for which data were available in France, Germany, Great Britain, and the United States. The general span covered is the 140 years from 1780 to 1920. He described the long-wave cycle for the average level of commodity prices as varying from 47 to 60 years in length. Kondratieff also studied interest rates on national bonds, nominal wages (cotton and agriculture), foreign trade turnover, production and consumption of coal, production of pig iron and lead, and private savings.

Kondratieff did not believe that the long cycle is as regular as clockwork, or that it is essentially independent of other forces. He saw the variability in cycle lengths reflecting the effects of many intervening events, and, in particular, wars and political events. He found that long cycles for the various factors tended to coincide in time, across countries and factor series, but, as with cycle lengths, not without reflecting national circumstances.

TECHNOLOGICAL CHANGE AS THE CAUSE OF ECONOMIC TURMOIL

Many economists and systems analysts who have studied global economies agree that technological changes create long-wave cycles. For example, Jay W. Forrester, Germeshausen Professor at MIT's Sloan School, using the Systems Dynamics simulation approach that he developed for analyzing industries, found substantial evidence that a long wave exists which is driven by technological change. The results were obtained from his System Dynamics National Model which is built up from policies used in 15 major sectors of the U.S. industrial economy.

In 1978 Forrester wrote:

I believe that we are at the top of a long-wave peak. If so, we are nearing the end of a technological era. Our present technology is mature. Since 1960 there has not been a major, radically new, commercially successful technological innovation comparable to aircraft, television, nylon, antibiotics, computers, or solid-state electronics. The things that are truly new do not fit into the present technological infrastructure; they must wait until the next great technological change.[20]

Kondratieff concluded that the cycles are related to "profound changes in the technique of production . . . preceded by significant technical inventions." Kondratieff said about the start-up of the wave: "It is clear . . . that the rising wave of a long cycle is associated with the replacement and expansion of basic capital goods, and with the radical regrouping of, and changes in, society's productive forces." He concluded: "one can find reasons why it cannot continue indefinitely, and why, at the expiration of a certain period, its turning point inevitably comes, and a downward wave sets in."[21]

Many others who have studied the long-wave effect generally agree that it can be attributed to major technological changes. Specifically, these long-wave economic cycles are attributed to the wearing out and replacement of major bundles of technology. Forrester explains in a remarkably concise way why it is tenable to consider that a long wave exists:

The long wave appears to depend on production methods that use capital equipment, on the life of capital equipment and buildings, on the slowness of moving people from one part of the economy to another, and on how far ahead people plan and the length of their memories of past economic disasters—both of which are substantially deter-

mined by the length of a human lifetime. None of these factors which give rise to the
long wave depends substantially on faster communications or details of technological
change. The policies and industrial structure that generate the long-wave capital-con-
struction cycle have changed very little since 1800.[22]

Dr. W. W. Rostow, former economic advisor to Presidents Kennedy
and Johnson, accepted Kondratieff's hypotheses concerning technological change as a means for identifying the economic performance of
industrial countries. Dr. Bruce Merrifield, a former assistant secretary
of the U.S. Department of Commerce, heading that department's Office
of Technology under President Reagan, stated that the department's
statistics supported the conclusion that a Kondratieff wave was at different
end stages in various parts of the world. He added that the United States
seemed to be further along in the process of replacing old technology
than was Europe.[23]

Major Technological Discontinuity

Peter Drucker talks about an age of discontinuity.[24] Forrester refers
to a time of technological discontinuity. Kondratieff's work called attention to the possibility that technological change over time may not be a
smooth process, with occasional minor distortions occurring. Instead,
minor forms of discrete and diverse technological changes—with new
technology replacing worn-out technology—come together, amplifying
each other in combination, until a major force, of unexpected power, is
unleashed.

The model that comes to mind is that of a river, fed by its many
tributaries. To understand how and why a river floods, it is necessary to
understand that the total river system is comprised of many interdependent waterways that are influenced by many of the same factors. For
example, heavy rains and melting snows are likely to cause many, but
not all, of the tributaries to experience high water levels. Rainfall levels
have one cycle, early spring heat waves to melt the snow on the mountain
tops follow another cycle. When the cycle peaks occur at the same time
(known as syzygy), the largest river overflows its banks with major
flooding.

Using a 54-year period, the years when major expansion reached a
peak were 1812, 1866, and 1920. Projecting backward would result in
the inclusion of 1758 in the series. Forward projection gives us 1974. It
should be noted that the series of years goes from peak to peak, and,
therefore, the troughs are roughly in the middle of each span of time. If

we assume that a 10-year plateau follows the peak, then recessions (also of about 10 years) would begin and end with the following years:

Begin	1768	1822	1876	1930	1984
End	1778	1832	1886	1940	1994

The actual dates of major depressions are the 1830s, 1890s, and 1930s. Taking into consideration the variabilities of cycle lengths, there is some semblance of a meaningful pattern.

Putting this into the context of Kondratieff's hypothetical long-wave model, there is reason to believe that the U.S. economy has completed the capital expansion and plateau stages of the long wave. Technological discontinuity has occurred. The economy is already well along into a major downturn. Meanwhile, the seeds are already planted and germinating for the next 30 years of investments in replacement technologies. The countries associated with the phoenix phenomenon are well along in the development of the new technologies. The United States must be prepared to play catch-up. Before it can do this successfully, the nature of the replacement technologies must be understood. It is hoped that Chapters 3 and 4 will help explain them.

The Nature of New Technologies

What kinds of technological changes are now occurring? How will they affect the way that people will live in the future? Alternatively, which of the old technologies are wearing out? By technological wearout, we mean that further capital investment in that technology is very unlikely to be profitable. How does the wearing out of technology affect the competitiveness of existing industries?

Kondratieff identified many of the important technological changes that characterized the 140 years that he studied (1780–1920). It is no surprise that many of the inventions he cites relate to applications of electricity and steam that are hardly thought about any more—although they fundamentally and irreversibly altered basic patterns of the way people live. To assure perspective, it is useful to understand a bit of the historical background.

The Long Wave, 1758–1812. James Watt (1736–1819) perfected the older Newcomen engine. Patented in 1769, the steam engine was first put into practical use in 1776. Its first commercial success occurred in 1785, which ushered in an entirely new era of transportation. Steamships and railroads began to move people and materials with speeds and reliabilities never before available. The most publicized technological discontinuity, called the (first) Industrial Revolution, began around 1775.

The Long Wave, 1812–1866. Michael Faraday (1791–1867) discovered electromagnetic induction, formulated the laws of electrolysis, and developed the first dynamo after he was employed by Sir Humphrey Davy in 1812. His work led to the generation of electricity and the design and application of electric motors. This was also an era in which steel and rubber were produced in volume by major corporations. The system of railroads was being built, with transcontinental connections being forged in 1869. Some say that a second Industrial Revolution began after the depression of 1830. In any case, it seems appropriate to note that technological discontinuity has appeared again in this period.

The Long Wave, 1866–1920. Starting at the turn of the twentieth century, Frederick W. Taylor (1856–1915) was the outspoken father of Scientific Management. His rationalization of the production process set in motion forces that have still not run their course. Taylor's work set the stage for Henry Ford (1863–1947), who in 1914 combined many technology developments in his Ford Motor automobile assembly plant. The Model-T Ford became a symbol of U.S. industrial strength. Ford's work emphasized the interdependencies of technology that he carried into manufacturing methods. It might be stated that after the Depression of 1890, a third Industrial Revolution began.

The Long Wave, 1920–1974. As the era gets closer to our present time, it gets increasingly difficult to pick out the highlights. It is tough talking about the characteristics of the immediately preceding economic cycle. Computers, jet aircraft, space feats, telecommunication satellites, and television might be cited as important inventions. To choose the names of the critically important people seems even more difficult to do at this point in time.

The Long Wave, 1974–2028. If we follow the pattern as set above, then the next long wave would be 1974–2028. One-third of it is already finished. What does seem quite clear is that the next wave will replace two kinds of technologies. First, old manufacturing equipment is obsoleted by the existence of computer controls that can instruct the machines as to what to do and how to do it. Second, old management methods have been obsoleted by the new manufacturing methods.

We are about to consider the two kinds of technological change that began coming into play in the 1980s. Using the rule of thumb that some entrepreneurs employ when evaluating the best time to invest in just-born technology, we should allow between 25 and 30 years. That takes us to 2005 or maybe 2010 for the solid part of the growth curve.

NOTES

1. Spoken by Sly Thomas in Nicos Kazantzakis, *The Last Temptation of Christ*, (New York: Simon & Schuster, 1960). Appropriately, the quote was brought to our attention by a book entitled *Cycles: What They Are, What They Mean, How to Profit by Them*, by Dick A. Stoken (New York: McGraw-Hill, 1978).

2. "Special" is meant to connote that present economic conditions fall outside of the stable system of variation that characterized past economic conditions.

3. Zenith Radio is a famous case developed by the Harvard Business School. The case shows how the managers of Zenith Radio did a thorough and careful competitive analysis of the TV industry in the 1960s. All of the major domestic brands were included (e.g., RCA, GE, Admiral) but foreign companies, such as Sony, were not mentioned. They were not even perceived as competitors.

4. The Commission chaired by John A. Young, CEO of Hewlett-Packard, produced the report, entitled *Global Competition: The New Reality*, for President Ronald Reagan. The report was published in January 1985 by the U.S. Government Printing Office.

5. The State of Tennessee has been very successful in attracting Japanese manufacturing industry with tax benefits and additional training funds. See Appendix A, "Japanese Managerial Practices in the United States—Alliances for Quality."

6. Operations research (OR) and management science had played an important military role during World War II. They had been used to rationalize military logistics for problems of inventory management, resource allocation, capacity planning, and maintenance policies. In the early 1950s, the practitioners of these quantitative decision sciences moved out of military commands into industry.

7. A notable example is the 500-point plunge in the Dow that occurred in October 1987.

8. At the end of October 1990, Philips N.V., the electronics giant based in the Netherlands, announced it would slash 45,000 jobs (16 percent of its work force) in a program to bolster profits and improve competitiveness. The annual dividend will be skipped. This certainly runs counter to the glowing expectations for the coming together of the European Economic Community, and the expected profitability of major firms after 1992.

9. As labor costs play an ever-smaller role in the costs of goods sold, the impact of labor productivity changes will become inconsequential. This same effect is driving a major change in the accounting methods used to determine overhead costs and profitability of various items in the company's product line.

10. In later years, the currency ratios were totally reversed so that it became cheaper to do things in the States than abroad. The reversal had no apparent effect on improving productivity growth.

11. The phoenix, according to Egyptian and Greek mythology, is a miraculous bird with a life span of 500 years. It builds a funeral pyre and dies in the flames, but then a new phoenix arises from the ashes. The 500 years is a truly long cycle—far longer than the Kondratieff long wave, which is about 10 percent as long.

12. The story of support for the recovery of the Japanese economy includes the assistance of engineers from Western Electric, which was the manufacturing arm of AT&T. The details have been well documented by Kenneth Hopper in several articles.

13. This saying as originally written in French was "plus ça change, plus c'est la même chose." We will make use of this aphorism again in Chapter 4.

14. From a survey of MBAs conducted by the Center for Operations, Columbia Business School, 1989.

15. Pogo was a famous cartoon character created by Walt Kelly, who parodied human failings through his animal characters. Pogo books are still very popular because they successfully satirize the human condition.

16. Philip A. Klein, ed., *Analyzing Modern Business Cycles*, Essays Honoring Geoffrey H. Moore (London: M. E. Sharpe, 1990).

17. The cotton gin (invented in 1793 by Eli Whitney) separated the cotton from the seeds. It created a period of prosperity in the Southeastern United States.

18. One of the more recent translations of Kondratieff's original work was published in 1984: Nikolai Dmitrievich Kondratieff, *The Long Wave Cycle*, translated by Guy Daniels, introduction by Julian M. Snyder (New York: Richardson & Snyder, 1984). Between 1922 and 1928, Kondratieff published various papers dealing with long economic cycles. The most fundamental was published in the journal *Voprosy Konyunktury* (Problems of Economic Conditions) 1, no. 1 (1925).

19. From the introduction to Kondratieff, *The Long Wave Cycle*, pp. 2–3.

20. Jay W. Forrester, "Changing Economic Patterns," *Technology Review*, August/September 1978, pp. 52–53.

21. Kondratieff, *The Long Wave Cycle*, pp. 94–95.

22. Forrester, p. 50.

23. From a speech delivered in 1986 by Dr. Bruce Merrifield, who was then assistant secretary of Commerce for the U.S. Department of Commerce, at a conference sponsored by the U.S. Department of Labor in Washington, D.C.

24. This book by Peter F. Drucker, *The Age of Discontinuity* (New York: Harper & Row, 1969), captured the elements of turmoil created by technological discontinuity, well before economists began to sense that something was amiss.

PART II

EFFECTS

Part II consists of Chapters 3 and 4. We will discuss the effects of special economic turmoil on the competitiveness of existing technologies, and on the adaptability of traditional management systems. Especially important, in this regard, are the effects of rapid and intense technological change on the competitive status of manufacturing processes (Chapter 3). Similarly important are the effects of swift and potent technological change on the methods and strategies for the management of organizations (Chapter 4).

CHAPTER 3 _____

Changes in Manufacturing Technology

There will never be a robot.
> Well-known American Science Writer (1927)

The Americans have need of the telephone, but we do not. We have plenty of messenger boys.
> Chief Engineer of the British Post Office (1876)

While theoretically and technically television may be feasible, commercially and financially (it is) an impossibility.
> Famous American Inventor (1926)

THE NEXT WAVE IN MANUFACTURING TECHNOLOGY

It may help to start with a question as follows: During the past decade, what old technologies are disappearing and what new technologies are starting up? The tendency to look for specific product or process innovations, such as computer numerical control machines might be misleading. We are looking for a broader viewpoint. The same kind of comment is appropriate for cutting-edge technological changes that stem from expanding chip memories and increasingly powerful software for flexible manufacturing systems. We are looking for the generalizations that include the details, a classification that subsumes a variety of computer-related changes in technology.

After studying hundreds of responses to our manufacturing surveys,[1] and discussions with companies, we conclude that two major classes of technology are undergoing significant change: (1) manufacturing technology (new machines and networks of machines), and (2) management technology (new ways of organizing the networks of people and machines). It is important to note that these two kinds of changes are interrelated. The first kind of technology change brings computers, machines for manufacturing, and machine operators together so that these components interact with each other. The whole behaves as more than the sum of its parts.

A change in management technology is necessary because traditional organizational forms of management established in the mid-1900s do not provide appropriate support for the new kinds of manufacturing systems developed after the mid-1980s. There may be some skepticism about treating management as a technology. Yet there is plenty of precedent for doing so. In the history of technology, management method and style have often been treated as implementational forms of technology. There is also a logical appeal to this approach. Managing the use of new equipment determines how this equipment will function. Poor repair and maintenance policies, for example, can sideline the new technology, reduce its impact, and destroy its effectiveness.

There is also considerable empirical evidence that successful global competitors treat the management of their production systems as a technology. Different performance flows from a competitive model based on the management of technology than from a competitive model based on the application of hierarchical power. Competitiveness would be improved if this point of view was widely adopted and consistently applied. The organization of business functions to achieve competitive goals is a fundamental part of management technology. New manufacturing technology cannot be used without changes in management technology.

Delving a little deeper into the pair of technological changes, we can rewrite these two points as follows: (1) changes in manufacturing technology—the use of information networks by people and computer-driven equipment (the subject of Chapter 3); (2) changes in management technology—the management of manufacturing technology, which focuses on blending the production process with human systems and procedures (the subject of Chapter 4).

To adapt to the future, both technologies are undergoing changes of considerable magnitude. It may seem peculiar to call management a technology. Inadvertently, technology has been associated only with the physical aspects of equipment. However, in its word derivation, "techno" is a combining form meaning "art, skill, and craft." The methods of scientific management pioneered by Frederick W. Taylor have often been listed as a technological advance. In any case, we treat the systematic body of knowledge for managing as a technology that is changing.

HOW MUCH HAS MANUFACTURING TECHNOLOGY CHANGED?

If this were a science fiction book we might have begun it with a prediction of the future:

In the 1940s, nobody could have guessed how much manufacturing technology would change by 1990. Using robots, 1990 factories doubled output—with half as many blue-collar workers—to match growth in consumer demand fueled by sharply lower costs and higher quality. Customers in 1990 dial the production process directly on their computerized telephones to set down their design specifications for the particular varieties of the company's products that they desire to purchase. Smart customers interact with smart factories to help design the goods and services that they want.

This is not a science fiction book, and "truth is seldom stranger than fiction." The idea that customers can use computers to interact directly with the production process was suggested by the Chrysler Corporation in the 1960s. It was more than an advertisement but less than a reality. The 1960s were a period when the "On-rush of Automation" was a cover story in *Time* magazine. A 1956 issue of the *Westinghouse Engineer* published an article describing a factory to automate the design of power transformers.[2] Most of the automation plans of the 1960s never made it. The point is that technological speculations can take many years to be translated into some form of reality.

It is surprising how little manufacturing technology has changed since 1940 in many parts of the United States and Western Europe. While computers are evident everywhere, they are not an integrated part of the production system. Robots are far scarcer in U.S. factories than had been predicted just five years ago. The expectation that new manufacturing equipment would decrease costs and increase demand came true on a global scale. But in the United States, total production output has remained fairly constant. The global market shares of various U.S. industries have decreased substantially. Many specific U.S. industries have experienced declines in domestic demand, as well.

For example, American demand for steel in 1985 was 107 million metric tons. In 1990 it was 83 million metric tons. Steel companies from all over the world compete fiercely for the shrinking U.S. domestic market. American mills have downsized and streamlined, but they are not producers in the vanguard of the newest cost-reducing, high-quality, technology. In general, costs of scrap metal and energy continue to rise. So the prospects for U.S. steel companies investing in new steel-making technology is nil without some kind of industrial policy to support such investment. And it is not at all clear whether such a policy would work. It might keep pace with the existing competition, but what about the competition that is yet to come?

As another example of declines in domestic demand, major U.S. automakers have closed many plants and significantly decreased output. The number of blue-collar workers continues to decline, but costs of production steadily climb higher. Quality of U.S. producers has improved, but global competitors set ever-higher quality standards. The new-wave goal of many firms to produce high-variety outputs in small lots remains elusive. Turmoil in the design of manufacturing processes shows no sign of abating in the immediate future. New computer capabilities are announced daily. Timing the decision to move from old to new technology is constantly going on.

A great number of large companies have some areas in their plants that are technologically advanced. Behind such showcase areas, many companies hide 70–80 percent of the plant's antiquated technology. It is remarkable to watch automated guidance vehicles (AGVs) move a car chassis from one welding robot station to another. They do away with the awkward constraints of conveyor belts. But the technology in the majority of U.S. assembly plants is an unbalanced mixture of the old and the new. Behind the showcase areas of the plant, there are paced conveyor belts that set the tempo for production output. JIT and kanban developments in the technology of management systems (see Chapter 4) have been obsoleting conveyors. Batch systems, which are described later, generally use forklift trucks to move work from place to place. In terms of floor space and investment, the old areas tend to predominate by a substantial margin. As far as achieving the production goal of smooth and continuous throughput, the old and the new eras of technology are almost never well-coordinated.

How can it be true that so little change has occurred in U.S. industry since computer technology is rich and abundant. It can be seen in plants and offices all over the country. It is fair to conjecture that there may not be a single factory in the United States where some form of computer-assisted machinery cannot be found. The answer is that computers bring about change only if they alter the way that work is done. Most manufacturing systems in the United States and Western Europe have not changed the way they work as a result of using computers. Instead, they have used computers to do what they did before in other ways. Thus, production processes have been only peripherally involved with computers. For example, computers may calculate machine settings more quickly than the workers can do it. But if the computer calculations follow the same procedures as the manual ones that were used before the computers, then the old systems are still in use.

The technologies that are wearing out include old machines that cannot produce to specifications. They also include machines that follow the old, manual procedures. However, the new technologies that are replacing the old ones are not simply new machines that can produce to specifications because their gears, cams, and bearings are not worn down. The new technologies reflect profound differences in manufacturing processes. Some examples are: (1) machines with linked computers that are responsible for changing them over from one job to another; (2) systems where machines communicate with each other through their computers to change process rates with the goal of minimizing work in process.

LEARNING TO MANUFACTURE

The number of industrial leaders who say that the United States must learn to manufacture is impressive. We will list just a few. Dr. W. Edwards Deming, educator, consultant, and author, is credited by the Japanese for helping them achieve their manufacturing success. Dr. Lester Thurow, dean of MIT's Sloan School, has set manufacturing revitalization as one of his school's major objectives. It should be noted that most business schools in America are hopelessly seduced by finance. Tom Peters, consultant and much-published author, has appeared regularly as a TV columnist. His emphasis tends to be on how to accomplish the changes in management technology (see Chapter 4) that must be achieved. John A. Young, president and CEO of Hewlett-Packard and chairman of the President's Commission on Industrial Competitiveness, tends to concentrate on industrial policies that will help U.S. industries become globally competitive. Each of these people have their own agendas. They share the same common objective, which is to revitalize U.S. industry.[3]

This sample of leading thought does not employ the notion of a new wave of technology sweeping like a storm across the existing establishment. Instead, it accents failure to continue to perform in a way that had been successful. As a result, the focus tends to be on slippage. The suggested remedy: play the game as well as you used to play it. According to this point of view, the competitive edge could be regained if management would work at restoring the competitive manufacturing situation that it once enjoyed.

The literature on competitiveness keeps stressing a host of "re-words," such as restoring, regaining, revitalizing, reawakening, renewal, revival, recapturing, and even renaissance (which means rebirth). The issue behind the re-words raises such questions as: Why is it that we once seemed to know how to manufacture, but now we no longer know how? Did we forget how to make great products? What has gone wrong and what should we do about it?

Our answer is: Managers in the United States and Western Europe may be able to alleviate, but they cannot solve their economic problems by going back to the way things were. The wheel of technological change does not roll backwards. Perhaps 20 percent of the competitive problem is management slippage—that is, not being able to do the job as well as they used to do it. This leaves 80 percent of the problem attributable to the fact that the competitors do things better than they were ever done before. If and when management regains and surpasses the 20 percent slippage, they still cannot play a winning game. Going back to basics is a nonsolution for the present situation.

The blueprint for success in the future will be drawn around invention and innovation. New ideas, not old recycled ones, are required to move ahead. Perhaps it is unfair to criticize the use of re-words. Some of them, like renovation and renaissance, could be interpreted to mean that invention and innovation are the important goals. The management of technology that worked in the 1950s stopped working because times changed. The essence of the problem was the fact that management did not adapt to these changes.

Waiting for the wheel to turn so that things would go back to the way they were was not logical. Cycles do not work that way. While the fundamental parameters of technological change—wearout → invention → replacement—are cycling, the particulars of the technology, such as steam engines to diesel engines, propeller planes to jets, batch production methods to flexible manufacturing systems, are continuously advancing.

How technological change causes economic systems to cycle through stages of peaks, plateaus, and recessions is a subject about which economists like to argue. Engineers, on the other hand, like to talk about the technological changes that cause the economic stages. Because 50–60 years separate similar economic events, it is understandable that young managers might conclude that what is happening to their firms has never happened before. Without the long-view perspective, there is an understandable tendency to think that unique conditions have been encountered.

Without knowing that there is a precedent, it may seem that things have never been so bad before. Being in possession of the long-range perspective enables managers to see crises for what they are.

Knowledge preexists that can help managers do what is best for the company. Thinking in terms of cycles should not be confused with waiting for the good times to return. Choosing strategies that are appropriate for the cycle stage is far more powerful than supporting the status quo while waiting for the good times to return. There are great penalties to pay for supporting the status quo in a period of technological turbulence. General Motors, in launching its new Saturn auto, advertises "It's amazing what you can do, if you are willing to start all over again." The Saturn auto plant in Tennessee lives up to this claim. It is a plant dedicated to new manufacturing and management technology. Nevertheless, it has experienced start-up problems that are attributable to the difficulty of shedding old management technology when using new manufacturing technology.

BATCH PRODUCTION SYSTEMS

When bureaucratic organizations support old manufacturing technology, batch production systems are the first to come to mind. In the United States, the predominant production method was, and continues to be, manufacture in batches. Does the advice regarding getting back to basics mean going back to batch production systems? This would mean eschewing advances into flexible manufacturing systems. Surely, that is not what is intended.

Advanced manufacturing technology is so recent that the timing for its adoption is at issue. Talking about competitive restoration implies relearning what we never knew. The United States was a master of what will someday be called "primitive" job shop production techniques. Perhaps "primitive" is too strong a term. Some managers will feel more comfortable if we called these techniques "unsophisticated." But 20 years from now, any form of noncomputerized manufacturing technology is likely to be called "archaic." With that notion is mind, can we settle on "obsolete" to describe the present situation?

Job shop production is the method of manufacturing in batches. Thomas Jefferson wrote a letter in 1798 to Governor James Monroe of Virginia describing Eli Whitney's gun factory in Connecticut, as follows: "Mr. Whitney has invented moulds and machines for making all the pieces of his locks so exactly equal, that take 100 locks to pieces and mingle their parts and the 100 locks may be put together as well by taking the first pieces which come to hand."[4]

How Defectives Are Produced by Batch Production Systems

There are serious quality problems associated with batch production. Because American manufacturing systems have always been primarily involved with batch production, American managers have developed an attitude in which some defectives are considered normal. We can best explain this by an example. Say that 100 pencils are to be produced by batch production. This means that a box of 100 pencil blanks (wooden cylinders with leads inserted) is moved from place to place on the plant floor.

To begin, the box of 100 pencils is moved to a machine that attaches the metal grommet onto the end of each pencil. Because of usual problems in setting up the grommet machine, say that two pencils are crushed. The box, now containing 98 pencils, is moved to the next workstation, where erasers are inserted into the grommets. Say that one of the erasers is too large and the grommet is crushed trying to insert it. This leaves 97 pencils. As a final step in this hypothetical example, the name of the pencil and the grade are to be stamped onto the side of each pencil. At this workstation, the stamping pressure is excessive at first and two pencils are split during this operation. As a result, only 95 pencils are completed according to specs. Since the order calls for 100 pencils, it would have been smarter to start with 105 blanks.

The batch production process is used by 70 to 80 percent of all manufacturing operations in the United States and Western Europe. The example shows how defectives are created, which account for about 5 percent of the materials and production costs of the defective pencils. There are other costs as well. The boxes of parts could have spent much time waiting for attention at each workstation. People, passing by, often pick up a unit as a trophy of production. Even when we ignore pilferage, there is the problem of damage of waiting goods.

Waiting Time Is Disruptive and Costs a Lot

Typical of the old technology (1920 and on), each batch waits at various workstations until other jobs are finished. Set-ups have to be repeated each time that a workstation has to switch from one job to another. Set-up costs can amount to more than 10 percent of the total costs. The cost of production being constantly disrupted is significant but difficult to determine. Lead time costs for materials from suppliers can add 10 percent to the costs. The costs of work-in-process are usually high. This is because waiting time is non-value-adding time. Another cost occurs if, because of delays, the pencils cannot be delivered on time. In addition to the cost of a lost order, the pencils are put into finished goods inventory where they rack up significant carrying costs. Overall, efficient production can save as much as 30 percent of the cost of goods and add these savings to the bottom line. Such production savings are not one-time; they are repeated over and over again.

The scenario just described is not atypical. How much extra cost is inherent in the use of batch procedures? The costs of defectives, and the costs of work waiting to receive value-added from the capital investment are generally so high that rational management would move away from the old batch technologies if they could do so. However, there is no pressure to change technologies if all the competitors are in the same boat. Phoenix industries would be irrational if they started up using old technology when they have the option to use new technology without the old-tech albatrosses around their necks. By being smart, start-up companies can obtain cost advantages of between 15 percent and 30 percent. Established companies have to dismantle existing systems to take advantage of the same benefits. The new technologies, when used by an efficient producer, can capture significant savings, which provide a lot of money for R&D, marketing, and allow lower prices to capture market share from technological dinosaurs.

Before the concept of interchangeable parts had been developed, each product was customized. Craftsmanship was the basis of production. Thus, one pair of shoes, or one musket, was made at a time. Each was its own work of art. The concept pioneered by Eli Whitney and Leblanc (in France) allowed parts to be made in batches and then assembled without worrying about which particular parts fit together. Subscribing to the principles of interchangeable parts, each job (batch of units) follows a particular routing through the various workstations. It is surprising how small the typical batch size is in the United States and Europe—averaging 50 units. It is not surprising that this small batch size intensifies the inherent disadvantages of batch production systems.

FLOW SHOP PRODUCTION SYSTEMS

Serialized production systems, which are also called flow shops, are another old technology process configuration. Henry Ford pioneered the design of sequenced assembly systems, which were implemented by the Ford Motor Company in 1914. Flow shops possess many cost and quality advantages over job shops; however, sufficient demand must be generated to warrant using them. Items produced by the flow shop come off the line, one after another. In contrast, customers must wait until the entire batch is finished by the job shop. The flow shop is caricatured by Charlie Chaplin's portrayal of mass production in *Modern Times*. Batch production, on the other hand, is familiar to everyone who has ever cooked a meal for a few friends. The office is a typical job shop. It is labor-intensive, costly, and inefficient.

Flow shop facilities use special-purpose equipment, designed to deliver the high volume of output needed. Job shop facilities use general-purpose equipment capable of being fitted with various tools, dies, and fixtures to do a large variety of jobs at the same facility. The job shop work force has to be able to do a lot of different kinds of work. As a result, job shop workers have higher hourly pay.

Flow shops prospered after World War I when demand was so much greater than supply that consumers would accept one option (say, black model-T Fords). Serious limitations to this form of production are imposed by the marketplace when competitors offer other models, other colors. Having only one option yields highly efficient production configurations, but unacceptable marketing opportunities.

The flow shop consists of a set of adjacent workstations. For example: the first puts a metal grommet on the pencil, the second inserts the eraser in the grommet, the third stamps the name and grade on the side of the pencil. At the fourth station, each 12 pencils are boxed. The inventory is then ready for shipment. The rate of production is set by a paced conveyor belt. The operations are performed repeatedly at each station.

FLEXIBLE MANUFACTURING SYSTEMS

The new manufacturing technology utilizes computers to change the settings of the equipment. This means that set-ups can be done quickly and correctly by remote-entry terminals. The variable costs of making the changes are negligible. The costs of the equipment are high, but once the investment is made, they can be considered as sunk costs. The major cost is involved in programming the system for each new product alternative. Often, the machines are grouped together in what are called "cells." Even larger groupings, connecting cells together, are termed "islands of automation." The equipment in such groupings shares tools in some mechanical way. Work is transported between the machines by means of mechanical arms and conveyors.

The new manufacturing technology is called flexible because many different kinds of products can be produced by the cell. There is, however, a high degree of commonality of the basic materials that the FMS uses for manufacture. The potential set of items that can be made has very high variety, but each variant requires its own programming. A simple modification in one program might suffice to produce another product variation. Generally, however, even small differences in the product require careful analysis and complex alterations of software. It is often costly and time consuming to debug programs.

Flexible manufacturing systems are hybrids of job shop and flow shop systems. Because set-up times are near zero, it is as inexpensive to make one item as a hundred items. When this theory is fully realized, it will topple the guiding principle of "economies of scale"—which underlies the pressure on manufacturers to produce high volumes by means of the flow shop. When variety—rather than volume—is the basis for manufacturing investments, then the guiding principle has been called "economies of scope." The principle of economies of scale is that per unit costs decrease geometrically as the production volume increases. The principle of economies of scope is that variety level increases geometrically as the average cost of set-ups decreases. Figure 3.1 illustrates these two principles graphically.

The counterargument, which must be taken into account, is that flexible manufacturing technology is filled with quirks and uncertainties. There is still a lot to be learned about how to make these systems work. Improvements of substantial merit are (so to speak) around the corner. Why not wait for the new model? The argument to adopt flexible manufacturing systems must be weighed against the counterargument for delaying adoption.

In a properly functioning FMS, some part of the system is always busy. However, every workstation is not fully engaged at all times—as is the case with the flow shop. Emphasis is on the production of variety—like a job shop. The relatively continuous stream of output from the FMS is similar to that of the flow shop. Product quality is comparable (or better) than that of the flow shop. FMS quality can be better because the variability of worker inputs is eliminated and the computer can set and monitor tolerances that flow shop equipment seldom attains.

How Much Variety Is Enough?

Flexible manufacturing systems will continue to replace job shops and flow shops because they have the ability to produce high levels of variety—at low costs—and with excellent quality. Studies have shown significant differences in the amount of variety that is utilized

Figure 3.1
Economies of Scale and Scope

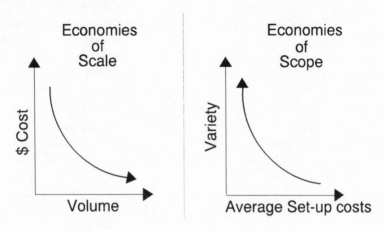

by companies in different nations. One report indicated that German firms achieve more than ten times the U.S. variety levels, and Japanese firms have more than three times higher variety levels than U.S. firms.[5]

Higher levels of variety require careful preplanning in which all of the options that might be desired are explored. To achieve higher variety, the idea of total automation must be compromised. In other words, human skills are interfaced with computer programming. Where the total use of programming logic would be too costly, people are assigned to interrupt when certain conditions arise. It has been said that the U.S. mind set to "do it all, if you do it at all" leads to low FMS variety levels because the total system of responses has to be programmed. Total automation is a costly investment. It results in less variety than a partially automated system. Also, the automated production system cannot be altered to conform to new market conditions. Before deciding how automated the FMS design should be, management must evaluate the costs and benefits.

FMS design features emphasize the combination of computer electronics and mechanical engineering. Both computer systems and the machine tools they control are undergoing continuous improvement. Therefore, timing the changeover from the old manufacturing technology to the new FMS is critical. Because a base of knowledge must be built to evaluate the situation, an on-going program of experimentation is warranted. A learning laboratory for FMS is worth considering.

A New Manufacturing Era Has Begun

FMS is not a fad or a transient invention of the moment. Awareness of this fact began to spread during the 1980s. It received attention by industry and government.[6] The advent of new manufacturing technology makes obsolete the old batch manufacturing approach. Being able to set up a machine rapidly so that it can do a number of different jobs in small lot sizes is the major breakthrough of the new technology. It changes the rules for manufacturing. Thus, those who say that "getting back to basics" will solve the present-day competitive problems are likely to be quite wrong. What must be accomplished to become globally competitive is to learn how to manufacture with the new technologies.

As technology changes, the job shop is likely to disappear first. It has so many wasteful characteristics and it lacks the efficiency of a serially utilized facility. The flow shop is more difficult to dismiss. It is a powerful manufacturing technology for achieving productivity advantages. The flow shop has an excellent cost structure and usually provides a powerful procedure for quality achievement. Unfortunately, it requires significant aggregation of demand volume to sustain the "mass production" advantages of economies of scale. It is probable that the flow shop will gradually absorb FMS technology, especially for suppliers to the production line.

When Japan first became a global competitor, it was by means of the flow shop being used in new and more efficient ways. They specialized in products having little variety, global markets, and price elasticity advantages. Once having established a foothold in markets, they used new technologies to increase the product line variety and special qualities. This enabled them to compete in markets where price elasticity favored the producer of nonsubstitutable goods.

HOW REAL ARE THE CHANGES IN MANUFACTURING TECHNOLOGY?

The first 75 years of the twentieth century have produced massive and pervasive changes in the way of life of a rapidly expanding global population, which has tripled since 1900. In the United States, the population has more than doubled since 1920. Yet in Europe and the United States, population is no longer growing. Between 1920 and 1975, methods of food production, transportation, communication, and health care have been revolutionized. In the 1990s, the rate of change seems to have decelerated to a crawl. Through the mid-1960s, U.S. exports grew at a rate that led journalists to proclaim that these were the "soaring sixties." Gross national product (GNP) doubled in the United States between 1960 and 1970. In the 1990s, these exciting changes seem to have slowed down, or even come to an end.

In the 1990s, entertainment is among the major American exports ($3 billion). Japanese companies, having secured 30 percent of the U.S. auto market and almost 100 percent of the TV and VCR markets, are moving in on the entertainment sector. Sony's purchase of CBS's record company and Matsushita's arrangements with MCA are indicative. Meanwhile, scrap steel and cardboard continue to be other major areas of export for the United States. The conquest of space captured the imagination of the planet in the 1960s. In the 1990s, space exploits are viewed with skepticism and TV coverage of any space event is far briefer than that of strikes or murders.

Opinion surveys indicate that Americans are more concerned with drugs, crime, pollution, elephants, whales, abortions, and fur coats than with the economic situation. New construction continues the longest recorded decline. Real estate values are collapsing. The budget deficit of the U.S. continues to mount. Members of the U.S. Congress seem to be more concerned with reelection than with developing a comprehensive solution to the deficit. Farmers in Europe and Japan pressure their respective governments for protection. An increasing number of big U.S. companies are forced into Chapter 11 bankruptcies. The stock market is extremely volatile. As people, all over the world, realize that a recession exists despite the inability of economists to agree when it started, concern about jobs continues to increase. With this background in mind, how real is the hypothesis that technology wearout is the real underlying cause of economic turmoil?

Manufacturing Technology Keeps on Advancing

Once upon a time, the machinery of manufacturing was driven by belts that were connected to a main drive shaft. These factories looked something like the inside of the shoe repair shop. Textbooks depicting the early history of technology provide pictures of factories in New England, where the earliest manufacturing boom in the U.S. occurred.[7] Many of these factories were located near rivers so that the main drive shaft could be driven by a water wheel, which was propelled by a natural or man-made waterfall. Later, the main belt was driven by an electric motor. The electrical power was often generated by a hydroelectric system of substantial size, such as Niagara Falls.

Computer Integrated Systems Are Replacing Human Controls

Belts disappeared as it became practical for machines to be powered by their own individual motors. Workers operated the machines and the skill requirements were considerable. Trained as apprentices, they positioned the tools and the pieces of work, setting feeds and speeds, as appropriate for the kinds of materials. Using micrometers and gauges, machinists cut metal to conform to the specifications of blueprints. In the 1990s, blueprints are drawn by computers using CAD programs (computer-aided design). CAM programs (computer-aided manufacturing) determine computer-machine settings in ways that the most skilled workers could not duplicate.

In the new technology of manufacturing, mechanical forces are guided and controlled by electronic systems. Designers of manufacturing systems began to replace gear and cam-type controls with electronic, computer-controlled systems. At first, the computer systems simply emulated the mechanical systems they replaced. Many of these mechanical systems required human skills to make adjustments. For example, a skilled machinist intervened in a variety of ways to compensate for mechanical variabilities. Electronic systems began to revise the way that mechanical work was being done by adding sensing and limited forms of decision-making. However, the shift from nonsensing mechanical systems to smart computer-controlled systems (capable of discernment) is only beginning to run its course.

Quality of Life Is Cyclical

The two paragraphs above may be so well-known that they are boring. At least they are brief. They simply recount the obvious continuous advancement of manufacturing technology. Economic conditions cycle; technological development does not. Technology advances at different rates, but it does not move backward. When investments in old technologies no longer pay, then capital starts moving to support the development and use of new technologies. Economic conditions change as capital flees from old technology. Those competitors who are in a position to ride the wave of new technology appear to be doing very well. However, there are risks of betting on any stage of new technology because it is developing so fast that tomorrow's designs may make today's achievements obsolete.

A very flexible position in new technology is warranted. There must be total willingness to be in a learning mode and preparedness to shift production configurations without paying off the outdated investment.

Established companies, seemingly stuck with large investments in old technology, are wracked with financial crises. Quality of life is related directly to the economic cycles. Individuals, faced with the loss of jobs because of downsizing and business failures, are bewildered by the fact that their quality of life does not improve with the advancements in technology. In fact, it is the improvements in technology that damage the quality of life for individuals.

Midsize Manufacturing Firms Successfully Adopt New Technology

The U.S. has been exporting manufactured goods with increasing success over the past five years, owing to the strenuous efforts of medium-sized firms. Using new technology in production and aggressive marketing practices, these midrange companies (with average annual sales of about $300 million) have become suppliers to global automakers, aerospace and construction firms, electronic and computer manufacturers, department stores, and food producers. While some firms work alone, many are involved with foreign associates in a variety of strategic alliances, including joint ventures. Still others are the relatively autonomous business units of large, decentralized firms.

The trade deficit of the United States would be far worse than it is if it weren't for the exports of these midrange firms, which have been averaging annual sales growth rates in excess of between 25 and 30 percent. Located all over the United States, these midsize firms have shown their adaptability by assimilating new technology at the right time, by producing high-quality products, and delivering better services at competitive prices. Especially noteworthy is the economic renaissance that has occurred in the U.S. "rust belt," spurred by the technological advances of midrange firms.

Many forces are at work that help to explain why the revenues of medium-sized organizations are growing. One of the most-often-mentioned reasons is the price advantage resulting from the currency ratios, which make the dollar cheap, thereby offering discounts to buyers of U.S. products. However, the currency advantage, by itself, is not a sufficient explanation of midrange company successes. It has not enabled many large U.S. companies to increase their exports. We must consider other explanations of why organizational size seems so important.

For example, midrange firms have to work much harder than large ones to get capital. Lenders require more evidence of probable success based on substantial innovations, as well as quality, service, and cost advantages. This kind of screening is bound to put better players on the field. Further, midsize business units have a close-knit communication advantage, which allows for better teamwork than large, bureaucratic organizations. We refer to this effect in Chapter 4 when describing how Japanese firms operate in the United States. Faster communication translates into superior timing, which means knowing when to adopt new technologies and when to stay with the existing systems. Also, the proportion of midrange firms that fail is large in ratio with the number that try to succeed, and the failures are relatively invisible. Most of these points apply to midsize firms all over the world, including those in developing countries, although the latter have many difficulties to overcome.

There are still parts of the world where production processes remain in the hands of artisans. There are even more parts of the world where the manufacturing equipment of the 1930s is fully entrenched. When the doors to Eastern Europe were thrown open, business people said that they were surprised to find that the manufacturing facilities were so antiquated. This seems strange until we realize that what really surprised those in search of business deals and strategic alliances was the uniformity and extent of the obsolescence.

What may have been most surprising was the lack of surprises. There were no special new-wave factories that had been hidden from view. The same observation undoubtedly applies to the People's Republic of China. The Western world should not be smug about this. Visitors from Asia, touring many of the long-established Western world's manufacturing facilities, might feel essentially the same surprise. How can the U.S. manufacturing system continue to ignore the new ways to use the new technologies? This is the pivotal issue. There can be banks of computers in place, but the paramount question is: Are those computers driving the system, or being driven?

It is understandable that the "phoenix countries" readily adapted their manufacturing systems to utilize the new technologies. It may seem less understandable that the change of technologies is successful in places that had been classified as developing economies. In this regard, it is worth noting that the countries that are successfully adapting the new technologies are those where the level of education is high, and where work disciplines are practiced even at the agrarian level of enterprise. Thus, the application of new technology systems of manufacturing are not constrained to industrialized countries. In fact, because the industrialized countries have so many large, established companies, the successful introduction of new manufacturing technology appears to meet with greater resistance.

Another fact of interest is that the new uses of computer-driven equipment in manufacturing are spreading from goods to services. Transport and telecommunications serve as excellent examples of highly technologized service functions. So does the fast foods service industry. Hospital activities, library functions, and even the dissemination of education are undergoing related changes. Service functions in manufacturing include hotlines to provide advice on contingencies, repair, and replacement. Integrated computer systems bring the customer up on the screen with a complete dossier of equipment characteristics and history of problems.

LIFE CYCLES OF MANUFACTURING EQUIPMENT

Another type of cycle that is associated with marketing describes the life cycles of products. How long does it take for a new type of toothpaste to go through the stages of start-up and growth, followed by the mature phase, and then the fall-off of revenues? Hopefully, long enough to recover the investment and earn a good return on the marketing expenses. Market managers say that the life cycles of consumer package goods have been decreasing. When revenues begin to decay, the company has various options, including withdrawal or restaging.

Life cycle speed-up has driven automakers to change models faster than they would like. The underlying question of the feasibility of change is always related to surpassing the break-even point associated with the investment required to make the change. The electronics and telecommunications fields are subject to the same kind of pressure as autos. Computers (both hardware and software) epitomize the most rapid life cycles that business has ever experienced. Because computers are the driving force in the long-wave changeover of manufacturing technology, it is clear that life cycles must influence a company's timing for the purchase of computerized manufacturing equipment. Should the production department buy 286-16 bit architecture or 386-32 bit architecture? The 486 is available, at a price. There may be a persuasive argument to wait for the sure-to-come 686.

Computer developments are occurring faster than similar changes in engine designs, which seemed chaotic during the long-wave period 1866–1920. Nevertheless, the pattern is typical of the early stages of the Kondratieff long wave. The chaos is caused by the simultaneous occurrence of old technology wearing out and a variety of new technologies that are competing for acceptance and implementation. The question is one of timing. How long should managers protect the old approaches? When do U.S. companies subscribe to the new ones?

It would be nice if we could settle the issue in terms of the bottom line. Unfortunately, the bottom line can only be calculated with any believability for the short term. Risk factors become increasingly unreliable as the planning horizon is extended. Because the future is not transparent, the old bureaucratic organizations can defend status quo strategies. Break-even considerations, based on present value calculations, will support the obvious. Established companies will support the status quo. New organizations, having no sunk costs, will attack the establishment.

LEARNING ORGANIZATIONS

If established organizations treated their investments in old technologies as nonrecoverable sunk costs, they would not go to great pains to defend these investments. This would free them up to learn about the new technologies. Then they could invest in replacements for the technologies that are wearing out as competitive sources of profitability. For example, steam power had been thoroughly exploited before being replaced by the power of the internal combustion engine. Markets for the existing technologies are saturated and organizations are competing with each other in terms of minor technological variations, whereas the new technologies are inchoate and offer significant competitive differences. For example, when commercial aircraft with propellers were first being replaced by jet engine planes, the airlines instituted a surcharge for jet travel. It was short-lived as the real competition turned out to be between different types of jets.

Periods of technological volatility allow learning. This provides an advantage to those firms that consciously invest in the learning aspect of new technologies. Normal accounting procedures will flunk the prospective technologies. Therefore, the accounting methods of innovative firms must be changed to reward knowledge acquisition above immediate bottom-line profits. It is well-known that accounting procedures do not readily dovetail with the operation of knowledge industries. A change of attitude is required to accept the fact that there is value in experimentation even if it can be measured only qualitatively.

Timing Is Crucial

The most compelling reason for experimenting is to determine the optimal timing for replacement of old technologies and implementation of new technologies. Timing has always been difficult to determine because of the exponential nature of the life cycles of technological development. It is difficult to project sales and shares when there is random oscillation around growth trends that are accelerating or decelerating. Also, technological life cycles can be further speeded-up when competitive pressures are effective.

The Mother of Invention May Be the Child of Necessity

We like to say that as the old technologies are used up, "necessity becomes the mother of invention." But there is ample evidence that the reverse is true as well—namely, invention is the mother of necessity. Before air conditioning existed, no one expected it. Some 40 years after it was commercialized, people take it so for granted that they will leave work if the "AC" fails. Invention mothered necessity.

Ampex developed the first commercial VCR. The Ampex managers visualized their market as being composed of the camera professionals of the TV industry. A broad-based market did not exist, nor did it seem feasible to develop it, among the TV viewing public. Sony developed the first household VCR. By 1990, about 80 percent of households in the United States owned at least one VCR. It might have been said that Ampex was reacting to necessity. TV professionals needed the ability to tape their programs. In contrast, Sony created the market for home VCRs.

Flexible manufacturing systems did not appear because of necessity. They appeared because:

- the state of the art had progressed to the point where FMS could be feasible—it is a new invention that is ready for commercialization, and
- the technologies that they were replacing had been exhausted as a good investment, and
- there were global investors ready to take advantage of the opportunities— the new tech is more competitive than the old tech.

PROCESS AND PRODUCT CHANGES AT THE BEGINNING OF A NEW WAVE

No matter how the cycles of technological change are named and categorized, there has to be an investment peak in the new technology that is followed by a period of decreasing profitability. Then, as it becomes apparent that investments in the old technology are not profitable, new alternative technologies begin to develop. Thus, the beginning of a new wave is characterized by many start-ups trying to capitalize on new technology, and many failures owing to inchoate or rudimentary stages of the new technology being replaced by superior developments. Studies of the weeding out of new process ideas show many cases taking 25 years or more. All kinds of bells and whistles are tried out.

A good example is the length of time that it has taken to develop industrial robots for the production process.[8] In Chapter 6, in the section entitled "Unimation: A Case Study of How America Missed Out on Robots," points out that 25 years were required to move from conception to general applicability. As the story shows, the Japanese won the market because Westinghouse Unimation Inc. followed the wrong fork in the road. They produced the wrong version of the product. There are many other examples of the turmoil that occurs during the initial stages of technological development.

Brand names come and go. Bowmar hand-held calculators replaced slide rules and all kinds of monstrous mechanical calculators and comptometers. Although their calculators were first into the market, Bomar is not a survivor. After all the fuss, things settle down. There is some degree of stability for the survivors—Hewlett-Packard, Texas Instruments, Casio, and a scattering of other brands from the Pacific Basin countries are the remaining contenders. Successful design distillation rewards those that have survived with increasing profitability, which may last for more than 20 years.

The point is that external economic forces that involve technological change bring about major economic turmoil and great opportunity for those who perceive the opportunities correctly. As in all of these waves of technological change, the principal advantage goes to those who recognize the production component involved with the start-up of new products and processes. There are tactical production concepts and strategic concepts that must be understood for the production function to prosper. Because of global changes in business, strategic alliances and joint ventures make it feasible for companies to survive and prosper during the turbulence of technological wearout and replacement. If you believe in cycle theory, these kinds of opportunities come only every 50 or 60 years, so it would be a shame to miss them.

WHAT MAJOR TRANSFORMATIONS ARE OCCURRING?

There are five main elements that capture the changes in manufacturing that are taking place:

1. there are fewer workers on the line, and
2. there are fewer supervisors for the line.

At the same time, there are

3. more smart machines,
4. more workers engaged in planning systems, and
5. more workers designing hardware and software.

Put in other ways, worker participation content in the line activities of manufacturing has decreased markedly. The ratio of worker content to machine content in the manufactured product has dropped. The blue-collar labor dollar content of the finished product is (on average) 15 percent or less.

Figure 3.2
Percent Distribution of Work Force
(Major changes from 1790 to 2000)

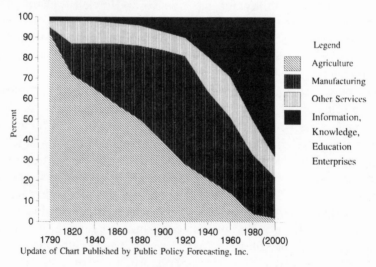

Update of Chart Published by Public Policy Forecasting, Inc.

In the United States the percent of workers engaged in manufacturing has decreased from about 45 percent in 1940 to less than 28 percent in 1980. In 1990 it is less than 20 percent, and heading down sharply. In the prior Kondratieff cycle, mining and agricultural labor content experienced similar sharp decreases. See Figure 3.2 for the percent of the U.S. labor force engaged in manufacturing, mining, agriculture, and services over more than 200 years.

At some point, the percent of (human) labor content dropped below a threshold that characterized systems and procedures previously used by conventional manufacturing technology to be competitive. At that point, the new technology cycle can be said to be accelerating in growth, and the old technology cycle is accelerating into oblivion. Not a lot is known about thresholds for change in business and human social systems. They are not crystal clear as in metallurgical changes from one structure to another; or even as evident as in epidemiology, where contagion factors can pass a threshold that signals the beginning of an epidemic. Nevertheless, the same kind of fundamental restructuring seems to occur, which explains why timing is so important in adopting new technologies.

NOTES

1. Sponsored by the Columbia Business School Center for Operations, 1989.

2. Marshall Middleton, Jr., "Product Design by Digital Computers," *Westinghouse Engineer*, March 1956, pp. 39–43.

3. The following publications will help to identify the four individuals that we have mentioned: W. Edwards Deming, *Out of the Crisis* (Cambridge, MA: MIT Center for Advanced Engineering Study, 1986); Lester C. Thurow, See Chapter 12, esp. p. 163, of the MIT Commission on Industrial Productivity, by M. L. Dertouzos, R. K. Lester, and R. M. Solow, *Made in America: Regaining the Productive Edge* (Cambridge, MA: MIT Press, 1989); Tom Peters, *Thriving on Chaos* (New York: Alfred A. Knopf, 1987); John A. Young, Report of the President's Commission on Industrial Competitiveness, *Global Competition: The New Reality* (Washington, DC: U.S. Government Printing Office, January 1985).

4. Jefferson also wrote: "Leblanc, in France, had invented a similar process in 1788 & had extended it to the barrel, mounting and stock. . . . Mr. Whitney has not yet extended his improvement beyond the lock." This letter appears in Jeannette Mirsky and Allan Nevins, *The World of Eli Whitney* (New York: Collier Books, 1962), p. 218.

5. Professor Ramchandran Jaikumar of the Harvard Business School reported in a 1985 study that out of 100 FMS systems that were installed and running, German firms with 20 FMS had an average number of varieties of almost 85; Japanese firms with 50 FMS had an average number of varieties of 30; and U.S. firms with 30 FMS had an average of only 8 varieties. "FMSs in this country are being managed for short-run interests in productivity rather than to exploit their full flexibility," says

Jaikumar. From David Kennedy, "Flexible Manufacturing, Inflexible Manufacturing," *Technology Review*, July 1985, pp. 78–79.

6. *Toward a New Era in U.S. Manufacturing: The Need for a National Vision*, Manufacturing Studies Board, Commission on Engineering and Technical Systems, National Research Council (Washington, DC: National Academy Press, 1986).

7. Lowell, Massachusetts, was the center for textile manufacturing. Waltham, Massachusetts, was the home of the Waltham Watch Company, which was one of the highest-tech plants of its era.

8. The word "robot" was first used as part of the name of a play written by Karel Capek in Czechoslovakia in 1926. The play was called *RUR* (Rossum's Universal Robots). Capek chose the word robot from the Slavic word *robotnick*, meaning "worker." Frederick W. Taylor (the father of scientific management) formulated the ideal bricklayer in terms that led his critics to claim that he was trying to turn workers into robots. Nevertheless, the derivation of the word relates to converting erratic human workers into consistently reliable machine-like entities.

CHAPTER 4 _____

Changes in Management Systems Technology

Plus ça change, plus c'est la même chose. (The more things change, the more they stay the same.)[1]

Alphonse Karr
Les Guepes, January 1849

When this well-known adage was written, industrialization in Europe, fed by a seemingly endless number of inventions, fueled the revolution of 1848 that drove Louis Phillipe, the citizen king, into exile. With this historical vignette in mind, it is not hard to figure out what Alphonse Karr meant. Behind the political revolution in France, which removed the last of the Bourbons, was the second phase of the Industrial Revolution. While the names and faces were different, human nature stayed the same. For the citizens of France, the governing bureaucratic organizations seemed unchanged.

Although ordinary citizens have always known the great difficulty of dealing with bureaucracies,[2] the perfection of this organizational form was considered essential for the success of both capitalistic and socialistic enterprises. In the early 1900s, bureaucracy was considered to be the most effective organizational form. It is even understandable why bureaucracies were preferred to the autocratic organizations of royalty, which had arbitrary and capricious rules. In the 1700s and 1800s, chaotic conditions prevailed in the everyday life of citizens. Therefore, it is understandable that being well-organized was considered to be a great advantage. Bureaucracy was viewed as the antidote for massive disorganization. The "inflexible routines" (part of the definition of bureaucracy) promised to end the era of capricious rulings and replace them with consistent direction and control.

There is no gainsaying the fact that bureaucratic organizations that developed in the United States and Europe became the most powerful companies in the world. But we should note that the manufacturing technology of this era was equally successful because it was so "inflexibly routinized." When manufacturing technology began to change into that of "flexible routinization," bureaucracy became a hindrance rather than an asset.

ORIGINS OF U.S. INDUSTRIAL SUCCESS

Because the traditional management approach worked so well for U.S. companies, what has changed? It takes a lot of persuasion to convince many managers that the time has come to reject the conventional management model. Therefore, it is beneficial to examine the question of what accounts for the prior successes and the present difficulties of the U.S. industrial system.

What is it that made the United States a great industrial superpower? A lot of reasonable suppositions can be offered, including the fact that U.S. arms and supplies were critical in two world wars. The production buildups during both World War I and World War II were converted from military outputs to consumer products. The supply of trained workers was without precedent. Factories were filled with a lot of general-purpose equipment and workers who knew how to use it. After World War II, chaos existed in Europe and Japan, but the U.S. industrial base had not been touched. Its industrial capacity had been expanding from 1914 to 1964.

A theory related to this scenario states that the U.S. economic advantage was based on the use of technology to convert abundant resources into products. This advantage ceased to operate when other nations in Europe and Asia began to tap their own resources. Eventually, according to the proponents of this point of view, manufacturing became less dependent on the value of basic resources (e.g., coal and steel), and therefore, the American edge was blunted.[3] The theory is richer and more complex than has been described; however, the essential argument is captured here.

The management of industry in the United States and Europe now faces a competitive challenge that pits the old establishment type of industrial organization against a new form of organization. The old systems of management are under pressure to change because technological wearout has made high volume, slow-changing production processes obsolete. The new technologies that are replacing the old ones stress flexibility to produce high varieties of output in minimal volumes. While new technologies such as FMS have the potential to be managed differently, they do not demand a change in management. They can be forced into a mold that emulates the old management systems. Therefore, to become globally competitive requires that the potential of the new manufacturing technology be realized by the existence of the new management technology.

WHAT IS MANAGEMENT TECHNOLOGY?

The key to understanding what management technology means lies in the definition of technology, and the applicability of that definition to management practice—as contrasted with the way that equipment and products work. The distinction that has to be drawn is between the systematic application of scientific principles to machines (such as engines and tools) and the systematic application of management policies to planning, organization, staffing, directing, and controlling the activities of a firm. The definition of technology includes both kinds of systematic treatment being applied in a practical fashion. Technology is often defined as the science of the industrial arts, which causes endless confusion because of the contradiction implicit in marrying science and art. This discrepancy is what manufacturing management must bridge. As applied science changes, and as the goals and values of people change, management technology is faced with new challenges and new opportunities.

The policies and procedures that management uses to operate its facilities can be written out in a manual. Often they can be graphically illustrated by means of flowcharts, blueprints, sketches, and load diagrams. Some parts of this management technology can be set down in mathematical equations that describe: [A] what is to be made, and [B] how much of it is to be made. The [A] part could be the chemistry of the product and the [B] part could be the analysis of make or buy, followed by a linear programming resource allocation. These methods and procedures are combinations of the art and science of formulating policies in as unambiguous a way as possible.

Process management is a technology that interacts with marketing and finance. The interactions are rich and complex. They deal with the differences between the qualities desired by consumers and those delivered by the firm. Management technology is sensitive to the relations between prices, costs, and profit margins. The entire system of elements comes together when a break-even analysis is performed. What percent of capacity must be utilized before the process under study begins to provide a profit? This question cannot be answered without knowledge about the technological coefficients of the process. The same reasoning applies to the market penetration parameters based on competitive analyses of costs and prices, advertising and promotion effectiveness, timing and campaign persistence, and so on.

THE TECHNOLOGY OF BUREAUCRATIC MANAGEMENT

As manufacturing technology changed, during the various phases of the Industrial Revolution, the technology of managing also changed. Changes in manufacturing technology tend to lead; changes in management technology tend to follow. One of the best ways to describe the system of management that is now under pressure to change, is that it uses the technology of bureaucratic management. Manufacturing technology is undergoing major shifts in capital investment that are driven by technological wearout. When that happens, changes in the technology of managing cannot be far behind.

Competition relentlessly seeks to improve both manufacturing and management technologies. However, for many reasons, a superior competitive system usually wins out only gradually. A firm has to be really bad to lose all of its customers in a short period of time. Inertia explains why some long-time customers choose not to switch to a new supplier. Habits change slowly. There are also rational reasons for preferring an accepted supplier (whose personnel are familiar and whose products have known characteristics) to a strange supplier (with a presumably better product). The costs of changing sources tend to protect the inferior producer, at least for a while.

Bureaucratic systems have worked out forms of management technology that tend to protect them against change. This applies to (1) the internal organization of the company, (2) the relationship with external suppliers, and 3) the interchange with customers. The internal organization (1) is the primary determinant of (2) and (3), but it is also affected by them.

CHANGING MANAGEMENT TECHNOLOGY

Many companies (especially large, established, and previously successful firms) recognize that inflexible policies, which are ingrained, weaken their competitive position. The inflexibility is translated into noncooperative and confrontational attitudes between employees of the same company. Instead of sharing a common goal, the employees act as though their main competitors are inside, rather than outside of the firm.

In an effort to shake things up, some long-established firms have introduced the notion that each individual in the firm acts as a supplier to others in the same firm. The underlying reason for this point of view is that outside suppliers must strive to satisfy their customers. If they do not make them happy, then a new supplier will be found. Thus, the supplier is beholden to the purchaser. When this model is applied internally, the hope is that each person will see themselves as providing service to their "customers," to whom they are beholden. It is hoped that everyone in the company sincerely believes that a customer must be pleased, and that it is very important to have satisfied and loyal customers. Will these feelings transfer to a fellow worker by calling him or her a customer?

Labels are known to be very important in our market economy. When sales begin to fall off, consumer package goods manufacturers relabel a product as "new." The same concept is at work with respect to converting adversarial attitudes in bureaucratically constrained firms into supportive and cooperative relationships. Changing a bureaucratic organization is nearly impossible. At least, theoretically, it is not impossible. It may be too early to tell for sure, but the efforts of big U.S. bureaucracies to shake off the shackles, to be free to soar as phoenixes themselves, show only the faintest glimmerings of being successful.

No Easy Alteration of Bureaucratic Management Exists

The first serious mistake is to believe that some simple panacea will cure the inability of bureaucracies to react vigorously. Being open to opportunities and responsive to competition are states of mind that we readily associate with entrepreneurs, not with curmudgeons. There are a few ways to revitalize curmudgeons, or, alternatively, to promote the entrepreneurs in the firm who can help to accomplish this difficult objective. Chapters 6 and 7 provide a few ways that seem to be working for logical reasons. These may not be the only ways to break out of the bind, but one must be cautious about flashy and faddish ideas that do not address root causes, raise false expectations, and may fail with dire consequences.

Many large companies that have used such fads show no new ability to shake loose the bureaucratic stasis in order to compete globally. The solution space is cluttered with journalistic and consulting treatments, such as quality circles, skunk works, touchy-feely management, zero-defects, management by objectives, discounted cash flow, kanban, JIT, participative management, everyone's a customer, and so on. There is nothing wrong with many of these one-liners if they are connected to a policy framework that integrates their systems' relevance and disciplines their application.

Downsize and Empower the Business Unit

The most important means for "shaping up," as opposed to "shipping out," is to downsize the organization and grant it relative autonomy. These steps encourage communication (with small enough size), and support intelligent risk-taking (with relative autonomy). Improved teamwork results because the organization is small enough that its parts are all visible; they are in touch with each other; and the system is empowered to do things differently, as needed.

As Chapters 5, 6, and 7 show, bureaucratic organizations that develop strategic alliances (especially in the form of joint ventures) have a good shot at improving teamwork and becoming better global competitors. If the internal supplier concept works to further these objectives, then companies should continue to make efforts to reward those employees who take the position that they are suppliers and, in turn, are supplied. Any technique or procedure that increases bureaucratic flexibility, or decreases bureaucracy, is worth encouraging in a period of relentless competition. The ability to alter the existing management technology to conform to new situations as they arise is essential for competitiveness.

In the long run, bureaucracies that attempt to resist change by protecting the older (outmoded) forms of doing business lose their customers to competitors that offer improvements. One form of protecting the status quo is to place emphasis on methods that do not work. An old trick is to create a diversion by upping the importance of the planning function. The position of strategic planner sounds good. A company doing strategic planning must surely be preparing for eventualities that it cannot avoid, as well as creating that part of the future over which it can exercise some control.

MANAGEMENT RULES—POSDiC

The MBA (master of business administration) degree that is offered by business schools in the United States and Europe is usually composed of a 20-course curriculum. All of these courses reflect management concerns, but only a few of these courses concentrate their teachings on management per se. These management courses systematize the way that executives function. This systematic treatment of the executive function is called management technology. Traditionally, it consists of the five POSDiC elements: *P*lanning, *O*rganizing, *S*taffing, *D*irecting, and *C*ontrolling. As normally used by large companies, these five administrative functions keep the status quo. They support bureaucratic intransigence. The five categories could as well be used to stimulate competitive change. It is how management uses POSDiC that can either free the firm to apply its administrative wisdom for change or, alternatively, increase the company's insensitivity to the realities of what creates competitive advantages.

TRADITIONAL VERSUS NEW MANAGEMENT SYSTEMS

The traditional approach was rooted in the Industrial Engineering concepts developed at the beginning of the 1900s by Frederick W. Taylor, Henry L. Gantt, Frank Gilbreth, and other famous founders of the production disciplines. At the same time, organizational theorists such as Chester Barnard, Henri Fayol, and Lillian Gilbreth paralleled the operational considerations with notions about authority, responsibility, leadership, and span of control. The company was viewed as a set of separate functions. Division of labor epitomized the organizational structure that was appropriate for the stage of manufacturing technology that existed. These old roots are still there, but everything else is changed or changing.

POSDiC as applied in the past by the old management system emphasized reducing direct costs and increasing productivity. Output volume was of paramount importance. Quality was considered to be of secondary importance and consequently its definition was limited to immediate utilitarian satisfaction. Issues of reliability, endurance, safety, extra features, and such were residuals of the planning process.

Planning

The First Rule of old-tech management is to stabilize the system. "If it ain't broke, don't fix it" is the colloquial saying that epitomizes the planning objective. Still widely practiced, this is a high-output-volume planning rule that accents throughput at the expense of quality. The underlying financial motivation is to obtain economies of scale. For production planning, it translates into the warning: don't stop the line. Planning is therefore aimed at the avoidance of changes that cause interruptions. This is recognizable as the status quo directive associated with bureaucracies.

Successful global competitors, responding to the capabilities of new manufacturing technology, have reversed the old planning rule. Japanese manufacturing systems are constantly being improved, subject to a broadly interpreted management dictum that planning for change is everyone's responsibility. All Japanese companies do not operate in the same way. This is evident from survey information that is presented in Appendix A. By and large, however, the idea to improve is not passive. It is not uncommon to perturb smoothly running production systems by reducing their feeder supplies, by running them faster, or by introducing a new product design.

The objectives of planning are entirely different in the old-tech and new-tech systems. Therefore, changing from the old system to the new one is all the more difficult. Further, with status quo as the modus operandi, the objectives, once chosen, are stable. With rejection of status quo, the search for objectives is dynamic and continuous. It is difficult to choose objectives that will enhance a firm's competitiveness, even when the economic environment is stable. Given times of great economic turbulence and uncertainty, which we associate with the end of one long wave and the beginning of another, the ability to replan becomes an important asset. A firm with built-in dynamics to shift objectives has an advantage over a firm suffering from "hardening of the categories."[4]

Organizing

The Second Rule of old-tech management is to design and support hierarchical organizational structures of many levels. The new-tech approach is to have the organizational structures as flat as possible. When deep hierarchical structures are used, each manager is responsible for fewer people than when flat organizational structures are used. Flat organizational arrangements make sense when the people reporting to the next level upward are able to do their jobs without requiring much consultation or supervision.

It is understandable why the managers of established companies resist changing the way their firms are organized. Hierarchical structures partition responsibilities among the major functional areas. By denoting who reports to whom, the organization is compartmentalized. This effectively cuts communication between people at the same level. The result is that information must be funneled upward, where it is the responsibility of the most senior executives to view the whole picture. Such organizational design secures power for those at the top and effectively denies power to those at lower levels in the organization. The principle is in keeping with the purposes of a bureaucracy to maintain the status quo.

Established bureaucracies have many hierarchical levels. These are epitomized by the traditional pyramidal organization chart, which partitions information and creates bosses over bosses, much like military organizations do it. There are many individuals (the troops or workers) at the bottom. The lines of responsibility converge as they move upward, until at the top of the organization there is a single individual (the general or CEO). The formal organization chart implies that an apex person is responsible for everything that the rest of the organization does. At the same time, everyone knows that an informal organization exists that is not represented by the formal chart.

As it moved toward employing new manufacturing and management technology, the Ford Motor Company slashed the number of levels between employees on the plant floor and the top management from ten levels to four levels. This matched the depth of Toyota's hierarchical structure. Ford found that quality was more readily improved, costs were lower, and productivity was higher. By means of this alteration of the organization's hierarchical structure, Ford had decreased the powerful bureaucratic grip that had taken hold of the company as it got bigger and older. Flattening the organization structure is helpful when an established company strives to become global.

For the same reasons that flattening the organization structure helps a large company regain competitiveness, small and medium-size companies possess an innate advantage. Without having to change themselves, their top management is much closer to the employees on the plant floor. There are fewer communication links to traverse. Information is broadly available, so power is disseminated. These smaller and mid-size companies find it easier to plan for constant change.

Staffing

The Third Rule of old-tech management is to staff by specialties. Specialists, separated by expertise in their respective functions, do not communicate well with each other. Cross-learning is discouraged. Individuals are pigeonholed, which means that once a shoemaker, always a shoemaker. As an example, a successful market research director was told that the senior vice president of marketing in his company was leaving. When he applied for the job, he was turned down because "market research is not marketing." For the same reason, MBAs are advised to avoid multiple concentrations (e.g., finance, marketing, production management, accounting, international business, etc.). They are being advised not to appear to be generalists. Knowing about many things is taken to mean that only a little can be known about each of them. In turn, to "know a little bit about a lot of things" is interpreted as superficial dabbling, or dilettantism.

The staffing rule for new-tech management embraces the systems point of view that everything is interconnected. This implies that all functional areas should be staffed by people with the broadest possible experiences. Cross-training and cross-assignments are highly regarded as means to achieve total communication between participants at every level and function in the company. As an example, the janitor, in one of the companies that we surveyed, noted changes in the character of the scrap that he was picking up every evening. He reported a possible machine problem in time to head off a severe malfunction with substantial downtime. The janitor was a retired machine tool operator from the company. In another company that we surveyed, the Japanese controller was an accountant who had spent 18 months working on the production line followed by 12 months with R&D. He also spent time in sales before returning to the accounting department.

One of the strengths of small and medium-sized companies is the fact that each person wears so many different hats that he or she can perceive problems from the company's point of view. Large companies tend to reinforce parochial points of view within each of the functional areas of the company. Individuals identify themselves as finance, marketing, production, or whatever, and defend their departments as if they take precedence over the company. But the rules for staffing are changing. Increasingly, staff persons are chosen who are systems oriented and cross-trainable. Managers who are excellent communicators can enhance information and knowledge flow between functional areas of the company. Supporting such people is another step of considerable importance in becoming globally competitive.

Directing

The Fourth Rule of old-tech management is to enforce the regulations. Since these regulations are the outgrowth of plans that set standards, they are themselves a form of the standards. The regulations are meant to detect deviations from standards and to remove them. Little or no latitude is given to managers for dealing with special circumstances that could be better dealt with on the spot. In fact, it is the lack of flexibility for managers to override regulations that make no sense in a particular situation that characterizes this fourth rule. Dogmatic adherence to the letter of the law, without regard to exceptions, is representative of bureaucratic directing. Managers are supposed to police workers, not assist them. In other words, the hierarchy is the blueprint of responsibility for carrying out the directives that upper-levels of management send to lower-levels. Military systems work in this way, and many established companies appear to follow the same model.

The new technology of management assumes that everyone in the company accepts responsibility for doing their jobs in the best possible way. Responsibility rather than authority flows from the top. The president of the company is responsible to more employees than anyone else. Managers are supposed to assist workers, not police them. Supervisors are considered to be consultants to their employees. Know-how is what distinguishes the foreman from the workers. Flexibility in interpreting the policies of the firm is crucial. This flexibility encourages problem-solving rather than problem-making. Special circumstances and exceptions are considered to be opportunities for managers to do a better job than had been envisioned by the planners. Oftentimes it is the "directing" function that brings the people of the company in contact with customers and suppliers. The changes in management technology are aimed at improving the quality of customer contacts and supplier relations.

Controlling

The Fifth Rule of old-tech management was to search out deviations from standards and remove them as soon as possible. As a result, controlling involved measurement of performance, comparison with the standards, deviation reporting, and steps to remove the deviations. This form of controlling carried out the intent of bureaucratic planners to set the standards and hold to them. Planners set the objectives. Directors carried them out. Controllers checked to see if the objectives were being met.

It should be noted that removing (reworking or scrapping) deviations is the way in which quality standards are met by many companies. At the final inspection, defective items are removed, thereby assuring the quality of the products being shipped. A problem arises when inspection is the method for assuring quality standards instead of using process control to find out and remove what caused the defectives. But the job shop with batch production did not lend itself to process control. On the other hand, the flow shop was a natural for process control. However, management technology was less concerned with quality issues than it was with cost control and productivity measurement.

What Counts is Changing

Accounting systems were designed to search out deviations from standards. They were institutionalized by bureaucracies because the cost and output information they provided were the core of the control function. The advent of new management technology includes major revisions to the old accounting systems. Labor accounting continuously loses meaning as the number of workers involved in manufacturing decreases (see Figure 3.2). Overhead accounting needs to be changed to provide information on what real profit margin is obtained from each of the company's activities. Overhead charges that are proportional to direct labor costs make no sense when direct labor is less than 10 percent of the total cost of goods sold. (This 10 percent, which is an average figure across different industry groups, continues to decrease so rapidly that 5 percent, or less, is a reasonable guess for 1999.)

Accounting for the costs and benefits of quality is another developing area that elevates the control function to a position where it can really advise management about what it is doing. A popular analogy compares the company controller to the driver of a car who steers the automobile by looking through the rear view mirror. With new management technology, we can do better than that.

Decision methods for investing in new manufacturing technology have to expand the vision of discounted cash flow analysis to include qualitative factors that are not captured by ordinary cash flow evaluations. Accounting for timing (time-based management, as discussed in Chapter 7) is a relatively new control area that is growing in importance.

Companies like Hewlett-Packard, for example, are analyzing the time required to break even for a proposed system alteration. Accounting and controllership experiments are commonplace. Changes in practice loom on the horizon.

Until accounting is altered to reflect the new realities of manufacturing, being in touch with what is going on in the organization will be an illusion. Since the new management technology emphasizes flexibility and variety, accounting controls must capture the costs of variety. The control function must react to the trade-offs between economies of scope and economies of scale. The appropriate management approach will provide these seven decision guidelines for controlling expenditures: purchasing FMS hardware, developing FMS software, making process changeovers to increase variety, achieving continuous quality improvement, motivating smart workers to work smarter, substituting team goals for performance evaluation, and managing the increase in innovation potentials.

INTEGRATED INFORMATION SYSTEMS

As we said in Chapter 3, FMS is at the heart of the change in manufacturing technology. Equivalently, at the heart of the new management technology is the revolution in information technology. The list of seven decision guidelines for the control function could be expanded to 17, or even 70. No matter how many, each item interacts with the other items in a substantial way. What is done to any one factor impacts all of the others. An information network is the only way to view the functional interactions that connect hardware, software, know-how and imagination.

Process Management Replaces Product Management

The invention, evolution, and impact of computers spans the end of one long wave and the beginning of the next one. Major technology changes take a long time to develop to the point where they become economically viable. The seeds are planted in the 1940s. The rooting process goes on for 30 years. Finally, in the 1980s the practical applications of computer technology begin to take hold. The real changes shake up manufacturing and management technologies during the 1990s.[5]

One of the repercussions of the shift from economies of scale to economies of scope is that the dominance of product management gives way to the new management focus on process management. This is illustrated by Figure 4.1 with respect to three different eras: pre-man-agement, traditional management, and process management.[6]

Product management is responsible for achieving and maintaining high sales volumes. By doing this, the company can obtain production economies, although this is seldom considered to be as important as maximizing the return on marketing expenses. In contrast, process management is responsible for achieving the optimal levels of variety, using the degrees of freedom available from the already installed flexible manufacturing systems. Viewed in another way, product management has the goal of keeping the system fixed and on target to maximize revenues or market share. Process management has the goal of using flexibility to maximize profits. Process management can deal with profits because it is sensitive to the costs incurred by all other parts of the system. Product management cannot deal with profits because it is only superficially connected to the rest of the business system. The change from product to process focus is proceeding at an accelerating rate, but it is still incipient. As the millennium changes to 2000, the consequences of the shift from one system to the other will begin to come clear.

The significance for the management of manufacturing systems is beginning to become apparent. The information transformations that computers accomplish have an architecture of their own. During the early stages of computer development, the architecture mimicked the existing information systems that had been installed by bureaucratic organiza-tions—that is, the old-tech rules of POSDiC, which have been discussed. This management process, aimed at removing variability, and focused on achieving standards, does everything possible to keep the product from being changed. Process management, on the other hand, is directed toward product change and product line variety. Consequently, process management cannot use the old information system. It requires a new architecture, which thrives on computer networking between various data bases.

Computer Integrated Manufacturing

CIM is a concept that has never been fully achieved. Far from it, the interesting speculation is: To what extent has it been achieved? Perhaps a fair guess might be that the record for the most advanced CIM to date is about 70 percent. This number was pulled out of a hat, but it was meant to characterize a person-free factory, where only the maintenance func-tion is required. How did this factory decide what to make, when to make it, and how much to make of it? Management must supply the plans.

Figure 4.1
Three Generations of Management Technology

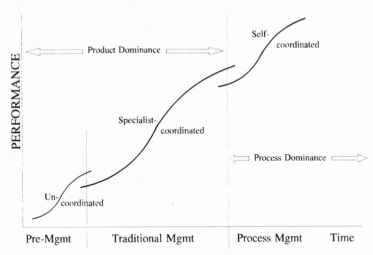

Source: Adapted from M. P. Hessel, M. Mooney, and M. Zeleny, "Integrated Process Management: A Management Technology for the New Competitive Era," in *Global Competitiveness: Getting the U.S. Back on Track*, ed. Martin K. Starr (New York: W. W. Norton, 1988).

CIM is the form of the organization that appears to be staffless, but this is unrealistic. Again, we encounter the difference between realizing 100 percent of the CIM concept and the reality. Therein lies the reason that the perfect CIM has not yet been realized. The idea that it falls 30 percent short of perfection is purely symbolic.

What is the perfect CIM like? It is a manufacturing system that receives all information that exists in the company, on-line and immediately. It has decision-making competence based on the assimilation of all relevant information. It has control capabilities and can react with optimal timing. The perfect CIM is pictured as a wheel with concentric cylinders surrounding the hub (see Figure 4.2).

The core function is manufacturing. The core is in communication with marketing, finance, R&D, human resources, accounting, distribution, and so on. In turn, all of the business functions are in communication with each other as they share their respective data bases. That is what is meant by "integrated," which is the middle I of CIM. It is difficult to come close to the perfect CIM. It is probably impossible to ever fully

Figure 4.2
A Computer Integrated Manufacturing Enterprise Wheel

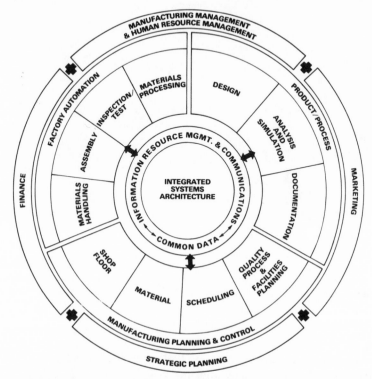

Source: CIM "Wheel" developed by the Technical Council of the Computer and Automated Systems Association of SME (CASA/SME)—Copyright 1985 CASA/SME, Second Edition, Revised November 5, 1985.

achieve it. But it is an excellent target to aim at in this period of technological transition.

Marketing and Production Interactions

Flexible manufacturing systems amplify the power of production to respond to marketing's request for increased variety. The amplification is so great that new relationships are created between marketing and production management. Planning to satisfy the demand of global markets requires balancing the costs of producing variety against the marketing advantages obtained. As far as production is concerned, new manufacturing technology makes set-ups for changeovers nearly instantaneous and cost-free. However, the design and software costs, as well as the administrative costs of variety (such as more stock keeping units to keep track of) can be considerable. As far as marketing is concerned, what is the value of variety to the customers—that is, how does it affect market share, how much are customers willing to pay for choice, and do increased choices simply cannibalize sales from previously existing options?

Operating under the umbrella of the old-technology systems, market demands drive production schedules. FMS have created a new situation. On the one (traditional) hand, marketing pushes production to make what it can sell. On the other (less conventional) hand, production pushes marketing. This occurs when optimum production schedules can yield cost savings that are so substantial that it pays the firm to manufacture products that marketing never requested. When production tells marketing what to sell, there has to be some understanding of what marketing can sell. Effective communication between the two functions is of critical importance. The old management technology that separates the functional areas of the company is passé. Management has the challenge and the opportunity to make the most of FMS potentials. No one can yet be certain about what the new changes mean, but we do know that old management systems have been outmoded by the transformed role of information systems.

SMART FACTORIES, SMART WORKERS, SMART MACHINES

Smart factories are not perfect CIMs. Smart factories are the best real approximation to what is really intended by the CIM concept. Perfect CIMs are impractical. With smart people around, there is no reason to strive for total replacement of the human brain by machine systems. Smart factories are practical, working systems that take advantage of the balance between smart workers and smart machines.[7]

Smart machines are the force behind economic turmoil. They are the essence of the new wave in technology. The advent of smart machines is the best possible way of describing the change in manufacturing technology that is taking place. In terms of nuts and bolts (we must add chips and programming logic), smart machines provide enormous memories, rapid computations, persistence that outstrips human endurance, and so on. When combined with good computer programming and adaptive mechanical systems, smart machines provide flexible manufacturing capabilities. Whether smart machines are artificially intelligent is a moot point that seems better suited for philosophical discussion than for any practical purposes. By smart, we mean that these machines can do things that otherwise require human assistance, especially in the form of mental skills such as memory and skill routines. Robots can sense certain situations, remember instructions, and they can be reprogrammed. Sometimes they can communicate with each other.

With smart machines fewer workers are required because the smart part of the machines does the work that formerly occupied any number of blue-collar workers. If the systems designs are effective, then the activities of the replaced workers are those that are less expensive when programmed than if the workers did them. Continuing in the same vein, good systems design uses workers where programming would be more expensive than employing well-trained people. That is why smarter workers are needed who are capable of programming and reprogramming the computers that control the mechanical and electrical components.

Smart factories employ fewer, but smarter workers. In addition, smarter managers are essential to take advantage of the new manufacturing technology. The way in which everyone gets smarter is by using information in new ways. All of the smartness is embodied in new aspects of integrated management information systems. Sharing information is the essence of CIM technology, which is the foundation of the new management technology. We can now characterize this new technology as the synthesis of smart machines, smart workers, and smart managers, which leads to smart factories.

Smart people are the critical resource. There must be enough of them, and they must get smarter all the time. That is what is really needed for success in the new technological era. Reading the daily papers, we find that education is slipping in the United States. Literacy is essential for basic performance. What are we to do if there are not enough smart people? The problem is real, but the shortage is not. Japanese transplants in Tennessee encountered literacy problems. They have offered all workers courses in English, which have been readily accepted. Most workers in Tennessee are smart. Those who couldn't read are learning to do so. Smart is better defined as the willingness to learn when there is reason to do so.

The General Electric Company (GE) has experimented with a smart factory in Salisbury, North Carolina, which reports major improvements in cycle time reduction. Value-adding time is increased. New projects are speeded up. The success of Salisbury, as a smart factory, has led to cloning efforts for other GE factories. The Honda Corporation of America has been a time-oriented company for a long time. It has not specifically called its factories smart, but it is clear that they are as smart as the new technologies allow. When new manufacturing technology and new management technology converge, the reported results are always related to time-based improvements. Time has become the crucial variable for competitiveness in the context of the next technological era. Chapter 7 deals with the time-based aspects of becoming a global competitor.

Smart management recognizes that transition is the condition that will prevail for the next decade. Established bureaucracies of the last era hated transition. Those management groups, of which many are still practicing, strove to get through with transition, much like navigating the tricky currents before entering the safe harbor with its calmer seas. The advantages of equilibrium and stability are not available during periods of major technological transition. Great opportunities exist for newcomers during these periods of transition, because those who enjoyed the halcyon days no longer have the stomach for the turbulence to start again.

REVISED HUMAN RESOURCE MANAGEMENT

At the center of the new approach to human resources is the fact that smart workers have more to contribute when they are not policed and regimented. They also have more to offer when they are given constant training and allowed to gain greater perspective about the operation of the company. As good as this sounds, there are some unexpected problems that arise as a result of the increased participation of people who work on the line and in the offices. The old military models never die. Often, these people are said to work "in the trenches."

Happy Workers; Reluctant Managers

As management bestows more freedom on the workers and, in effect, empowers the people on the line, the workers get happier and their managers get perplexed. Undoubtedly, managers are confused because they have been brought up with the stereotype that exists in the U.S. culture for the smart, authoritarian manager and the lucky workers who have such a good boss. In a number of U.S. firms, the Horatio Alger story of the boy who makes good has changed significantly. Managers are no longer called managers. Instead, they are called associates, coordinators, facilitators, or consultants. What workers are called in these companies has also changed. They are called members, or associates, or other names that remove elitism from the workplace. This kind of change is the effect, not the cause, of the change that is taking place in management technology.

The changes that are taking place tend to make the workers happy. Unfortunately, the cause of the workers' happiness, which is more freedom, power, and participation in group decision-making, appears to backfire on making managers happy. Our surveys of manufacturing employees, especially for those in large bureaucratic firms, indicate that managers have problems with the enhanced position of the line workers. Control has been passed from the managers to the workers. Managers have less responsibility because the workers have more. This applies to on-the-job decisions, but also to other areas related to work schedules, bonuses and payroll, the working environment, food service and coffee breaks, and so on. Managers who have to discuss these kinds of issues with workers seem to get less job satisfaction out of organizational arrangements that make them feel as if they are on the same level as the workers. The MBA education is hardly adequate preparation for managers. It does not help MBAs to see the advantages of empowering line personnel, which although decreasing their power, benefits the company.

Research Results on Some Japanese Firms Operating in the United States

At this point, we provide a brief summary of some of the characteristics of changing managerial styles gained from research done by the Columbia Center for Operations, which is part of the Graduate School of Business at Columbia University. This research provides in-depth observations of five Japanese firms operating in the state of Tennessee.[8] A summary of this research is presented in Appendix A.

Here are a few statistics. Total Japanese direct investment in Tennessee exceeded $2 billion by the beginning of 1990. This was approximately 4 percent of all Japanese investments in the United States. Tennessee was host to 71 Japanese firms, including 41 manufacturing facilities and 30 sales and distribution centers. There are 12,650 employees on the payroll of Japanese employers, with only a few hundred coming from Japan. The largest of these plants operating in Tennessee that employ more than 500 people each include Nissan, Bridgestone, Sharp, Calsonic, and Toshiba.

The five Japanese factories included:

1. An electronic components plant, owned 50-50 by two Japanese companies
2. A heavy industrial equipment plant, a 50-50 joint venture with a large American company

3. A large truck and car tire manufacturer, 100 percent acquired and owned by a large Japanese firm since early 1983

4. A major auto component producer, 100 percent owned by the Japanese

5. A TV assembly plant, 100 percent owned by a large Japanese electronic corporation

We also used research based on tracking studies of foreign affiliated firms operating in the United States. Appendix B presents one of the most recent of these studies.

The research indicated that American employees working with (mostly) American managers in Japanese-owned firms with Japanese top management produced fewer defectives, worked harder, and had lower absenteeism and turnover. Generally, they were more satisfied than Americans working for American firms. A number of them contrast their level of job security with that of workers doing similar jobs for American firms in Detroit and elsewhere.

Furthermore, Americans working on the plant floor of the Japanese-owned firms consistently have been improving their performance. They consciously make the effort to produce fewer defectives, decrease their absenteeism, achieve higher productivity, and so on. They are rather stable in their expressed satisfaction with their workplace situations.

BREAKING AWAY FROM TRADITIONAL WORKER-MANAGEMENT RELATIONS

In July 1989 the workers at the Nissan plant in Smyrna, Tennessee, voted on the question of whether or not to join the United Auto Worker's (UAW) union. They voted 70/30 against joining the union. This is a concrete example of the preference of U.S. workers to stay with the Japanese-style management policies with which they were familiar. Another related example occurred three years earlier, when the workers at the Honda plant in Marysville, Ohio, turned down the UAW bid to organize production workers.

In both cases, workers said they rejected unionization because they felt more secure with the existing situation. To be sure, not all workers voted with the company. Also, some workers referred to the expansion plans of both companies in terms of job security. But overall there was a definite indication of trust in the management system that employs American managers to carry out the policy directives of the Japanese owners.

Our studies do not specifically refer to these companies. But, across the spectrum of companies that were studied, there was definite evidence that while the workers in Japanese-owned plants were satisfied, the American managers in the same firms (who were carrying out the directives of the Japanese owners) were uncomfortable with their situation. The workers felt they had more control over their destinies; the managers felt they had less control. Often, off the record, the managers expressed frustration with their situations. This trend has appeared in studies since 1982, so it is not a fluke of any one survey.[9]

Why is it that while the workers prefer the Japanese management style, the managers themselves are not nearly as enthusiastic? If these managers are not enthusiastic, why do they stay? They do not all stay. Managerial turnover is higher in the Japanese firms than it is for European-American firms and for strictly U.S. firms. Those managers who stay with the same firm as long, or longer, than the overall U.S. average of three years say they feel they are learning something that will be of great value to them in the future. Many of them—especially those in human resources, marketing, purchasing, and accounting—say they get involved with a different mind-set. We would paraphrase that mind-set as a systems view of company problems, and a different orientation toward technology and quality.

One of the major gripes, heard even from Japanese managers in the U.S. foreign-affiliated firms, is the lack of clear managerial control, including the ability to fire workers. The Japanese managers explain that this need is appropriate in the American situation. Another negative factor is the support for small but continual changes that take place in the production process, usually because of worker suggestions and minor product design changes. Although often stated last, perhaps the most important point is the difficulty of moving up the career ladder, which is custom-made in a typical American hierarchical organization structure and frowned upon by Japanese management policy. To emphasize this point, there is the fact that Tokyo retains the final say in all major matters.

It is important to note that the policies that underlie the Japanese management style are carried out by the American managers who are instructed in the ways of the Japanese. So, in the examples given below, American managers are doing things that please the Japanese top management. While they make the workers happy, they do not fit their American-based images of being personally successful. There are very few MBAs in these management groups, although this number has been increasing, in a limited way, over the past five years. As an example, the Sony Corporation has made a concerted effort to find ways to give MBAs a sense of career opportunities.

Bearing in mind that the four points below can be criticized for broad generalizations, here are some of the things that workers have said they like, and that managers have said that they do not like:

1. Workers like the fact that managers are expected to spend time on the plant floor in an advisory capacity. American managers do not enjoy plant floor duty. They prefer big, upstairs offices with minimum interruptions. Plant floor workers and office workers like the open-space plan, which puts managers without walls right onto the floor. Most managers prefer the privacy of their own offices. They feel more efficient with walls to protect them from the noise that makes telephoning difficult, and protects them from constant interruptions.

2. Workers like flat, decentralized organizations that are small enough so that everyone knows each other, and people are on a first-name basis. American managers prefer deep hierarchical organizations so there are many assistants below them on the organization chart, and so the potential to rise in the hierarchy is substantial.

3. Workers like the fact that they can introduce continual incremental changes to improve their work processes. Managers prefer stable and nonchanging systems. They consider their jobs to be more important when they spend their time on "big issues" involving major investments.

4. Workers feel good that they are partners with managers, sharing in responsibility for product quality and for output rates. Managers in the United States and Europe have seldom been indoctrinated to a system where they are viewed as facilitators and coordinators. Yet, in small and medium-sized firms, managers traditionally assist workers in attaining their quality and productivity objectives. In managerial terms, workers enjoy the control they have over tactical issues, whereas managers prefer dealing with strategic considerations.

If such ideas are part of a new management technology, it seems apparent that human resource managers will have to hire and train both workers and managers in a distinctly different way than is common practice today. Is there any recipe for getting American managers to enjoy following the precepts of the new management style? This is not likely in large, hierarchical organizations. On the other hand, the owners and managers of small and medium-sized U.S. organizations have already adapted to the demands of smart workers, smart machines, and, thereby, smart factories. This is because managers who take action with the power of ownership have a sense of purpose that matches that of any globally successful company.

Team Play Is a Matter of Size

The key concept for Japanese firms in the United States seems to be "team play." Large, bureaucratically run organizations do not have the communication systems or the will to cooperate that team play requires. Smaller organizations that have the team orientation appear to have happy workers. Those that also provide, in one way or another, the power of ownership, avoid the frustration of management, so apparent in the Japanese success stories.

This fact raises the question of why we call this style of management Japanese when it occurs all over the world. It is apparent in small and medium-sized (including family-run) organizations. It has appeared in decentralized units of large organizations. When technology changes, these small units are the first to adapt to the new situation. Simply stated, when there are few managers in an organization, they know every worker and get involved in all functions. Decentralization of large organizations, which cuts the hierarchical structure down to size, fosters the management style that makes both workers and managers happy. This is even more evident when managers really participate in the ownership of the firm.

The Japanese are doing something about managerial dissatisfaction in their plants in the states. They are providing more upward mobility for American managers and transferring more authority to their (increasingly decentralized) subsidiaries. If anything, they are further flattening their U.S. organizational structures. The Japanese are pleased when they see workers assuming more power, which means that managers have less power over workers. Our studies show increased expenditures on worker training. Managers continue to be considered as advisors to workers and not policemen. If the new formula works, it may set a model for American firms to make the workers and managers happy at the same time. For management to be willing to share power, they have to be part owners of the firm. The reality is that there is just so much power to be shared. The very things that make the workers happy seem to make the managers feel impotent. With the workers getting a greater percentage of power, necessarily the managers are getting less of it, unless the managers are so busy that they appreciate the assistance of anyone who relieves their overburdened schedule.

A second source of managerial dissatisfaction is that Japanese systems are based on teamwork, whereas what American managers want is rewards for aggressive, individualistic behaviors. It may be that power sharing is not really at issue. Rather, it is know-how sharing that lies at the heart of the Japanese management success. Americans are good team players. If top management believes this, can the know-how sharing culture be made to work?

THE EFFECTS OF NEW TECHNOLOGY

Peter Drucker concluded his excellent article about manufacturing by pointing out four areas of conflict that have troubled twentieth-century plant management.[10] Each of his pairs has a yin and a yang aspect in that they complement each other, but they attempt to dominate each other as well. We see these dual terms, not as old and new, or before and after, but as the past in transformation toward the future.

The first of these word pairs points to the management conflict in dealing with people and machines. The past (era) stressed people. The future (era) will stress smart machines. The resolution of this conflict can be seen in action. (GE and Honda are mentioned, but there are many other places to study.) The conflict is resolvable by changing the traditional relationships; as machines become smart, the fewer people that use them become smarter, faster.

The second conflict is (and we reverse Drucker's order for the pair) money and time. In the past, money had the upper hand. Time was second best. As we move into the future, this relationship is reversing. Time is crucial because it secures advantages that will never be measured by money. Smartness, survival, adaptiveness. longevity, loyalty, control over destiny, and power to implement are some of the terms that defy being measured by money. So, in the era that is coming, time-based management is replacing money-based management.

The third point of conflict is standardization versus flexibility. The accomplishment of the past was the development of superbureaucracies. The bureaucratic goal of inflexible routinization is passé. Established companies are trying to go through another metamorphosis in order to be present in the future. The means by which some companies are succeeding in doing this is the subject of Chapters 5 and 6. Many companies will not be able to accept the fact that transition, not equilibrium, has become the standard operating condition. Flexibility is the way to adapt, and to survive and prosper in an epoch of transition.

The fourth of the word pairs points to the management conflict that arises between functions and systems. The job of each function is not at issue. The job must be done, but not as it has been done in the past. In our terms, the compartmentalization of functions is the essence of routinized inflexibility. In the future, the systems view will prevail because the winning global competitors use it. It wins because it integrates the information and knowledge of all functions by means of continuous communication. It wins because it learns faster than any other approach, and the technology is now there to support it. Perfect CIM is an ideal model for manufacturing systems, but any approach to a CIM-type system is bound to be smarter than rigid policies that are out of date before they are programmed.

NOTES

1. Another translation of this oft-quoted saying by Alphonse Karr is: The more the change, the more it is the same thing.

2. The dictionary definition of "bureaucracy" reveals its roots in government: a system of carrying on the business of government by means of departments or bureaus, each controlled by a chief, who is apt to place special emphasis upon routine and conservative action. The definition is extended to organizations in general, as follows: a system which has become narrow, rigid and formal, depends on precedent and lacks initiative and resourcefulness. *Webster's New International Dictionary* (Springfield, MA: Merriam-Webster, 1959).

3. Gavin Wright, "The Origins of American Industrial Success, 1879-1940," *American Economic Review*, October 1990.

4. Winston Churchill is reputed to have said this about Lady Astor in describing "her only fault." The intended association is with the sclerotic condition identified with old age, namely, arteriosclerosis, which is hardening of the arteries.

5. Martin K. Starr, ed., *Global Competitiveness: Getting the U.S. Back on Track* (New York: W. W. Norton, 1988, for the American Assembly, Columbia University). See Chapter 5, "Integrated Process Management: A Management Technology for the New Competitive Era," by Marek P. Hessel, Marta Mooney, and Milan Zeleny. Also see Chapter 7, "On Waiting for Neither Godot Nor the Apocalypse: Practical First Steps to Move U.S. Managers Toward World Class Managing," by James A.F. Stoner, Arthur R. Taylor, and Charles B. Wankel.

6. *Global Competitiveness*, Chapter 5, p. 140.

7. See Shoshana Zuboff, *In the Age of the Smart Machine: The Future of Work and Power* (New York: Basic Books, 1988).

8. Martin K. Starr, and Zhuang Yang, Principal Investigators, "Report on Japanese Managerial Skills and Practices: Based on the Study of Five Factories in Tennessee," Survey Report sponsored by the Center for Operations, Graduate School of Business, Columbia University, July 1989. Appendix A provides a brief summary of this research.

9. At the conclusion of Chapter 5, some ideas are presented for achieving new levels of cooperation between unions and management. These notions were put

forward by the managers of various companies, with long-standing union relationships, that are making efforts to move away from confrontation with new organizational arrangements.

10. Peter F. Drucker, "The Emerging Theory of Manufacturing," *Harvard Business Review*, May-June 1990, pp. 94–102.

PART III _____

REORGANIZING

Part III consists of Chapters 5 and 6, which deal with strategies for reorganizing the company. Changing the way you do business might be essential if the old way is not succeeding. However, before managers can redesign their organizations, they must understand what is happening to that system and, especially, what is going wrong. Before they will decide to change the system, the force of dissatisfaction must overcome the costs (including nonmonetary costs) of giving up the status quo. Chapter 5 provides a number of ways of approaching change, and includes the description of a model that elucidates the preconditions necessary to change oneself.

Chapter 5 explores tactics and strategies available to companies that are trying to compete for global markets. Companies have invented a variety of competing and cooperative strategies fashioned to fit their own unique situations. Some of the competitive approaches discussed are continuous quality improvement, being first bringing new products to market, downsizing the organization by decentralizing managerial responsibility, increasing the firm's value-added, and so on. Chapter 6 examines partnerships. This includes the use of cooperative organizational arrangements such as tactical and strategic alliances, mergers and acquisitions, keiretsu, and joint ventures to take advantage of synergies and symbiosis.

CHAPTER 5 _____

Transforming the Existing Organization

So who is us? The answer is, the American work force, the American
people, but not particularly the American Corporation.

Robert B. Reich[1]

The Japanese manage to incorporate a huge amount of change and yet
remain stable[2]. What is meant by this? Japanese managers we have
surveyed don't think that much has changed at all. Their perception is
somewhat akin to that of a tightrope walker. If you make a mistake you
fall off. Practice long and hard; learn to keep your balance. But, if you
do fall off, which is likely to happen, make sure you have a safety net.[3]

ERAS OF BUSINESS COMPETITIVENESS

Technology has always played a profound role in determining the
character of competition. When technological change is moving along at
a fast rate, then the technological component is at the cutting edge of
what constitutes the competitive advantage. When technological change
begins to slow down, other factors that make one company more
competitive than another come into play. While there are no hard and
fast dates to give for the exact beginning or end of particular eras of
competitiveness, the list below provides a fair approximation of basic
changes in the forces that dominated competitive success at different
points of time over the past 70 years.

Production (inventions)	1920–1950
Marketing (high volume)	1950–1970
Financial (investments)	1970–1990
Technology (systems)	1990–2020

The production era that started about 1920 was dominated by inventions for the job shop (stand-alone machines like turret lathes and milling machines). There were also inventions for the flow shop. Sequenced assembly manufacturing (which Henry Ford started in 1903) was still a new idea in the 1940s when Henry Kaiser built Liberty Ships for the U.S. war effort on a flow shop basis. Process inventions were used to make steel and rubber, find and refine petroleum, move people and cargo across the country by auto, plane, truck, and railroad.

After World War II, marketing was stressed because of the need to move large volumes of product. By 1970 the growth of companies required as much capital as could be obtained, so financial managers began to take over the reins of corporations. The investment business flourished almost like a board game, where companies bought and sold other companies whose product lines were not even known to them. One might suppose that it was the financial excesses of junk bonds and leveraged buyouts that caused a shift in focus during the late 1980s. However, it is more likely that the change in technology to information-driven, flexible manufacturing created the need for top management that was oriented toward putting it all together with the systems viewpoint. The fourth era, just starting, is concerned with the interconnectedness of new technology, and the effect of systems thinking on management practice.

THE CHANGING CHARACTER OF BUSINESS COMPETITION

To make an organization more competitive, it is necessary to understand the various forms that competition has taken over time. Since we have talked about the phoenix countries rising from the ashes of defeat with competitive advantages, it seems fitting to start with the Phoenicians establishing Carthage about 810 B.C. The greatness of Carthage is attributed to its competitive success in international trade. Queen Isabel had international trade on her mind when, in 1492, she agreed to underwrite the expeditions of Christopher Columbus. David Ricardo, an English political economist of the free trade school (1772–1823), explained that one country would trade to another those things that it had some advantage in making. It would receive back, in turn, those things the other country had an advantage in making. Thus, each country exported what they made the best, and imported what the other made the best. Ricardo called this logical economic process "comparative advantage." Taking advantage of comparative advantage, the Dutch and the British developed colonial empires for trading purposes. The British Commonwealth was a special kind of trade association.

At the end of World War II, the United States became the volume producer for a broad array of products on a worldwide basis. This was a time of mass production with acceptable quality and reasonable prices. In the United States, the need to increase demand to absorb expanding productive capacity led to development of multinational corporations and to emphasis on marketing both domestically and internationally. We can call this the "production capacity era." It was epitomized by mass production concepts pioneered during the war for such diverse items as canned Spam and Liberty Ships.

By 1960 a new era was under way, which can be called the "consumer value era." Japanese industry was reconstructed with the emphasis on quality level at the best possible price. At first, the opportunity was epitomized by low-cost products (such as autos), which were not luxurious but more reliable than the competition offered. As discretionary income increased on a worldwide basis, the consumer was presented with up-scale luxury items, still at the highest value received. The notion of value received is difficult to formulate, because it involves qualities delivered divided by the prices that must be paid for those qualities. The consumers' values for a set of qualities must be measured in terms of perceptions, which means that market research is needed to measure value received. The global competitors in this era measured success by sales and market share, which means that they accepted the risk of bringing out a new product and then being wrong about consumer reactions. We will discuss both the U.S. penchant to measure perceived quality before bringing a new product to market and the alternative, which is to make cosmetic changes rather than fundamental changes.

By the end of the 1980s, a new era was well under way, which we can call the "technology-driven era." The consumer was now offered high quality at low cost, and there was also the opportunity to upgrade user technology with capabilities not yet anticipated by users. This meant that a stream of innovations needed to be incorporated into the production capabilities of the company. At the same time, major changes were occurring in the relations between the USSR and the United States. The Cold War was coming to an end and economic factors seemed to dominate the world situation. Some called it the end of history as the world had known it—that is, the end of military might and the beginning of economic competition on a global scale. That position led to such statements as: "In the new era, economic performance will replace military might as the measure of a nation."[4] Seven months later, problems of war and peace in the Middle East had quieted such speculation. Nevertheless, the planetary economy will inevitably dominate the energies of nations.

BECOMING MORE COMPETITIVE

Bureaucratic organizations are difficult to change. As these organizations age, their bureaucratic responses become increasingly ingrained. Their managers are more likely to perceive opportunities as deviations from accepted practice that must be avoided. Efforts are concentrated on cost control. Direct labor costs are decreased by reducing the work force. Productivity is increased by demanding more output from those workers that remain. Increasing plant utilization is considered to be another way to increase productivity. This approach increases work-in-process and finished goods. It also raises the number of defectives and the amount of rework.

Traditional Performance Measures Can Be Counterproductive

If the wrong standards are used to measure performance, then the better you get by these standards, the worse off you become. It may be counterintuitive that by increasing plant utilization, a firm can be stubbing its toes. Keeping people and machinery busy is fine as long as the demand exists, at a profitable price, for what is being produced.

The domino effect is nowhere more apparent than in the case of competitive slippage. Manufacturing goods just to keep busy raises inventory levels. Price cutting is used to increase inventory turns, which slash profit margins. The banks and the market don't take kindly to this so they decrease your credit ratings. This means that competitors pay less than you do to get the funds to buy new machinery. A fundamental competitive advantage exists for those firms that can change their technologies at a lower cost. This scenario is intended to show that the additional stock-on-hand, which was produced by the desire to look good on utilization measures, carries a far steeper penalty than the cost of idle employees and underutilized equipment. By using the wrong measure of performance, the firm becomes less and less competitive.

Another example of a counterproductive measure of performance is related to downsizing by work force reduction. Starting around the mid-1980s, the United States has gone through a period of sustained downsizing. It may be partly true that downsizing by firing is a way to become more competitive. There are substantial cost savings. As proof that something good must be happening, consultants often warn their clients: this is going to hurt. It does hurt, and the pain does damage to the competitiveness of the firm.

Fewer people on the payroll cuts costs. However, although the payroll is smaller, there is still "hell to pay," which is a slang expression for the fact that a hidden penalty of substantial size has not yet been taken into account—that is, the cost of poor morale, if it could be measured, would be huge. Poor morale and fear inhibit the creative pursuit of new sources of revenue.[5] This results in further erosion of revenue, market share, and profitability. The problem is actually worse than it seems. Competitiveness is diminishing, which is reflected by the decrease in market share. But market share is a relatively weak surrogate measure for a company's competitiveness.

Valid measures of competitiveness are tied to customer loyalty. One measurement standard that cuts to the heart of the competitiveness issue is based on the comparison of competitive products with respect to their appeal to customers. This standard of competitiveness can be rooted in product qualities (what it does, how it looks and feels, how long it lasts, how safe it is, who repairs it, etc.). Product value is determined by each customer based on what those qualities are worth and how much they cost. This kind of competitive standard is difficult to measure, especially when the competitors are constantly improving the product. Then, the competitive standard is a moving target that gets tougher to measure, rougher to match, and near-impossible to beat.

The use of financial standards to assess how well a company is doing in competitive terms is misleading. It is also subject to manipulation. The same criticisms apply to marketing performance standards. That is why we advocate the use of product-to-product and service-to-service comparisons. Through the eyes of customers, these comparisons can help a company understand what is causing its competitive problems. Then it has a chance of being able to correct the situation before it slips below the point of no return. Market research can help to generate the kind of information that is relevant for assessing the perceptions of customers to their product choices. Engineering standards are also helpful, but only after knowing how they relate to customer attitudes. Many companies rely on customer complaints. While this can be helpful, it is skewed and incomplete information. A very small percentage of customers complain in a meaningful way. The real problems may not be the ones that customers mention. The key to discover is what really motivates customers to value the product and the company that makes it.

Intrapreneuring—Downsizing for Innovation

An attractive alternative is to use idle time to create new revenue-generating ideas and activities. Statistically, and logically, the innovative process is bound to produce more failures than success stories. Since bureaucracies abhor failures, it is unlikely, in most large firms, that the agenda to use idle time for creation of new forms of revenue will get off the ground. On the other hand, by empowering separate groups to intrapreneurship,[6] it is possible that management will circumvent the constraints of the overly established firm. Intrapreneuring is a term cleverly coined to represent entrepreneurial efforts inside the firm. Of all the terms that connote business striving to be innovative, entrepreneurship leads the pack.[7]

As we have noted, the term "downsizing" is usually taken to mean a reduction in the size of the work force. The reduction is aimed at decreasing direct and indirect labor costs. In a different sense, downsizing can be achieved by breaking up the large, hierarchical organization into smaller components. This is done to get everyone into the act. The smaller group size improves communications. The expectation is that by gaining the small-group advantages it will be possible to overcome the bureaucratic stasis. In this sense, intrapreneuring becomes a form of downsizing without firing anybody. The counterintuitive part of all of this is that downsizing by firing is likely to deteriorate competitiveness, whereas downsizing without firing is likely to improve competitiveness.

The group that is commissioned to develop new products or processes is self-contained. To be effective, it must be empowered to act like an independent company. It cannot function successfully if it is penalized for failures by its parent. But it has to be awash with incentives and replete with motivations to be successful. An example of success, along with a description of the difficulties encountered, was reported by Tom West for the development of a new Data General Computer.[8]

When properly designed, the intrapreneurial group has some of the characteristics of a joint venture. What it lacks in the synergies to be gained from partnership with other firms (different markets, know-how, resources, etc.) it may make up by avoiding the problems of developing familiarity with strangers. Such effects are described in the sections on joint ventures in Chapter 6.

If the intrapreneuring process is really supported by top management, it may have a chance. This means that management anticipates many more failures than successes. Therefore, failures are not penalized. As successes occur, the firm becomes more competitive. Since all of this is as obvious as it seems to be (and many managers we have surveyed know about it), why aren't firms discarding the wrong performance criteria and changing to the right ones?

The measures are wrong only if competitiveness is the goal. The measures are appropriate if maintenance of the status quo is the goal. It is more difficult to change the goals of an established bureaucracy than any other form of organization. By analogy, bureaucracies have been designed to protect their goals with an immune system that effectively eradicates the virus of change. It is their strength in stable times. It is their weakness in times of change.

CREATING SMART PILOT PLANTS

There is no way to change the zebra's stripes. But a company that earnestly would like to move from the old-tech to the new-tech framework is able to experiment with the concept of a smart factory by setting up a pilot plant operation. A pilot plant is a scaled-down model of the full-size system, used to experiment with concepts of the full-size system without the costly risks. Ideally, the smart pilot facility will be a separate division that is kept physically apart from the rest of the company.

The next step is to avoid the trap of thinking that new-tech equipment must be purchased immediately and installed. First, a new idea must be instilled, which is that labor is composed of relatively interchangeable individuals. The workers cannot be considered as commodities by management, and unions (if they exist) cannot be treated as adversaries. The smart factory is a learning facility. Training is an on-going function in which everyone participates. All employees help to define what kinds of training should be available. Eventually, all employees can apply for any of the jobs in the factory. A fair and reasonable basis for reviewing applications should be determined with the help of all employees. Open access to all data bases is a goal. What should be in these data bases is, therefore, a question of concern to everyone.

The above description sounds as though everyone is messing around in subjects that they cannot possibly know anything about. A crucial point is that people should not be expected to participate in considerations and decisions that lie outside their areas of competence. Since the smart factory is a learning organization, there is no restriction about who listens in, but there are requirements as to who makes decisions. Among the first decisions that must be made is what kind of smart equipment should be brought into play to augment the present production system.

Since computer systems are the foundation of smart machines, computer training has the highest priority. What has been learned from experiments that are at present under way is that contrary to what had been expected, the trend to fewer employees does not downgrade the required participation of workers. Rather, it increases the need for smarter workers who could interact with the smarter machines. Supervisors as policemen began to be replaced by supervisors as consultants to the workers. Also, a cadre of designers and planners becomes essential to utilize the capacity of the smart machines. This establishes priorities for learning.

PRIORITIES FOR LEARNING

The priorities for learning focus on making changes with least disruption. Keeping the existing system running is important, but has a lower priority than changing the existing system. The words that carry the highest priorities for learning are: innovative quality first and after that, in no special order, variety, speed, cost, and productivity. The issue of producing a variety of product innovations quickly enough, places emphasis on:

1. changing the system continuously, so that:
   a. quality levels continuously improve, and
   b. constantly surpass the competition, but
   c. production must remain smooth

2. producing a large variety of products that:
   a. marketing can sell, and that
   b. production economies dictate

3. speeding new products to market, often by working with customers and suppliers, so that:
   a. quality is not compromised, and
   b. timing is just right (see Chapter 7)

4. removing waste and maximizing value-added to obtain the lowest costs of production

5. having lower break-even volumes than competitors.

If quality levels are to improve continuously, it is essential to be able to live with change. Many devices are used to facilitate this goal. For example, suggestion systems are set up with a variety of reward systems for those who come up with ideas.[9] Quality circles have been tried with some success and some failures by a great number of manufacturing and service companies. The secret of success is well-known, but that doesn't mean it can be emulated. Superficial improvements, like requiring that pencils be used down to the nub, are ultimately counterproductive. The changes that must be made are organizational. There must be pride in the company's product, and both monetary and psychic pay for achievement of quality goals.

Willingness to innovate and improve continually are organizational attributes. Downsizing by means of decentralizing the power structure and the communication system are reasonable first steps. Alliances, as described in Chapter 6, are sometimes the means to the end. The eye on the ball, in this case, is to design products and services that everybody wants, and to produce them with diligence to the precept that value-added is the ticket to success. This prescription is futile if the organization is too large and too bureaucratic to respond to the challenge. Management has to be able to see both the details, and the whole, expanding its vision by systemwide management to improve short- and long-term performances.

These new management systems decrease the need for internal supervision and increase the need for management interface abilities. The interfaces include "loyal" customers, "trusted" suppliers, and smarter factories, which by means of telecommunications extend their reach all over the globe.

MANY DIFFERENT KINDS OF COMPETITION EXIST

Competitors are, by definition, those who are competing with each other for some part of the world's total disposable income. The mission for each company is clear: the pie is out there, get the largest slice you can—or, put in another way, capture as much market share as you can. We prefer to talk about gaining loyal customers. Loyalty takes care of the present and provides for the future.

Language is replete with words that describe conflict: compete, vie, contend, strive, struggle, challenge, rival, battle, and fight. Each carries its own nuances and derivations. One of the most interesting of these is "rival," which is derived from people living on opposite shores of the river. In the present time, rivals are as apt to live on opposite shores of distant oceans as they are to be on opposite corners of a busy intersection. In the past, rivalries were more likely to be focused on military issues than on market shares. This is changing, especially among the industrially developed countries of the world. For the developing countries, military situations may still be more appropriate than economic competition. Ultimately, however, the rivalries of the twenty-first century will be played out in market penetration and cash flows.

Competing by Emulation

We hear a lot about "simulation," but emulation is a concept that has not been similarly discovered. "Emulation," by dictionary definition, is (1) to try to equal or surpass, (2) to imitate (a person or thing admired), (3) to rival successfully. Emulation is a form of "competition" that brings to mind another competitive description, namely, that of the "underdog." The competitive implication of emulation is that the underdog attempts to equal the leader's performance before striving to surpass it. The underdog, for reasons that are usually obvious, is operating under a disadvantage. At the same time, being an imitator carries certain negative connotations that emulation avoids.

A class of influential marketing models shows how an imitation of the market leader's products can provide handsome profits to the company that copies the successful product of the company that was first into the marketplace.[10] The emulator can wind up having the second-best share of market. Winning by mimicry is not the kind of imagery that a powerful company would like to associate with its ability to pull off a competitive coup. It does, however, illustrate how complex competitive strategies can be for a company that innovates in some areas and imitates in others. In this case, the copycat firm has extra money to use for marketing promotions, price reductions, or for further innovation of the "me too" product. By being the emulator, this firm has not spent the time and money on R&D that the originating firm has spent. It has also been spared the expenses required for the introduction of a new product to the marketplace.

All firms are to some extent imitators. Industrial systems' know-how has been transferred back and forth around the globe by multinational corporations as users, by equipment manufacturers as producers and sellers, and by consulting groups as teachers and facilitators. Nevertheless, emulators are usually considered to be the underdogs in the business arena. Competitors that are viewed as underdogs provide some interesting insights. The Japanese were considered to be underdogs when

General MacArthur's economic mission was to resurrect Japanese industry. The same concept applies to the use of the Marshall Plan, where aid was supplied by the United States to help European reconstruction.

Price discounting with high quality is a viable strategy. There is a great deal of uncertainty about how people will react to the underdog. Probably the response is directly correlated with the attractive qualities of the underdog. In general, it can go either way. Sometimes they are given a break; at other times they are kicked around. Strategists for candidates to political office have to evaluate how many votes their candidate will get, and how many they will lose, by portraying themselves as an underdog. The underdog gets votes out of sympathy for someone struggling against the obvious winner. Underdogs have been known to score resounding victories when the leading candidate has been painted as arrogant and cocksure, which turns away votes. Similarly, people often root for the underdog team or the underdog player. But, when it comes to making purchase decisions, customers do not choose the underdog out of sympathy. Customers opt for the best valued items within the set of choices that they consider substitutable. (Best valued means the highest ratio of qualities to price.)

Competing as an emulating underdog can be effective when price discounts are of interest to the customers. The imitations must be of the same high quality as the imitated. Discounters of all kinds have built enormously successful businesses by picturing themselves as a no-frills outlet. Service is the only compromise in this case. The products that are sold are the same as those that could be bought in the high-price frilly department stores. In fact, service is the only way in which the frilly department stores can win back customers from the discounters who are selling the same merchandise. Early Japanese successes in the auto markets were the result of bargain-basement prices.

When Japanese exports first started making inroads in the United States, their manufacturers were accused of imitating ideas that had been developed by American engineers and designers. It was said that by using cheaper labor they could undercut the U.S. market prices to obtain market shares. As the costs of labor rose in Japan, the price cutting allegation disappeared. The accusation about imitation did not. After many years, it became entirely clear that the Japanese prospered because of their superior methods of process engineering, which were not imitations.

It is useful to summarize this important point with a few examples. TVs, VCRs, and compact disk players (CDs) were created in the United States. There was nothing wrong with U.S.-made TVs, but they were far more expensive, less reliable, and of lower quality than the TVs made by Sony, Panasonic, and other Asian firms. The idea for the VCR was American. Ampex and Sony made professional models for use by the TV studios. There never was a practical U.S.-made, household VCR. Sony introduced the first Beta models and Matsushita's Panasonic Division competed fiercely with Sony by introducing a different format (VHS). As time went on many innovations were introduced (e.g., lighter and smaller sets, remote wands, on-screen programming, freeze and slow frame controls, four heads, stereo).

The innovations were part of a competitive battle that was fought exclusively between Japanese companies. The same history of developments applies to radios and CDs. The Sony Walkman evolved from the transistor radio, which was developed in America. The United States got out of the radio business more than 30 years ago. The Wankel engine was developed in Germany. Until Mazda's RX-7, no company in the world was able to employ it. The Japanese started with someone else's basic ideas. Then, by means of design changes and a superior manufacturing process, they won the customers' loyalty. The same recipe works over and over; improvements in product quality follow from continuous design improvements and better manufacturing methods.

Reverse imitation occurs when U.S. firms emulate Japanese business systems. In fact, it was not feasible for U.S. firms to copy Japanese business systems. The one exception was the production process, which could be emulated because it had more to do with technological factors (which travel well) and less to do with cultural differences (which do not transfer easily). But even so, imitation of the superior production systems has not been easy for large American companies. To understand why this is so, we should note that continuous improvement is built into present-day Japanese production systems.

Competitors Using Continuous Improvement Methods

In the early days of development, as one improvement led to another, the Japanese institutionalized the procedures for continuous improvement. Japanese business units operate on a systems basis, meaning that all of the functions talk with each other, and there is an effort to reach a real consensus. These procedures result from cultural forces that support cooperation between members of an organization and reject adversarial behaviors between them. As a result, Japanese production methodology includes integrating the design of products and processes. Japanese production planning is synchronized with marketing and distribution. Since the bureaucratic structures of large U.S. companies are directed to protect inflexible routinization, it is clear why emulation of the Japanese production system is not a simple matter to attain.

Long before any technological change of manufacturing started coming into play, the Japanese utilized the economies of scale derived from serial (flow shop) production methods. This was the original MITI plan.[11] To aggregate large and therefore economical production volumes required aggressive participation in world markets. Thus, production demands pushed marketing into a global role, and distribution of products from Japan to places all over the world was the connecting linkage. Thus, originally, the Japanese were successful as low-cost, high-volume, global competitors.

Later on, as new flexible manufacturing technology made changeovers from one product to another inexpensive, the Japanese incorporated these ideas in their already smooth-flowing, continuous production line. With careful planning of their product designs and production processes, their companies moved into the next technological era as the leading global contenders. Because of the emphasis on continuous change, it has not been easy for the large U.S. companies to imitate the Japanese production methods. But, on the face of it, no great objections arose from any sources for U.S. firms to utilize this form of reverse imitation. Small and medium-sized firms do not seem to have any trouble making it work. The largest companies have been the first to analyze and apply the Japanese production methods. But these organizations have had lots of difficulties with many of the fundamental features of continuous improvement systems.

COMPETITIVENESS AND THE SIZE OF THE BUSINESS UNITS

When intrapreneuring was discussed as a means of downsizing without firing, it was apparent that organizational size was an important competitive variable. One of the advantages of start-up firms is that they are small enough to enjoy the communication advantages that are denied to large firms. Start-ups can move quickly, but that doesn't mean that they all do so. Failure rates for start-up firms are very high. Many reasons account for the high mortality, but one that we like the least is the idea of random selection for bad luck. Much that is published about new firm failures treats the start-ups as though they were the hordes of tadpoles that must work their way upstream while being devoured by myriad predators. At last, a few survive to become frogs, and begin this process over again.

Small business units that survive are different from those that fail. They all have the potential advantages and disadvantages of being small. One of the disadvantages is that it is more difficult to obtain capital. Another handicap is that the new product or service may not have been as well researched or designed as a large organization can do it. That is why the large organization that is willing and able to break itself into smaller units can gain substantial benefits. The small business units have access to the capital and research/design know-how of the large company. At the same time they have the small organizational advantages of flexibility and creativeness.

It is worth noting that in world markets, it is the small and medium-sized manufacturing firms that are the most successful exporters from the United States to Canada, Europe, the Pacific Basin countries, and South America. Without them, the U.S. trade deficit would soar because manufacturing exports are the only entries that balance out the huge amount of imports being brought into the United States. They are the fastest growing segment of American business. These small and medium-sized manufacturers have the best track record for converting R&D dollars into profitable ventures.

REORGANIZING: MULTINATIONAL AND TRANSNATIONAL CORPORATIONS

Multinational corporations (MNCs) have a clear record of being adroit with international finance. They have benefitted from differences in capital markets, currency shifts, and tax advantages. MNCs have shown less deftness with respect to international marketing and almost no flair at all for international production. Marketing has been successful to the extent that it has emulated the national model. Plants for manufacturing in foreign countries have a strong tendency to look and to act like all other run-of-the-mill national plants. So, when we think about how a company should reorganize itself, the MNC-model is not likely to be anyone's first choice. It may, however, be their second choice. The first choice will be a modification of the basic premises that, in the past, have worked so well for the multinational corporation. We call these modified MNCs transnational corporations (TNCs). The TNC appellation has been used quite interchangeably with MNC, but it is a different form of doing business. TNCs are companies without a specific home-country affiliation.

In the 1950s and 1960s, multinational corporations were innovators of substantial merit. In the 1990s, the major complaint that can be leveled about MNCs is that they have aged like their parents. They have become arthritic and slow. MNCs have become MNBOs—multinational bureaucratic organizations. In general, they are not as routinized or as inflexible as the home-grown variety of bureaucratic organizations. This is because MNCs tend to be run by foreign nationals who speak the two languages of the parent and the subsidiary, and who are sensitive to cross-cultural issues and problems. They are living in the global community while the parents are not.

When a multinational corporation is no longer identified with the nationality of its parent corporation, it becomes (in our terms) a transnational corporation. Ideally, the personnel of TNCs can operate effectively in all of the countries that form its network. Language may inhibit free movement from a plant or office in one country to that in another. If the company's orientation is truly systems-based, then office and plant interchanges are no more traumatic than transcountry moves.

We hope this description makes clear the fact that TNCs transcend the characterization of the home-based parent. Some very large organizations, such as IBM and Sony, appear to be transforming themselves into TNCs. While not there yet, they are striving to fulfill the reality of the model, which includes freedom of communication between all locations and levels. Bureaucratic inhibitors are evident in both organizations. These inhibitors constrain creativity and replace it with inflexible routinization. In concept, TNCs are truly global companies. Appendix B presents data that show many companies losing their national parent affiliation by dint of strategic and financial alliances. Chapter 6 explores such partnerships.

The special features that made MNCs so successful, at one time, are still evident, although old age has slowed them down. Instead of worrying about which country gets the profits, TNCs are defined by stockholders, employees, customers, and suppliers who are themselves transnational— that is, they come from every part of the globe. TNCs are the essence of what "becoming global" means. The achievement of being a TNC is aided by strategic alliances and joint ventures as described in Chapter 6. Because they are composed of global components, total communication ability is essential. To be successful, the network of cooperating entities must have a time sense for continuity, concurrency, and synchronicity. These are turning out to be the hallmarks of world-class competitors.

We can expect that the performance of TNCs will be recognizable by the following characteristics:

1. ability to attract potential employees for all kinds of jobs, from a global pool; ability to attract capital from global sources; flexibility in finding and choosing suppliers from all over the world

2. appeal to customers from all over the world fostered by imaginative, aesthetic, and reliable product designs that are constantly being up-graded.

The international dimension of flexibility is one of the most difficult to define. Achieving international flexibility will be one of the greatest challenges for new companies and those that are attempting to change themselves in order to gain or regain the global advantage.

HOW TO BRING ABOUT CHANGE

Changing an existing organization to become globally competitive is a large order, even when the CEO has stated unequivocally that this objective has top priority. Understanding what is involved in bringing about change is essential. Once the mechanism of change has been explained, it becomes clear why an executive order will not suffice.

Dr. David B. Gleicher developed a change model that has been received with enthusiasm by many individuals who have different perspectives.[12] His model was used to structure the agenda for a three-day American Assembly held at Arden House in Harriman, New York, November 19–22, 1987. The conference title was "Running Out of Time: Reversing America's Declining Competitiveness." It was attended by representatives from industry, labor unions, government, the media, and academia. The conference participants were charged with the mission of preparing a final report, which was published in an edited book of papers that provided background for the meeting.[13]

The Gleicher model states that three factors must be present to allow an organization to change. These three factors have a multiplicative effect on each other, so that if one of them is zero, then there is no force for change. Further, when all three factors are greater than zero, their product must be greater than the cost of changing the situation. The three factors are: dissatisfaction with the present situation (D), vision of what the future can become (V), practical first steps to achieve the vision (P). The model is: $D \times V \times P > C$, where C is the cost of changing.

Spelling out the three factors in a little more detail, one would expect dissatisfaction with the present situation for those firms that are consistently losing market share and customer acclaim. U.S. automobile companies are great candidates for being dissatisfied. Although their advertising might belie the fact, the top executives of these companies are discontented. How can they change to regain their competitive dominance? They have taken steps to improve their quality and to reduce costs. The problem is that their bureaucratic organizational form remains and it continues to constrain what they can do. They can shed this inhibiting organizational form and replace their "anachronistic factories."[14]

Becoming a successful global competitor is the vision of what the future can hold in store. But the problem is that the turmoil created by the change in technology has led many American firms to take a defensive posture. Machine tool companies are working with products that symbolize the new technologies that are at the cutting edge of tomorrow's factories. Their vision is reflected by their actions. They are downsizing by firing, and closing plants instead of spearheading new product innovations, and building new state-of-the-art plants.

Practical first steps to achieve the vision make no sense if the vision is retarded, inward, and defensive. Even if the glimmerings of the vision are there, the problem is that no small steps are likely to work. Realizing that this is true may be the most important constraint on change for American manufacturing giants. Chapter 6 begins with a quote from Lloyd George, who said that is impossible to jump over a gorge in two leaps. The alternative formulation of this concept, that half the distance is better than none, does not work when critical thresholds exist. You can't get half a moon rock by going halfway to the moon.

A lot of effort to transform an organization will be wasted if the threshold principle is not understood. Whatever steps are taken, they must produce results that overpower organizational inertia, which, like a sponge, can absorb far more weight than its own. Exceeding threshold levels can be done with innovative moves that take advantage of experimentation and joint venture. All of this brings to mind the story (from Greek mythology) of Sisyphus, a greedy king who is doomed in Hades forever to roll a giant stone up a hill; but the stone never gets to the top and always rolls down again.

We can explain why bureaucracies have so much difficulty changing themselves: the costs of changing loom very large. Dissatisfaction is minimal for those who are powerful enough to make the decision to change things. Supporting change is not realistic until the CEO gives up power and pay. In large organizations, each employee is being paid, and usually well enough, for the time being. Those who find themselves unemployed are usually shocked because they always thought that someone else was expendable. Stockholders have high dissatisfaction, but they can do little about that. Customers who are not happy find that the cost of changing to a new supplier is too high for them to switch.

As far as vision of future possibilities is concerned, many executives believe that if you wait long enough, the future will cycle back to be like the past. The confusion is one that we have mentioned before. Economic conditions cycle as a result of the technological waves of wearout and replacement. These dynamics stress the company's ability to adapt to change. If the company does not adapt, it will fail because the consumers' expectations are not cycling. Rather, the customer expects continual improvement as the marketplace absorbs the new technological potentials. Management that waits for "the good old days" is itself an anachronism—that is, out of its proper historical time. Operating under the pressure of turbulent economic conditions, the quality of life for management and the financial well-being of the stakeholders do not cycle. But change can be started if the vision of becoming a multinational corporation, or, better yet, a transnational corporation has enough appeal to get everyone in the company started together on this new path.

The practical first steps are not obvious. The phrase implies that the first steps are small. Common sense says there are no such opportunities. But then, as Stuart Chase once pointed out, common sense is "that which makes us think the world is flat."[15] There are relatively small steps that can be taken that include the intrapreneurial pilot experiments described in this chapter, and the use of joint ventures described in Chapter 6.

THE POSDiC REVISION

Applying the POSDiC concept (Planning, Organizing, Staffing, Directing, and Controlling), which was developed in Chapter 4, the first requirement for transforming an organization is to alter the planning goals. Move to niche marketing all over the globe, and plan for the implementation of flexible production systems that can furnish the variety required by the marketing potential of the product design plans. Find innovative arrangements that put unions and management on the same team.

This means giving up on the old system, which focuses on achieving high volume equilibrium production and marketing situations. Organize and staff so that people are happy to eliminate the inflexible routines. Reorganize the controller's function so that it encourages experiments aimed at destroying standards of mediocrity. Shift primary activities away from the removal of deviations and toward innovations that, when successful, will alter the way that everything is done. The new staffing criteria is to bring in employees who are uncomfortable with stability and who enjoy change, not for the sake of change, but for the sake of long-term competitive success.

COOPERATIVE ARRANGEMENTS WITH UNIONS

Possibly one of the most important areas for new organizational developments to take hold is between unions and management in the United States and Europe. To discuss the type of cooperation that is possible—as a form of reorganizing the company, or transforming the existing organization—we can refer to the Nissan Company's defeat of the UAW bid on July 28, 1989. While this defeat was taken as another sign of the crumbling power of unions in America, it should have been recognized as the signal of a new opportunity for unionized American auto manufacturers.

While many factors account for the workers' rejection of unionization, the Nissan Company's slogan, "One Team," symbolizes the ability of management to convince workers that Nissan, as a company, was better-suited to protect workers' interests than the UAW in the 1990s. Nissan's solution of "One Team" highlights a seldom-considered condition that afflicts unions these days: namely, that a redundancy of functions has developed between union and management bureaucratic organizations.

Not long ago, unions were a natural counterpoint to those managements that viewed labor as a commodity that could be exchanged for machines. Unions arose to protect workers' jobs against speed-ups, layoffs, and various grievances. Management was responsible for profits and unions for wages. The functioning of the production system was balanced by this adversarial relationship. This system could be fine-tuned because there was great stability in what was being produced. Adding to the stability was the fact that product line changes came slowly and production processes were developed that could be characterized as labor- or capital-intensive. Such descriptions are misleading now because of the continual changeover to new manufacturing technology, and the correlated decrease in blue-collar inputs, as was shown in Figure 3.2. The traditional struggle in manufacturing is passé. There are new rules that outmode the traditional standoff to the status of an argument about who is going to hold the buggy whip. These days, the talk is technology, as software and hardware interact in complex ways to meet the demands of volatile markets on a global scale.

Production systems are now responsive to market needs. This means that production processes are embedded in the organization's strategic response system. They are not a white elephant, or a sunk cost. They are as dynamic as any other part of the whole. In this new functional interactive organizational arrangement, management is forced to assume a different role—a role that is more involved with the production function and, therefore, one that is supportive of workers as crucial functionaries in the production process. Nonproduction managers seldom know how to produce the products. Even engineers are too specialized and so far removed from the production process that they cannot stand in for the workers on the line. Management complacency, derived from the belief that it knows more than the workers about the production process, has evaporated. All of the players are dependent.

NEW OPPORTUNITIES FOR UNION-MANAGEMENT RELATIONS

As a "One Team" mentality emerges, we are seeing more worker training and cross-training for different jobs. Because workers are valuable production system resources, rational management strives to reduce absenteeism and turnover by increasing wages and benefits, in spite of cost-reduction pressures. Job security is enhanced and there is increasing focus on participative management to capitalize on the potential contributions of worker know-how.

Workers at the Nissan plant (and at the Honda plant, three years earlier) indicated their belief that management supports them. Management recognizes their role in achieving continuous improvement of the production system. Even more significantly, the workers rejected the idea of two management teams looking after their interests. Under these circumstances, unions seem isolated in their traditional role of jousting with management in a win-lose contest. Then what legitimate function is there for the union when management usurps the old, traditional union role? Alternatively, what justification can be found by management that would permit them to include participation of unions in their strategies?

Let us generalize what we have been discussing to any manufacturer operating in the United States. In light of the Nissan vote to have one unified management team, there are only two strategies that make sense. The first, which many companies, including the Japanese transplants, tend to use is to avoid unionization. There are many strategies for doing this, including locating plants in nonunion regions of the country. Going nonunion is not at all restricted to Nissan, and not even to Japanese transplants, but it is not our first choice. Going nonunion is more readily available to start-up companies, whether or not their industry is typically unionized, than it is to established companies such as U.S. automakers who are already deeply involved with unions. In that regard, the presence of the UAW in the U.S. auto industry has a long and time-honored history that could be turned to a real competitive advantage for U.S. companies.

The second solution is to have the unions join the management team in pursuit of becoming a successful global competitor. Working together, not as adversaries, but as teammates, union and management could each do what each does best. As will be described in Chapter 6, this is one of the primary requirements of a successful alliance. The union-management alliance would be engaged in a win-win effort. Both groups win when the company wins. Competition is focused on outside companies. Energies are not wasted with internal struggles.

What's the quid pro quo? Management needs the knowledge base about production processes, and how to make a better product at a lower cost. MBA courses in finance do not supply that kind of unique production know-how, which is increasingly more valuable as technology becomes smarter. Workers need to be given the constant training that will create a learning organization. Workers count on management to understand the financial and marketing issues that support selling the product that they make. In all the surveys that we have done, there has never been any indication that workers would like to take over that aspect of running the business if they don't have to do so. Thus there is quid pro quo—the attributes of the union members and management complement each other in the kind of harmony that promises an organization that can compete successfully.

Let's go into this alliance agreement a bit deeper, by considering the reality of the present predicament. Aside from small and medium-sized companies, much of U.S. management lacks knowledge of how to obtain and use production leverage to gain competitive advantage. Further, U.S. management shows no inclination to become production-oriented. Corporate managers more readily identify with activities centered around planning, budgeting, advertising, marketing, and strategizing.

In these major U.S. firms, what is sorely missing is management ability to take the initiative in productive creativity (which includes the design of the product and the process). Even when CEOs come out of the production department, in large companies their hands are quickly tied by the culture of the company and the stress that must be placed on financial and legal issues, marketing, and governmental impingements. Meanwhile, MBA course preferences epitomize the situation. One financial crisis after another since October 1987, has barely dampened the desire of these graduate students in business to prefer jobs in finance to any and all others by at least two to one.

Also, there are some compelling reasons why unions are well-equipped to team up with company managements that traditionally eschew the plant floor. Union managers know how to release the competence and creative capabilities of the blue-collar workers. They are themselves the blue-collar contingent that understands production processes. They respect the value of total training. They admire the achievement of quality. They hold in esteem the pride of good workmanship. They are ashamed of shoddy work even when it seems to make sense to someone on the basis of a financial analysis. They know how continual improvement is secured. The MBAs do not. They seem to come from different worlds, which is the basis for the greatest alliances. Alliances work when people need each other and know that they need each other. Because they know their respective strengths and weaknesses, when they get together they can make quite a team.

NOTES

1. Robert B. Reich, "Who Is Us," *Harvard Business Review*, January–February 1990, p. 54.

2. "The interesting thing is how the Japanese manage to incorporate a huge amount of change and yet remain stable," said Robert Alan Feldman, economist for Salomon Brothers. "This is something for the West to consider." New York *Times*, January 1, 1990.

3. The safety net is analogous to contingency plans.

4. *Fortune* Magazine, January 15, 1990.

5. One of W. Edwards Deming's 14 points from *Out of the Crisis* (Cambridge, MA: MIT Center for Advanced Engineering Study, 1986), is "Drive out fear."

6. See Gifford Pinchot III, *Intrapreneuring* (New York: Harper & Row, 1985).

7. The characteristics of entrepreneurship are well spelled out in Peter F. Drucker's book, *Innovation and Entrepreneurship: Practice and Principles* (New York: Harper & Row, 1985).

8. Tracy Kidder, *The Soul of a New Machine* (Boston: Little, Brown, 1981).

9. The Paul Revere Company's dealing with service quality established all kinds of rewards for good suggestions and improvements in general. See Pat Townsend, *Commit to Quality* (New York: John Wiley, 1986).

10. Stochastic models of consumer preference distributions can be found in marketing and market research journals and textbooks. A major commercial model, developed by the Hendry Corporation of Croton-on-Hudson, New York, has been utilized by major marketers all over the world.

11. MITI is the Japanese Ministry of International Trade and Industry. It has played a major governmental role in shaping the Japanese industrial complex. Over the years, U.S. government figures and industrial leaders have alternately cited it as an example of the powerful effectiveness of industrial policy, and railed against it for

supporting unfair practices. MITI pushed Japanese export industries to develop highly cost-efficient, serialized production processes throughout the 1960s and 1970s. In the 1980s, MITI took a less apparent role in export industries, but it strongly supports the development of computer capabilities for flexible manufacturing systems.

12. The Gleicher model is described in some detail in R. Beckhard and R. T. Harris, *Organizational Transitions: Managing Complex Change* (Reading, MA: Addison-Wesley, 1977).

13. See the "Final Report of the Seventy-fourth American Assembly" in the book sponsored by the American Assembly, *Global Competitiveness: Getting the U.S. Back on Track*, ed., Martin K. Starr (New York: W. W. Norton, 1988).

14. This is a term coined by Wickham Skinner, a professor at the Harvard Business School, whose contributions to manufacturing knowledge are legion.

15. Stuart Chase, *The Tyranny of Words* (New York: Harcourt, Brace, 1938).

CHAPTER 6 _____

Forming New Kinds of Organizations

> The most dangerous thing in the world is trying to leap a chasm in two jumps.
>
> David Lloyd George

MANAGING FAR-REACHING CHANGE

When it comes to chasms, gorges, ravines, and abysses, mountain climbers move about with care. Transforming an organization is similar. Crossing the gap between what the organization is now, and what it will be after transformation, can be as fatal as staying put. This warning about how dangerous it can be to change things gradually is attributed to Lloyd George, who was prime minister of Great Britain during chaotic times.[1] Its relevance to political and military decisions is not in doubt. How does it apply to business?

Faced with major decisions about making far-reaching changes in manufacturing and management technology, planners might well prefer to make the transition gradually through off-line experiments with other organizations. (By off-line, we mean that the new organization is not directly involved in the day-to-day business of the company.) But, while the gradual approach might not mobilize enough energy to bring about change, the new cooperative arrangement with another company is sure to have some repercussions. It might even shake things up.

The term "alliance" is employed in many different ways by company executives, journalists, and academics. The literati call it a "dressing

136 GLOBAL CORPORATE ALLIANCES

gown," a word that hides a lot of meaning beneath its folds. A cooperative arrangement is a simple way to describe an alliance. But then, cooperation is itself another dressing gown word. Some of the cooperative arrangements that can be used are limited commitments of company resources, such as joint ventures, a subject we will be exploring. The problem is that limited solutions, even when successful, might not influence the companies that participated in the experiment. Nothing lasting might ever come of the limited approach. Still, alliances intended to change the way that an organization behaves are worth trying even though there are no guarantees of success.

COOPERATIVE ORGANIZATIONAL ARRANGEMENTS (COAs)

Lloyd George's admonition is most appropriate to explain why cooperative organizational arrangements are now receiving so much attention from large, long-established, and mature companies. The chasm that these firms face seems to have opened up suddenly, like a giant fissure from an earthquake. This is analogous to the widening gap between the old technology of routinized systems and the new technology of flexible process control. The analogy continues with management of the old technology stressing the removal of deviations and the maintenance of unwavering standards. Management of the new technology is still learning how to use smart people with smart machines to make smart factories.

The deepening abyss (or gradually widening gap) was there to be seen for many years. Recently, it has become abundantly clear that competitive events are moving faster and faster. The chasm must be crossed now by firms attempting to survive severe technological wearout. As the process of change accelerates, the ability required to cross the gulf from the old tech to the new tech becomes increasingly demanding. Figure 6.1 provides a humorous interpretation of the required transition.

Throughout the nineteenth and early twentieth centuries, royalty, politicians, and generals dominated the alliances among nations. These cliques made the overriding arrangements that determined the distribution of global power. Within nations, royal families interlinked ruling connections through marriages. Kings and queens held sway with succession determined by their offspring princes and princesses. Military alliances dominated the major and minor wars that repeatedly drained the energies of the world. To exemplify the preponderance of these types of alliances, journalists described the opposing sides in World War II as

Figure 6.1
Management Attempts to Jump to the New Wave

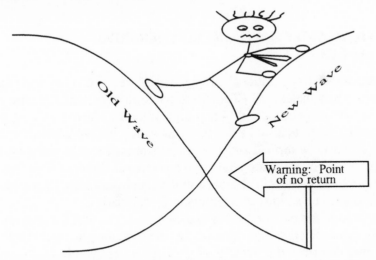

the Allies (United States, Britain, France, USSR, Australia, Belgium, Brazil, Canada, China, Netherlands, New Zealand, plus six other countries) versus the Axis (Germany, Italy, Japan, Hungary, plus two other countries).

A major change in the global power elite began to occur about 1975. Companies that formed economic alliances started to emerge as cross-boundary power brokers. Royal families had been losing stature since the end of World War I. Kings, queens, princes, and princesses were fast becoming symbolic tokens of gentility. Military alliances were being replaced by global business arrangements. The rise of Japan as a major economic power sent a signal to the world that national interests could be best served by growth in exports and foreign investment rather than growth in armaments.

In 1990 the USSR acknowledged that its commanding military arsenal could not stem the economic erosion that was debilitating the nation. The revision of priorities for all of Eastern Europe sent another signal that return on investment had become more important than military offensive capabilities. The USSR has serious economic problems and so does the United States. The Cold War is gone, but on the economic front, the two superpowers are in trouble. This is not sudden; the handwriting has been on the wall for a long time. Consider the following quote, written in January 1985 by the President's Commission on Industrial Competitiveness: "Our ability to compete internationally faces unprecedented challenge from abroad. Our world leadership is at stake, and so is our . . . standard of living."[2].

TACTICAL AND STRATEGIC PARTNERSHIPS/ ALLIANCES

Cooperative organizational arrangements are as diverse as crystal patterns. Nevertheless, all COAs are some form of partnership arrangement between two or more different organizations. The overall category could be called tactical and strategic partnerships, but preferred common usage seems to be tactical and strategic alliances. This chapter suggests that by means of such cooperative organizational arrangements, ailing and moribund bureaucratic business organizations can reconfigure themselves to become serious competitors in global markets.

One reason for partnerships is to create synergies where the partnership is more effective than each of the partners acting alone.[3] Another word that describes the benefits of partnerships is symbiosis. Derived from biology, symbiosis occurs when by working together the partners gain mutual benefits. Many kinds of biological symbiosis have been recorded; much less is known about the various ways that companies can work together. This is not for a lack of examples. Some good books and papers have been published.[4] What makes study difficult is the rapid changes that are taking place in the regulatory approaches of different countries all over the world. Also, companies are changing the ways that partnering is done, but there are some fundamental patterns.

Alliances are cooperative arrangements, made between firms for mutual advantages. The mutuality of the advantages will be different for each partner, but on their individual scales of perceived value, the advantages to one must be balanced against the advantages to the other. If that is not true, and one partner is getting more than the other, the alliance is unstable and likely to dissolve. Worse yet, if one partner feels "ripped off," then the alliance is bound to fail. In many ways, alliances are like marriages. It helps to realize that they succeed and fail for the same kinds of reasons that cause couples to split up.

Alliances Alter Hierarchical and Regulatory Constraints

Alliances introduce new communication patterns and new relationships into an organization. The degree to which this occurs depends on the kind of alliance that is developed. For example, in a merger the hierarchical layers of two or more organizations must be folded into each other.[5] At each level, leadership questions arise. Underlying any specific hierarchy is the hierarchism. These are "the principles or authority of a hierarchy." The hierarchy of an organization may be well-known, but its hierarchism is often less certain.

In military organizations, the hierarchism is clear and well-known. If the captain of the ship is killed in battle, all on board know the chain of command. Government hierarchism is spelled out, but there are ambiguities, and the principles are not well-known. Few business organizations have any idea of their hierarchism, even though their hierarchies are elaborate and usually spelled out by the company organization chart. Therefore, when an alliance occurs, there can be a clash of hierarchies. Ultimately, there must be a meshing of hierarchies, and a resolution of where authority lies for each level and function. The process can be beneficial by altering bureaucratic constraints.

Alliances between companies of different nations fall into a special category. These multinational alliances have opportunities to call upon the regulations of whichever country has the most favorable rulings. This can be a great advantage when it comes to international trade. Goods can be manufactured, assembled, and warehoused by the partner's country that exacts the lowest toll. Taxation and customs differences are other factors that multinational alliances can exploit. There is also an intangible factor, which has to do with potential conflicts in the application of two nation's laws. Knowing that, the members of the alliance, working together, choose to invoke whichever country's policies seem most beneficial. The dual-country affiliations tend to keep regulators off balance. It is noticeable that those in charge of taxes, tariffs, and fees are confused by the situation, and they look the other way. The noninterference preference can be felt at all levels in the U.S. government administration and right up to the doors of the U.S. Congress.

Organization Chart of Alliances

The forms that these partnerships can take include both strategic alliances (SAs) and tactical alliances (TAs). For analytic purposes, it is convenient to depict tactics as a separate branch of alliances. This is the case in Figure 6.2, which shows an organization chart of alliances. In real life, tactics are to strategies like the hand to the glove. Both must be included as a working part of any reorganizational arrangements.

Figure 6.2
Structure of Alliances

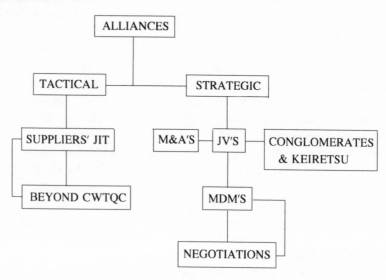

As shown in Figure 6.2, the first level for partitioning alliances is SAs versus TAs. The left-hand branch of Figure 6.2 deals with tactics, which are the methods for accomplishing the strategic objectives of the firm. Tactical alliances are partnerships formed to increase the firm's value-added by improving the product line and the production process.[6] The emphasis is on methods to reduce defectives, work-in-process, delivery quantities from suppliers, and so on. We have called these topics Suppliers' JIT (deliveries are made just-in-time) and Beyond CWTQC (meaning that the use of companywide total quality control includes everyone who has anything to do with the company). They are discussed in Chapter 7, which deals with time-based management. The time orientation includes a conceptual framework and a set of methods for achieving fast response and timeliness. Time control has become one of the most important tactical competitive factors. Time planning has become one of the most influential strategic components.

The right-hand branch of Figure 6.2 deals with strategic alliances, which are business partnerships involving financial interchanges, market-sharing, know-how-sharing of production technology and R&D. In this category, we will consider mergers and acquisitions (M&A). Alliances are defined as close associations (of companies, or nations, or families by marriage). If one company acquires another simply to sell off its parts, that hardly qualifies as an alliance. The definition of "merge" emphasizes that someone's identity is lost by being absorbed. Commonly, when we "acquire" something, no identity protection goes with the deal. Consequently, the degree to which a partnership prevails with some M&As is open to debate. However, the majority of M&As are efforts to blend the best of each business unit, and some aspects of each partner usually endures.

Other forms of strategic alliances include conglomerates, keiretsu, and joint ventures. Conglomerates are financially driven aggregations of diverse companies that used to be far more popular in the United States than they are today. Keiretsu are families of firms engaged in diverse activities that are coordinated by powerful Japanese leaders. Joint ventures (JVs) are new business units that are usually dedicated to particular, well-focused, and limited objectives. Because they are created by the partnership of two or more companies, JVs necessitate negotiations between multiple decision makers (MDMs) selected by each of the participating partners.

SAs and TAs are agreements between two or more firms to work together for some mutual advantage, which is usually a combination of tactical and strategic benefits that are different for each partner. For example, a firm that has several suppliers for some important component that it uses approaches one of these suppliers with a proposal for a long-term, high-volume contract for the component. The buyer is taking a risk by moving from many to one supplier. The buyer thinks the risk is worthwhile because of the special trust relationship that promises to provide a better product at lower prices. The supplier is taking a risk by spending money to bring new technology into the plant, and by guaranteeing quality levels that must improve over time. The supplier thinks that the risk is worthwhile because of the special long-term relationship with a customer. The buyer wants smaller quantities of constantly improving quality, with more frequent deliveries, at guaranteed prices.

The two firms have to work out many issues that are of mutual interest, such as what happens if the supplier's costs of materials increase—that is, how much gets passed along? Similarly, what happens if a union-management agreement that will be up for renegotiation leads to a strike situation? How will the risk that the supply could be cut off be handled? These and many more questions need to be addressed. Many of the issues that surface are ordinarily not thought of, or they are ignored by companies that are too involved putting out fires to think about contingencies. By taking the position that a strategic alliance is being forged, an entirely new perspective is developed. Thus, SAs augment transaction effectiveness for all participating partners.

MERGERS AND ACQUISITIONS

Mergers and acquisitions are one of the major classifications of SAs. That is true when the participating organizations contribute their special know-how, preserve and endow the new merged entity with elements of their unique character, and retain some of their original personnel. If the arrangement is strictly a takeover of physical resources or market distribution, then the M&A is not an alliance, and the SA description is misused. M&As are fraught with problems of organizational blending and balancing. Fear is everywhere and human resource problems abound. But if there is a real desire to have the people of each organization cooperate, then some partnership advantages can be found. Note how in the "Case of Unimation," which will be described later in the chapter, even though management wanted to make the buyout synergistic, it was unable to do so because the social norms of the two organizations were so different.

Alliances in Name Only—Hostile Takeovers

Mergers and acquisitions can create unbalanced situations that have the potential to damage the new partnership. When these are accomplished by a hostile buyout, the advantages of an alliance are indeed questionable. There are many examples of unfriendly takeovers occurring in spite of the fact that this practice runs counter to common sense.[7] The belief that there is more to it than we can appreciate is belied by the number of failed systems that result from antagonistic acquisitions. Many of the people who represent the collective know-how and wisdom of the company flee to other firms. Those that remain do so because of constraints, and are not likely to become enthusiastic partners of the new management. If the buyout is not for people, but for property, such as production process techniques and patents, then hostile buyouts might be justified. However, even when takeovers are friendly, there are many pitfalls to confront before the new association can be made to work.

Somehow, the conviction developed that process and markets that are purchased (as part of an alliance package) can function effectively without the support of their people systems. This notion, which can be found in MBA cases, books on management, and in common parlance at executive programs and business conferences, should be carefully scrutinized. There is overpowering evidence that the assumptions are incorrect. One of the premises of new-wave technology is that management technology is of considerable importance to becoming global. The cooperation of people is essential in that context.

In the 1980s, many M&As were driven by one party having a power advantage over the other one. The more powerful partner takes control. The fact that the acquired company does not object is no assurance that a hostile takeover is not in process. The acquired puts up no fight because it has no hope. Never mind, says the financial community. These takeovers are the best thing that ever happened to American business, because the companies that are taken over are marginal producers. After the takeover, the new management will set things straight and bring back efficiency to the company. The takeover artists are the tailors who clothe the famous emperor. They create such an illusion that the emperor is forced to doubt his own senses. He goes out in public naked.

There are many different motivations for doing M&As. One party wants entry to a foreign (unknown) market. Another wants to learn about new process technology. Access to talented people, limited resources, acquisition of know-how and an infusion of capital are other reasons. Foreign buyouts of Hollywood studios such as MCA, MGM, and Columbia Pictures are examples of big investments seeking creative talents to produce, direct, and act in pictures. The advantages of alliances—including mergers and acquisitions—can be realized when mutual benefits are really shared and synergy occurs.

As a result of working out arrangements for mutual satisfaction, the inflexible elements of bureaucracies can be removed. Both parties to the alliance start out being bureaucracies, and yet, the new organization can be flexible, and ready to be smart. The POSDiC rules of management (which were explained at the beginning of Chapter 4) can be developed to fit new-tech opportunities, and the old-tech rules can be discarded when both parties insist on achieving synergy. But, if the new alliance is a power play takeover, then the more powerful company's bureaucracy will prevail.[8]

Are there different meanings for the M and the A? The various motivations do not explain why there are different words for mergers and acquisitions. The etymology of these words, as used by lawyers, accountants, and the financial community, is not clear. Why are these two words always teamed together with an ampersand? If they mean the same thing to a financial person, specializing in M&A, why isn't one of these names enough? Are there any Wall Street investment firms with a department that is simply called "Acquisitions" or, alternatively, "Mergers"? If, in a practical sense, they don't mean the same thing, which one is preferred and for what purposes? There is also the legal matter having to do with the way that the stock is bought up and redistributed.

There is no intention to be facetious. Each alliance is quite special. It is not possible to sort them into the two classes, Ms and As. The category belies the fact that to be successful, these kinds of alliances need to be guided by smart managers of smart people using smart machines in smart factories and smart offices to provide levels of efficiency and innovation that match those of the global competitors. Financial arrangements and legal issues are not the stuff of which customer loyalty is made.

Conglomerates: Financial-Based Mergers

Large-scale conglomerates were one of the early forms of M&As. Their popularity soared in the United States during the 1960s and 1970s. They are no longer regarded with great favor, but important conglomerates remain, which explains why they are included in Figure 6.2. A few of the biggest ones are mentioned later.

What accounted for the surge in the formation of these organizations? The motivation was to buy up companies having financial problems, no matter what their industries or products. The tax laws benefitted both parties. But the centralized management of these myriad business organizations could not cope with their diversity. Various studies showed that the profitability of conglomerates was substantially lower than the average company operating with a product focus. Conglomerates, with their emphasis on financial acquisitions, in general, achieved the reverse of synergy. As a result of poor performance, many conglomerates ended up selling off most of their unfocused units. For example, Beatrice Foods, whose locus was plainly indicated by its name, found it difficult to manage a plumbing supply house that had been purchased during the stage of rapid acquisitions. Still, ITT, GE, Procter and Gamble, and other U.S. giant conglomerates continue to operate multiple units, and some with high degrees of success.

KEIRETSU

Keiretsu (an industrial group of companies with a family affiliation, such as Sumitomo and Mitsubishi) are a Japanese form of conglomerate. This said, it must be emphasized that the similarity to conglomerates in the United States lies only in the aggregation of disparate companies. Keiretsu have been operating in Japan, almost like feudal fiefdoms, for many years. Before World War II, the zaibatsu were the powerful leaders of the major keiretsu. They controlled the banks, the major industries, and were instrumental in national planning. After the war, the zaibatsu were gone, but the keiretsu regrouped and are among the most powerful companies in the world.

Unlike U.S. and European conglomerates, the hundreds of companies in each keiretsu are highly decentralized. While being separate and independent, they are part of an incredible communication network that allows them to cooperate with each other when there is mutual advantage to do so. Member companies can, at the same time, be competing with each other in one venture and cooperating in another.

In each keiretsu group, there is almost always a major bank, which can help members finance long-term investments that might be considered too risky by U.S. standards. For the most part, there is cooperation within the keiretsu family, but between the different keiretsu there is intense competition, both within Japan and worldwide. Americans think of competition between General Motors, Ford, and Chrysler as examples of domestic competition. By keiretsu standards, the competitive relations of these auto companies to each other would be considered as softball, rather than hardball. In any case, domestic competition has honed the competitive skills of the keiretsu companies. There are those who say that the Japanese competitive skills in the United States, and in world rivalries, are related to their fierce domestic competition.

The keiretsu groups find expansion to the United States compelling. The dollar is so weak relative to the yen that purchases of property, plants, and labor are a bargain.[9] At the same time, the U.S. trade deficit is large enough to cause concern about protectionism. To defend themselves against tariffs and other regulations that would keep out their exports, they invest heavily in the United States. Another set of equally good reasons can be offered to explain large keiretsu investments in Europe, which is no longer a series of small markets, with its emerging economic community. Consequently, the marked worldwide impact of the keiretsu organizational arrangement will continue to grow.

Let us consider a few of these keiretsu. There is the Mitsubishi Group, with 28 core members and hundreds of other Mitsubishi-related companies. When dealing with Mitsubishi, it might be wise to drink Kirin beer, use a Nikon camera, and take your life insurance with Meiji Mutual. With the Fuyo Group, you can drive a Nissan and use a Canon copy machine. Toyota and Toshiba are part of the Mitsui Group.[10]

Unlike the U.S. conglomerates, which accent financial management, keiretsu are oriented to cooperate in accord with whatever contribution a family member can make to help the other family members. Business units may be cooperating as suppliers of parts, lenders of capital, contributors of production know-how, or providers of access to markets. All of this happens quietly. It takes a lot of digging to find out who is supplying what to whom. Even then, many of the arrangements cannot be uncovered. Most of the agreements will never be known. Keiretsu behavior epitomizes cooperation based on mutual advantage. Keiretsus actively seek out joint ventures with a broad range of partners, all over the world.

JOINT VENTURES

One of the most successful forms of strategic alliance is that of joint ventures. With JVs, the partners agree to form a new business. By careful prearrangement, each of the partners contributes various resources, people, facilities, and money. They all share in the agreed-upon missions of this new company. However, they do not all have the same objectives.

The partners have created a new entity, much as parents having a child. The arrangement between the partners is more like a marriage of convenience than a marriage for love. This is because the partners enter the arrangement with specific goals and purposes in mind, which can include a termination agreement. For example, a joint research project might be concluded after the project is completed. In other situations, the new business might be nursed along until it is able to make it on its own. At that point, the JV will be given independence, and the partners will be stockholders in the new venture with all of the expectations for dividends and capital gains. In some cases, after a period of time one of the partners will take back the joint venture and run it as part of its own company.

As in all alliances, the motivating force is one of mutual benefit. Special to JVs is the fact that each partner usually has different reasons for wanting to cooperate in this way. One partner may be interested in gaining access to a market, while another partner wants to learn about manufacturing technology. The two major forms of joint ventures are those that focus on making and selling new products. In various ways, the partners share costs and contribute resources in line with their particular strengths. To a greater degree than with other forms of strategic alliances, joint ventures are a shared responsibility.

Sensitivity exists to failed expectations within JVs. The expectations of the partners should be realistic and fully understood by all participants. Professor Kathryn R. Harrigan of the Columbia Business School has pointed out that setting realistic expectations for the joint venture is a major factor in achieving success.[11] She also discusses how the selection of partners can lead to the successful negotiation of working agreements. A poor choice of partners is evident when their expectations are contradictory or conflicting, unrealistic, unattainable, or unnegotiable. What works at the beginning may change. Professor Harrigan warns that it is vital to be able to recognize when the system is no longer working.

Although they are difficult to handle, multinational joint ventures are proving to be worth the trouble to their partners in ownership. However, unless they are carefully designed, with a great deal of forethought about what can go wrong (contingency planning), they can end abruptly in a court of law. What the preagreements cannot take care of is insuring that good "chemistry" characterizes the relationships of the people working together in the new venture. A primary cause of JV failures is a lack of trust between the representatives appointed by each partner. Once hostility appears, the venture is unable to address head-on many of the problems that it will face. Understanding and respect between people can be particularly difficult to achieve when the joint venture partners come from many different cultures.

In a matter of a few years, the ownership of many firms that formerly were clearly identified with one country or another has blurred. A study completed in 1989 revealed that many joint ventures have so many partners participating in special ways that employees are no longer certain about the nationality of the company for which they are working. As an example, one company was a joint venture operating in the United States, ostensibly a 50–50 arrangement between an American and a Japanese company. However, the American company was partly owned by a Belgian firm, and the Japanese partner was the subsidiary of a British-Japanese venture operating in Canada. In another case, there was a complex cascade of alliances between producers, suppliers, and customers from all over the globe. The hybrids were composed of firms from the three major sectors of North America, Europe, and Asia.

Characteristics of Joint Ventures

Many of the characteristics of JVs will also be found in strategic alliances as a general class. However, the special characteristics of joint ventures come from the following facts:

1. There is limited scope to the JV operation. Only a small amount of capital and resources are involved for each partner. Thus the risk levels are contained. Failure does not carry major consequences. JVs are preferred to mergers when the necessary synergies can be realized with

the involvement of only particular areas of each firm.[12] Further, the duration of the agreement can be limited. Codevelopment is a usual limitation, such that a specific "product or technology development is the purpose of the joint venture. Projects for a specific goal are characteristic of joint ventures but not alliances.

2. It is possible to learn about and enter new markets with limited risk. Later, when NUMMI is described, it will be evident that Toyota was able to learn about, and become comfortable with, the U.S. auto market, not as an importer and not with a major investment, but as a partner in a limited-investment joint venture. The same can be said about the opportunity to gain first-hand experience with American employees and their unions. At NUMMI, Toyota tried out various hiring and training strategies with UAW unionized employees. The learning was great, the cost low. This is not usually available with other forms of alliances.

3. Another form of learning should be mentioned. That is, gaining know-how about new technology is a common objective of U.S. and European companies that team up with Japanese firms in joint ventures. The reverse is also true. Japanese companies have made strenuous efforts to learn aerospace technology through joint ventures. They have encountered great difficulties because various U.S. interests are leery about losing another industry to Japan.

4. Joint ventures are a way for companies to obtain much needed capital. If the firm that needs capital maintains a limitation on its participation in the joint venture, it can utilize profits from the joint venture to change its technology. It also maintains its identity for further bargaining. If it enters fully into the joint venture, it is essential that it brings as much bargaining power to the table as the other partner. In this regard, the auto air bag venture of National-Standard, which will be described later, is very interesting.

5. The partners that form the JVs exchange managers, expertise, and capital. They give these to the new entity as a dowry, and generally provide relative autonomy for its use. So to speak, the child is on its own; but because it is such a limited commitment, JVs tend to be unstable. The conditions for partnership are dynamically changing all of the time. JVs are seldom formed with the profit motive being the primary goal. Rather, learning, market entry, capital acquisition, technology acquisition, and regulatory facilitating are the primary purposes.

With respect to learning, each party seldom wants to learn the same thing. For example, one party may want to learn about advanced production processes, while the other wants to learn about labor conditions and other factors that play a part in the decision to open a plant in the other party's country. (Toyota in Fremont, California, moved on to near Lexington, Kentucky, and now plans a third assembly plant in the United States.)

With respect to facilitation, the main issue is how to gain market entrance so the JV is created in one party's country with that obvious purpose; but what has the other party to give? Usually, it is the product design or the production process that is used, such as the National-Standard air bag case.

Three Case Studies of Joint Ventures

The NUMMI Joint Venture Case—GM and Toyota

In the early 1980s, General Motors and Toyota agreed to restart GMs Fremont, California, plant (under the New United Manufacturing Motors, Inc. name). The Fremont facility had been classified as one of the worst auto plants in the United States, and had been closed down by the lack of employees reporting to work. The agreement between Toyota and GM was carefully worked out, including the union contract. All GM plants are unionized by the UAW, and GM reasoned that the union would insist that its joint venture be unionized also.

Toyota agreed to operate GM's plant. A limited number of GM managers were allowed in the Fremont plant, but strictly as observers. Toyota took about eight months to start up production of the Chevy Nova and Toyota Corolla (the Nova was essentially a Corolla).

It has been generally speculated that what General Motors hoped to get out of this joint venture was information about Toyota's latest technology. Also, Toyota wanted to learn about producing cars in the States with American workers. Toyota got what it wanted, but GM got something opposite to what it had expected.

During the long start-up period, Toyota used in-depth interviewing for employee hiring and eight months of training per employee instead of computerized machine and robot technology, which GM had been expecting to learn about. For reasons that are entirely consistent with their joint venture plans, Toyota experimented at Fremont by changing management technology (Chapter 4), rather than by changing to flexible manufacturing technology (Chapter 3). Perhaps 30 percent of the work force was sent to Japan for indoctrination and training.

After it came on-line, Fremont was rated as one of the best U.S. auto assembly plants. Because of these results, General Motors was said to have revised its plan to employ massive amounts of new technology in its effort to restructure. In 1988, Toyota opened its first U.S. plant in Georgetown, Kentucky. On November 28, 1990, the *Wall Street Journal* said: "Toyota plans to nearly double the size of its car-assembly complex with a second plant at a time when the Big Three auto makers are sharply paring their own operations."

There is a lot to be learned about joint ventures by studying NUMMI. There is no doubt that General Motors learned a great deal from this joint venture; however, what has been learned is difficult to apply because GM continues to be a giant bureaucracy, and Fremont's success exemplifies decentralized management. The Toyota management system empowers the autonomy of the local authority. Japanese terminology calls this "glocalization." Conjecture exists that Toyota will take over the Fremont plant when the agreement with GM expires.

The Air Bag Joint Venture Case

In September 1990 a joint venture was consummated between a wire manufacturer in Niles, Michigan, and the American trading arm of a Japanese steelmaker. The wire producer, National-Standard Company, and a consortium of Japanese companies in a similar business, led by Toyota Tsusho America, announced an agreement to build a plant in the United States.

The plant will turn out stainless steel wire cloth, which is used to filter and cool the gas that inflates an air bag in a fraction of a second after the initial impact of a crash. National-Standard's 50 percent equity in the joint venture gives it access to Toyota Tsusho's high-speed manufacturing technology for making wire cloth. In turn, Toyota Tsusho America and its Japanese partners expect to gain from the American company's commercial ties as a supplier of wire cloth to the world's two largest air bag manufacturers—TRW Inc. of Cleveland and Morton International of Chicago.

National-Standard's financial troubles forced the company to find an equity partner willing to invest in new equipment. The shortage of capital from U.S. sources has plagued many American companies. Without the capital to invest in new manufacturing technology, the risk of falling behind, as air bag demand takes off, is not a risk at all; it is a certainty. National-Standard had repeated operating losses over four years. In effect, this joint venture saves a company that common sense tells us should not have needed saving. Capital infusion may seem to be the issue, but management ability to deal with technological change is the crux of the matter.

Unimation: A Case Study of How America Missed Out on Robots

The name "Westinghouse" was a household word in the 1940s and 1950s. It stood for a major brand of light bulbs, solid dishwashers, reliable refrigerators, and a host of other products for households and industrial customers. The Westinghouse Electric Corporation, a heartland American company with home base in Pittsburgh, was also known for its advertisements about how much research it was doing to make things better for America's households. The General Electric Corporation had a similar product line and used the same kind of advertising approach. To consumers, Westinghouse and GE were perceived as being head-on competitors, of about equal size and importance. Unlike GE, Westinghouse sold off its consumer products businesses, including light bulbs and appliances. The company policy was to move out of consumer products in order to better serve its industrial customers.

Joseph Engelberger is widely acclaimed as the inventor of practical hydraulic robots. He founded Unimation, a U.S. corporation, to make these robots for sale to manufacturers in the early 1960s. By 1982 Unimation had almost 45 percent of the U.S. robot market. Forecasts for the industry envisioned significant growth for the coming decade.

As far back as 1968, in an effort to generate cash flow, Unimation had licensed major elements of its hydraulic technology to Kawasaki Heavy Industries, Ltd. At the same time, Kawasaki was developing electric robotic technology on its own. Because of its continuing need for capital, a merger was arranged with Westinghouse. As part of its shift to industrial products, Westinghouse bought Unimation, expecting that the robot industry would give it entree into factory automation, which it believed would be a billion-dollar industry. There appeared to be good reasons for an alliance on the part of both companies. Thus, Westinghouse Unimation came into being in 1983.

Unimation once controlled almost 50 percent of the robot market. It no longer exists. Japanese companies have taken over the robot market, which once had hundreds of contenders in the United States and Europe. Too many things went wrong to be able to list even most of them. However, there are several crucial points that reveal the difficulties that large U.S. companies face in dealing with new manufacturing technology.

First, Unimation and Westinghouse were both fixated on hydraulic robotics, even though Japanese competitors were emphasizing electrical power and control systems. Both large and small companies experience great inflexibility for quite different reasons. Small companies are dominated by the owner-inventor, who has done everything to get the company going. There is no time for such a person to enjoy the luxury of exploring alternative routes. Joseph Engelberger's contribution to robotics was "larger than life" already. And yet, Unimation might have found it easier to change its perspective than Westinghouse. When it acquired Unimation, Westinghouse entered into an unbalanced alliance, in which it dominated the new venture. Only a small part of Westinghouse but all of Unimation were merged. Westinghouse had bought into hydraulic robotics, and with the typical inflexibility of successful bureaucracies, it would justify its choice by rejecting the possibility of doing anything else that might raise questions about the soundness of the Unimation deal.

There were serious drawbacks to the hydraulic systems that vibrated and leaked. The fluid systems needed frequent repairs by plumbers and electricians. In union shops, this meant two kinds of repair people having to work together. Customer complaints were numerous and serious. It was on the record that many buyers were waiting for corrective designs before making additional commitments to this company. Meanwhile, Japanese robot manufacturers had persevered with electrical robots because there was clear user preference for them. Costs of operating and maintaining the hydraulic robots was many times higher than the costs associated with electrical robots. This case illustrates a well-documented bureaucratic response: repel forces for change before analyzing them.

Second, the Westinghouse culture was that of a large company. This was incompatible with the culture of the much smaller Unimation. A joint venture between the two organizations, where Unimation had kept its unique identity, might have succeeded if all of the details had been carefully worked out. As it was, people were not happy with the situation, and both sides were damaged. The Westinghouse bureaucracy was anathema to the innovative engineers and designers of the much smaller Unimation. The organizational arrangement failed to bring out the best in both companies. Instead of learning and synergy, both organizations were damaged by the acquisition, one fatally. Unbalanced alliances are more likely to fail than to sail.

Global Joint Ventures

A long and interesting story can be told about each of the global joint ventures listed below. The first set of 14 relate to the auto industry. The second set of 13 are manufacturing ventures with metal goods and pharmaceuticals. The third set of 12 relate to food manufacturers and service industries such as banks, hotels, movies, airlines, and department stores. The fourth group of 7 are chip and computer manufacturers. The fifth group of 5 appear to be venture failures. JVs with serious problems abound, but as in the case of GM and Saab shutting down their joint showcase factory in Sweden, general conditions of economic turbulence can be blamed.

Sample List of Global Joint Ventures

Toyota/General Motors—NUMMI
Chrysler/Mitsubishi—Diamond Star Motors
Ford/Mazda
Ford/Volkswagen Minivan for Europe
Ford and Nissan's Minivan
Ford/Jaguar
General Motors/Isuzu—Isuzu/Subaru
Nissan-Smyrna,Tenn./Subaru of America
GM with 50 percent of Saab-Scania
Renault/Volvo accord creates problems
Honda Motors with 20 percent of Rover
GKN's Working Partnerships with U.K.'s Racing Industry
Mitsubishi/Daimler-Benz
Chrysler/Maserati, Ferrari and Lamborgini

Xerox/Fuji
Alcoa/Kobe Steel
General Electric/Tungsram Hungary
Otis Elevator of United Technologies/East German Elevator Co.
Sikorsky of United Technologies/Korean Airlines—Helicopters
Corning Inc.—Objective: "Global Network"
Olivetti/AT&T/Xerox/Volkswagen
National Standard Co., Niles, MI/Toyota Tsusho America—Air bags
National Steel/NKK of Japan
Bridgestone/Firestone—Michelin/Uniroyal Goodrich Tire Co.
Elan PLC/Marion Labs—Cardizem
Airbus Consortium (Britain, France, Germany, Spain)
Du Pont Merck Pharmaceutical Co.

Matsushita (JVC) et al./MCA Inc. (Universal Studios)
Sony/CBS Entertainment
Bass PLC/Holiday Corporation—North American Hotels

Seibu Saison/Intercontinental Hotels Inc.

KLM/25 percent Northwest Airlines—British Airways bid for 15 percent of United Air Lines—Failed

Swissair/SAS Cooperation

Bat Industries Ltd./Saks Fifth Avenue and Marshall Field

Kikkoman/50 percent of Del Monte—Obtained from RJR Nabisco

Grand Metropolitan PLC/Pillsbury Company

Barneys of New York/Isetan Company of Japan

Daiwa Bank/Lloyd's Bank (U.S. Branches)

Federated Department Stores and Allied Stores/Campeau Corp.

IBM/Toshiba—Lightweight Screen

Apple Computer/Sony—Notebook Laptop

Canon/17 percent of Next

Texas Instruments Travelmate 2000/Sharp PC 2600

Goldstar/Zenith Electronics

Bull, France/Honeywell

SGS-Thomson/Siemens/Philips—Chip Manufacturing and HDTV

Motorola/Hitachi—Settled lawsuit

General Electric/Daimler-Benz—Settled lawsuit

Philips drops out of HDTV Consortium

Du Pont and Philips end their JV because of different goals

Borden, Inc. and Meiji Milk Products (with over 50 percent of Japan's premium ice cream market)—ended their JV

Joint Venture Advantages of Being Small

Joint ventures could be characterized as decentralized decision systems with centralized information and capital formation systems. When used properly, this gives the joint venture access to power without losing flexibility and speed required to become a global competitor. In the traditional, large-scale organization, how does the apex person communicate with everyone? As information moves upward, it must be condensed. Bureaucracies edit the immense volume of information by routinizing the system so that only exceptions are transmitted up to the next level.

Bureaucracies have become so effective at editing that eventually all anomalies are removed, and the head administrator never hears from below. This would be something like the captain of a ship issuing navigational instructions without knowing the state of the ship, where it is, and where it is going. The person at the top of the organization is really isolated if the formal system of communication is not backed up by an informal network. It is as if the people who steer the ship have no vision. This kind of system becomes a liability when fast reflexes provide a competitive advantage.

The technology of bureaucracy owes a lot to Alexander Graham Bell. The telephone was not wired into a pyramidal network, but it has been used as if it had been wired that way. A worker on the plant floor of a big company is not about to call the chief executive. So, even though any phone can reach any other phone, bureaucratic practice effectively cuts the line between most pairs of phones. The patterns of phone calls that are actually made in any organization represent only one aspect of the hierarchical constraints on communication.

Have computers (which have been present since the 1960s) altered the technology of bureaucracy that personalized phone communication created? In large companies, each group tends to access its own programs and data bases. Even when sharing information is permitted, the effect of the old bureaucratic telephone network continues to compartmentalize people and separate organizational functions and levels. Under the old-tech system, no one is encouraged to break out of the prescribed routines. Computers were configured and used in line with the old systems and procedures. And that's not so different from face-to-face communications, which tend to be stylized and limited in large organizations. Meetings in the hall are an obvious opportunity for people to talk about their work-related problems, but most large organizations use architecture and space assignments to further constrain who meets whom and, thereby, who has an opportunity to communicate with whom. Even if the stock clerk and the CEO meet in the cafeteria (which is unlikely if there are separate dining rooms), social pressure constrains the stock clerk to a greeting of the day.

The joint venture has the small and medium-sized company advantages of fast communication in a well-connected network. Everybody knows everybody else. Decentralization can work effectively for large companies trying to gain the size advantage. But the large company must be willing to let go, and to permit the managers of the joint venture to make their own decisions about product designs, process changes, marketing moves, and so on. The problem of being small and run with an iron hand by the owner-inventor is also bypassed by the joint venture, which has two partners that share their visions in many ways.

Joint ventures are based on power sharing. They need to balance the interests of all partners. This requires attitudes of cooperation, accepted interdependence, and coordination. Confrontational management style, so readily sanctioned by established companies in the United States and Europe, is repudiated by joint venture management. Internal competition is not likely to spawn an organization that can compete successfully on a global scale. Adversarialism weakens the organization's problem-solving abilities. Problem-solving is the forte of joint ventures. Like the offsprings that they are, both in and out of trouble, they can call upon their parents when the going gets really tough.

MULTIPLE DECISION-MAKERS AND NEGOTIATIONS

Alliances, and particularly joint ventures, involve a unique form of decision-making. It is called decision by multiple decision-makers, or MDM. In a typical firm, there is one person who has the responsibility to make critical decisions. It is not unusual for that person to have many advisors, but the "buck stops at the top." At every level, there is one person who is authorized to make decisions at that level. The individual is always looking upward, to his or her boss, for their approval.

In a joint venture, the partners share the power to make decisions. In business cultures of the United States and Europe, there is a need to learn how to do this; it does not come naturally. During the start-up stages of the joint venture, and even after success has been achieved, there may be liaison functionaries whose job is to tell the parent companies what is going on. The intermediaries may serve as more than a conduit to pass information from the joint venture to the parents. They may convey approval and disapproval from the parent back to the joint venture's management team. Some intricate patterns for decision-making have to be worked out, not only at the top of the organization, but at every level in the new joint venture. For example, questions of quality are viewed as being of the greatest importance in many Japanese joint venture transplants. If a supplier fails to meet standards, the Japanese parent company might view this as a top management issue, whereas the American counterpart might view it as a statistical incident.

To avoid problems of this sort, it is essential that careful negotiations must precede the start-up of the JV. Agreement can be made as to which partner is responsible for which type of decisions. Generally, decision responsibility is assigned to each partner's representatives in line with the special knowledge or expertise that is that partner's contribution to the joint venture.

For example, the partner whose firm pioneered the use of robots to manufacture will make decisions about how to employ new manufacturing technology. The partner whose company knows the home market will be responsible for decisions in that area. Because the joint venture is of small size, both partners will discuss their decisions, allowing any interactions to occur that might change their respective points of view.

Negotiation is the mechanism by which agreement is reached about the structure and organization of the joint venture. This negotiation is used to set down the ground rules for making decisions in the joint venture. These rules envision the kind of situations that might arise. However, everything that will happen cannot be anticipated. Negotiations must also be part of the on-going dialogue, and competence to negotiate must be inherent in the organizational design.

Consequently, there has to be a mechanism for negotiation after the joint venture is under way. When each partner feels that their company should make the decision, the first step is to find out if they both do indeed have equal expertise. There is also the problem encountered when two or more decision-makers do not agree about some decision. Then, the reason is often differing utilities and values. Some way has to be found to arbitrate the issue, or settle by some other means. There can be a vote of senior executives to iron out a difference of opinion. But, most often, the partners each have their own strengths. They know them and willingly defer to the specialist among themselves.

The Learning Organization

What are the strategic and tactical factors that make the joint ventures into successful global competitors? JVs provide an excellent organizational format for companies that are striving to become global players. Partners coming from different parts of the globe make the first steps easy. Where else can so much knowledge about two or more cultures be assimilated into a practical agenda for marketing and operations?

The size of the JV is appropriate to maximize learning. There is no need to downsize, and decentralization is accomplished automatically. Assuming that all parties have clear objectives in mind, and that they each contribute about equally, there still remains the need to get everything spelled out concerning who should make the various types of decisions. Everything needs to be spelled out unambiguously. We are not talking about legal documents to resolve ambiguity. In fact, the less that lawyers are involved, the better. The issues are those of managing a business system. The terms of the understanding relate to employees, customers, and suppliers.

The ground rules are not legal, but human and technological. If they have not been carefully thought out, the joint venture is bound to founder. If the homework for agreeing about what to do with disagreement has been done, then a powerful new form of organization is likely to develop. This charting of new waters is the steepest part of the learning curve. Some forgetting is also required, since each partner may be coming to the joint venture with their own respective bureaucratic hang-ups.

Each partner brings conventions long practiced, which must be changed if they are going to get along with each other. The right agreement allows both partners to break old habits, and in this way, the alliances encourage learning. Joint ventures are particularly well-suited to learning—if the chemistry is right for the partners. Learning is one of the primary underlying reasons that companies enter joint ventures—the NUMMI case being one of the best illustrations of this point. The old rules that were accepted as truth in the past are not likely to be mutually agreeable.

Advantages of Joint Ventures

At the risk of some repetition, it seems useful at this point to summarize the benefits to be derived from JVs:

1. Properly configured, joint ventures are small enough to enjoy the systems perspective, and they have the advantage of multiple cultures working together.

2. They have to do a lot of work familiarizing themselves with each other, early on. This sort of indoctrination activity normally does not occur with a company start-up in the United States. The result is that JVs are better prepared for contingencies as they arise. These organizations can move faster than their opponents.

3. Each party knows their particular strengths and those of their partners. Specialists in areas are given autonomy to reach decisions quickly within their domains of expertise.

4. Smoothly running joint ventures learn how to create demand rather than to follow it with adequate supply.

5. Strong joint ventures gain access to markets through innovative product designs that otherwise are protected by the normal barriers to entry established by large companies.

6. Strong joint ventures, in turn, create new barriers to entry by securing market niche loyalties, which decrease the attraction of volume markets that the large firms try to access.

7. Joint ventures provide the comfort of a risk-sharing situation that allows them to experiment with product innovations. Even when not high tech,

they are still able to employ the new management technology. When high tech, they are flexible manufacturers with knowledge about producing and selling variety that is not commonplace.

8. In addition, joint ventures often have access to two or more labor pools, and two or more separate markets.

9. Joint ventures can trade information about suppliers, formulating a single list of "accredited" companies.

10. By studying comparative government regulations, joint ventures can choose the most favorable situations with respect to taxes, tariffs, and other restrictive conditions.

Formula for Success

A concluding statement about joint ventures seems in order. All over the world new JVs are being created. They are a new and popular form of entrepreneuring. What's new about them? The partners share in the decision-making process. Negotiation rather than ownership characterizes them. The key for success is mutual participation rather than domination by one party over the other. When the partnerships work out, there are many kinds of payoffs; when they fail there are great penalties. Failed ventures, which are beginning to appear with increasing numbers, can lead to legal actions (e.g., Motorola and Hitachi), which is wasteful and debilitating. Because the penalties are high, U.S. firms need guidelines concerning how to make JVs work.

NOTES

1. David Lloyd George was the prime minister of Great Britain from 1916 to 1922. World War I ended in 1918 and was followed by a period of much uncertainty and change. According to Kondratieff, the year 1920 marks the end of one long wave and the beginning of the next one. Putting the two facts together, one can understand why Lloyd George was worrying about falling (or failing). Kondratieff's paper entitled, "Long Economic Cycles" was delivered in Russia on February 6, 1926.

2. From the Report of the President's Commission on Industrial Competitiveness, *Global Competition: The New Reality*, John A. Young, Chairman, Volume 1, January 1985.

3. Harvey L. Shulman, chairman of Ramsey Fabrics Company of New York, at a Columbia Business School seminar on The Use of Partnerships, expressed the belief that all business organizations are enriched by good partners. Individual entrepreneurs should make every effort to find at least one compatible partner, if need be a spouse. The quality of management improves when there is dialogue and mutual responsibility. A partnership enhances perspective and keeps individuals from being power-driven, or accepting all responsibility. It makes for better planning, decision-making, and implementation. Internal partnerships might even improve bureaucracies.

4. Kathryn R. Harrigan, *Managing for Joint Venture Success*. (Lexington, MA: Lexington Books, 1986).

5. The word "hierarchy" is derived from the Greek root for leader: *hieros* (sacred) + *archos* (leader, ruler).

6. Value-added is zero for purchased parts and materials. It is also zero for inventories. Value-added starts to accumulate as work is done by the firm to transform raw materials and purchased components into finished goods. Therefore, the cost of goods sold less costs of purchased goods is what is meant by value-added. When work sits around waiting to be serviced, which is typical of the job shop, no value is being added. One of the best tactical measures of a firm's efficiency is the average percent of time that value-adding is going on. Studies have shown that this number is often less than 5 percent of the time.

7. The *Wall Street Journal* of December 4, 1990, said: "From a plodding conservative company whose stock was recommended for widows and orphans, American Telephone and Telegraph Co. has turned into an aggressive predator." In a hostile buyout attempt, AT&T, the U.S. communications giant, offered $6.03 billion for the NCR Corporation. The management of NCR, a niche computer manufacturer in America, rejected the offer. Analysts speculated that the people responsible for NCR's success are most likely to leave the company, which would substantially decrease its value. It is worth noting that Unisys, which is the name of the alliance formed when Burroughs purchased Sperry for $4.8 billion in 1986, has shrunken to a much smaller and less successful company since the acquisition. The issue revolves around the question: What is the contribution of people to making alliances successful? In the old-tech systems, the answer was clear that people, like commodities and baseball players, can be traded. In a powerful bureaucracy, "no one is indispensable" really means "everyone is disposable." Based on empirical evidence, this position is not recommended for becoming a successful global company.

8. Reference is again called to the Unimation Case.

9. The management of U.S. companies does the same kind of thing. Mexico has been one of the most-favored countries for U.S. industry since 1985, and it continues to be so in the early 1990s. Many U.S. companies have set up assembly plants, called *maquiladoras*, across the border in Mexico. At the beginning of 1989, there were about 1,300 such plants, employing more than 325,000 Mexican workers. Their wages at the time ranged from about US$ 0.90 to US$ 1.30. The boundary for these maquiladoras runs from Juarez, Mexico, across the border from El Paso, Texas, to Tijuana, Mexico, across the border from San Diego, California.

10. *Business Week* lists the major keiretsu as Dai-Ichi Kangin, Fuyo, Mitsui Group, Sanwa, and Sumitomo. The publication states that "cross-share-holdings, interlocking directorates, joint ventures, and long-term business relationships . . . create a family of companies that do not depend on formal controls, but rather recognize their mutual interests." September 24, 1990, pp. 98–107.

11. One of the best books that has been written to date about joint ventures is Harrigan, *Managing for Joint Venture Success*.

12. From Alan I. Murray and Caren Siehl, *Joint Ventures and Other Alliances: Creating a Successful Cooperative Linkage* (Morristown, NJ: Financial Executives Research Foundation, 1989).

PART IV ————————————————————

TIMING

Part IV consists of Chapter 7 alone. It deals with time-based strategies, including a sense of timing and an awareness and responsiveness to timeliness.

Analysis of global competitors—with established records of winning performances—indicates that they do not make strategic decisions based on short-term financial objectives. These firms have elevated fast response capabilities, and the timeliness that fast response allows, to the top of their wish lists. This represents a major shift by the leading global corporations in the design of their competitive strategies.

The shift makes sense in terms of the new technological capabilities that manufacturing has experienced. Because it is well-known that Honda is a fast response organization, it was no surprise to the managers of U.S. car companies and their air bag suppliers that "all U.S. Hondas to get air bags by Fall of '93. . . . What may be most remarkable about Honda's announcement is how swiftly the auto maker will switch from mostly automatic belts to air bags" (*New York Times*, September 25, 1990).

CHAPTER 7 _____

Time-Based Management

> Time driveth onward fast.
>
> Alfred Tennyson
> *The Lotus-Eaters* (1833)
> "Choric Song," Stanza 4

THE FOURTH DIMENSION

The name "time-based management" could easily be misleading. It sounds as though time alone is the basis for reaching managerial decisions, and for planning, organizing, staffing, directing, and controlling. But this is not what is intended. Instead, the point is that time, which so often is taken for granted, is explicitly included—as one of the main objectives—for all management thinking. Cost must be managed, quality must be managed, why not time?

High school science starts out with the three dimensions of space and the fourth dimension of time. In this context, time is purely academic. The dimensions of competition are less tangible than length, width, and height. But time is not academic. It is a driving force behind competitiveness. We could aptly speak about time-driven management.

The time it takes to finish a project can be crucial in getting into the market first. But the critical notion about time is not speed as much as timing. Getting the timing right is what counts in life, golf, and motor cars. Could it be any less true for business? Everyone knows that timing plays a part in being a successful competitor.

There is a quality to time that is inexorable when it is in synchronization with major forces. Farmers march to the seasonal drum. Fleets wait until "the tide has turned." Poets write that "time and tide wait for no man," which is impressively true at syzygy with a neap tide. Time has been the touchstone of philosophers and authors of maxims. It is the enigmatic domain of Einstein's relativity and Heisenberg's uncertainty principle. With such credentials, why has time been taken for granted by business? It is to the credit of the bureaucratic organization that it found a way to make time less important by refusing to let things change. The currency of time is change.

Until recently, business did not have a sense of urgency about the explicitness with which time issues were addressed. Now that change is rampant, time is right up there in importance with cost and quality. Under some circumstances, it is necessary to deal with the time factor in order to understand and to solve the cost or quality problem. In the new-wave way of doing business, timeliness has been elevated by global competitors to being the first dimension of competitiveness. Time drivers are often more sensitive to the real business factors than are cost drivers. Presumably, that is why no one is startled when they hear that old refrain: time is money.

TIME AND MONEY

Time-based management has been the subject of numerous management studies. Over the past ten years, various names have been used, but the most popular has been time-based management.[1] There are certain points worth noting about the use of time as a major business variable:

1. For old-tech management systems, time enters the picture indirectly. Bureaucracies are dedicated to preventing change and maintaining routines and standards. When variations occur from the standards, the effort is made to remove the causes of the variation, as quickly as possible. For example, when machine utilization drops to 70 percent, then management strives to bring it back to full utilization. How much time will it take? If a machine breaks down, how long will it take to return it to operation? Many of these issues are of interest to new-tech as well as old-tech management systems.

2. For new-tech management systems, flexibility is of paramount importance. Since flexibility refers to the adjustability of the process to changes in demand, the time concept is already built into it. Management's goal is to produce in small lots. To do this, the entire system must be geared to changeover of the production system. Time

management is crucial to achieving these objectives. How much time between changeovers? How long does it take to change over? Is changeover time different if you go from A to B, than if you go from B to A? Many of these issues are of interest to old-tech as well as new-tech management systems.

3. For both the old and the new management systems, project management is a time-based activity. Project Evaluation Review Technique (PERT) is a project management approach that has been used since 1950. The primary PERT variable is time. However, as flexibility of the production process is stressed, new forms of project management have emerged. These issues will be covered in the material that follows.

4. The relationship between time and money is not a simple matter to analyze. There are occasions when moving faster can spell the difference between failure and success. Alternatively, there are situations where being first brings no benefits, or even penalties. There are circumstances when eliminating wasted time can improve cash flow and returns on investment. In other situations, it makes no difference while costing money.

Each situation must be evaluated as a unique set of circumstances. But to ignore the potential impact of time and timeliness is fraught with danger. High marketplace variety and new manufacturing flexibility reinforce the likelihood that time will be a major competitive variable. It becomes perilous to overlook the potential impact of time factors on competitive advantage. Although the effects of delay and idleness have become magnified, the penalties of a casual attitude toward time are not always obvious. If management does not know where to look, no one in the organization will realize that it is bleeding.

The altered role of time first became noticeable in the high priorities given to time management by global firms. However, for many years before global forces became evident, marketing managers emphasized the speed-up in product life cycles that was taking place domestically. This accelerated through the 1970s and 1980s. By the 1990s, global competitors seemed to gleefully outmode their own product lines. In this competitive environment, the status quo is bound to be a losing strategy.

Fast response organizations (FROs) have significant competitive advantages. FRO is an acronym for organizations that can move rapidly. We will be discussing them in the section devoted to synchronicity. But, for the moment, let us note that fast response is not meant to represent high velocity management (HVM), where speed for the sake of speed is rewarded. FROs employ time as a resource. They can use more or less of it as is warranted by the circumstances.

Size and response times are related, which is not unexpected. Smaller organizations move faster than larger ones; this applies to alliances in several ways. Decentralized business units can exercise control over time in spite of the size of their parent company. The connection: new alliances enable large companies to decentralize business units that would otherwise be constrained by the inflexible routines of the overgrown parent.

CATEGORIES OF TIME-BASED MANAGEMENT

There are different ways of classifying the effects of time on management. The most logical first step is to use the categories of tactics and strategies that were previously developed to describe the fundamentally different divisions that alliances can follow. Referring back to Figure 6.2, we note the two main branches. The left branch traces the tactical alliances; the right branch traces the strategic alliances.

Time-Based Tactical Alliances

One of the main driving forces for tactical alliances is that they permit the supplier and the buyer, as partners, to get closer to the production issues of quality and reaction time. With such coordination of activities, both firms are able to assert time-based management principles. Recently, gaining the time advantage has become the primary motivating force for tactical alliances between firms that utilize a great deal of purchased content (such as the automobile industry). Only the left branch of Figure 7.1 is filled in, because it deals with tactical alliances. Refer to Figure 6.2 for the entire chart.

Tactical time advantages can also be classified in terms of "continuity of the production process." We will use this category for our discussion because continuity represents a basic concept for time-based management. The point to keep in mind is that

Production Process Continuity = Tactical Time Advantages

Another type of continuity is related to the strategic benefits of project management—for example, new product development, or process improvement. There is a time driver in project development that relates to continuity, as follows:

Project Development Continuity = Strategic Time Advantages

Figure 7.1
Tactical Alliance Structure

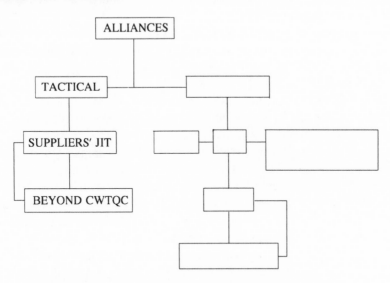

The Holistic Approach Merges Strategies and Tactics

"Do the right thing; then do that thing the right way." This phrase that business should live by has been said by many people. However, although it is widely known and often stated, it is not followed by most organizations. The reasons for this reluctance to "do as I say, and not as I do," is best explained by referring to the Gleicher model for achieving change in Chapter 5. There are inertial forces in nature that are inimical to change for both physical systems and organizations of people. There are counterforces that lead to change, but friction and bureaucracy both work in their own ways to impede these pressures.

Tactics are the "do the thing the right way" part of the initial phrase. Although they are critically important, tactics must always be subordinate to strategies. If you can't find the right things to do, it doesn't matter how well you do whatever you do. However, when it comes to fast response systems, the fact is that you cannot separate strategies from tactics. The ability to move quickly and effectively is a holistic issue.

Strategies can create new product opportunities that are flubbed by the company with poor tactical follow-through. As an analogy, think of the team that has a coach who always knows the right plays, but no one on the team can run or throw. It is hard to characterize in a few words the reasons for success or failure. Nevertheless, no explanation for Japanese economic success with its products in export markets would be complete without noting the importance they place on tactics. In a few words, good strategies backed up by an addiction for perfection in tactical matters provides a winning combination.

Part of this pattern lies in the tactics of project management. Having the capability of improving the project goals is a major advantage. Having the tactics to carry one project after another to success is another major boon. Being able to develop new products and processes quickly after learning about market opportunities is another score for those who know how to play the game. Learning how to adapt emerging technological developments is another skill that helps to win the day.

The strategic-tactical approach to being a fast response organization is related to being able to solve quickly a series of problems such as: When there is product improvement, what do you do with the old versions? Are they obsoleted, or can they be sold at a lower price? What is the best time to release the new version? How do you incorporate process innovations? What is the best timing for major moves such as relocating plants, acquiring companies, forming alliances? Overall, the holistic approach, shown in Figure 7.2, provides a distinct competitive edge in trying to resolve questions big and small, so that the answers are constantly being related to each other. The questions and their answers are like different facets of the same diamond; a pretty analogy for systems thinking.

THREE MAJOR THEMES

The discussion of time-based management will be explored using three different major themes: continuity, concurrence, and synchronicity. While these words are understandable in a general sense, their meanings are specific to time management and will have to be explained in this context. We will give a flavor of the meaning at this point.

1. Continuity
    *   of the production process: the continuous flow of materials on a non-stop basis
    *   of project development systems: a cascade of projects with on-going team management

2. Concurrence
    *   of project development systems: parallel development of project stages rather than sequential

3. Synchronicity
    *   of the total management system: orchestration of all functional players (production, sales, etc.), to achieve optimal timing

Figure 7.2
Strategic and Tactical Aspects of FRO Systems

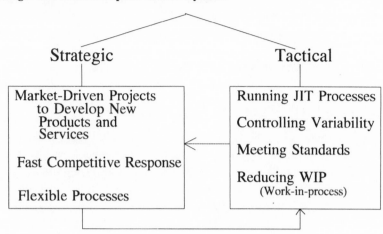

Continuity is the first of the time variables adopted by new management technology. As has been previously mentioned, continuity, in its management context, is of two kinds: (1) *Tactical*, which relates to the operation of the firm's own production process and its relationships with suppliers. Overall, this raises the issue of being efficient as possible with a fixed strategy of products, processes and demands; (2) *Strategic*, which involves using the project development system to create new products and processes. We will first talk about time-based tactical aspects of the production process. Then, two sections follow that deal with the temporal aspects of project development systems. The first section treats methods for establishing project continuity. The second section examines the concurrent management approach for project development.

CONTINUITY OF THE PRODUCTION PROCESS

We have described the continuity of the production process as the continuous flow of materials on a nonstop basis. This is a production objective that aims at eliminating waste to improve quality and reduce costs. We use time flows to manage the system because time is a powerful surrogate in this respect.

Production process continuity deals with scheduling of production, workflow, and shopfloor control. The ideal situation is to have zero work-in-process inventory and to have all materials flowing continuously through the plant. In that way, value is always being added to the materials and components that have been purchased. Again, the ideal is to transform the raw materials and subassemblies into finished goods, which will be shipped out the factory door as they are completed. There is no mystery about all of this. Enlightened management knows that continuous flow is the lowest per unit cost method of manufacturing. It is also the foundation for achieving a maximum value-added system.

Increasing Value-Added with Time Management

By logical extension, the firm would like suppliers that practice as the firm preaches. These suppliers will deliver products with maximum value-added benefits. Furthermore, the link between the supplier and the producer is a potential weak spot. Too many goods being delivered at one time sit around. Someone has to pay for the space to store them, for insurance and other costs, and for the inventory carrying charges that must be levied. That is where the JIT-link for suppliers is forged. This is shown in Figure 7.1, as is a box labeled Beyond CWTQC.

If the supplier delivers a product on a JIT basis, then every item delivered must be of acceptable quality. Defective goods have to be subtracted from the total shipments. To compensate, the supplier can add some items to cover the defectives that are expected. Here we see a breakdown in the goal of continuous value-added manufacturing. For example, repair, rework, and rejects that must be scrapped are value-added drains. To deal with this, a trust relationship must be developed between the producer and the few suppliers that are so chosen. Design changes of both product and process might be necessary. Working together, both companies can have no secrets. All offices have open doors, and files have open drawers. These relationships can test the mettle of those having the best of intentions for establishing strong tactical alliances.

Quality attainment is expected. Quality enhancement is to be worked on together. Constant improvement is of mutual interest. This kind of relationship is "beyond the concept of companywide total quality control," because it is as if the supplier was part of the buyer's company. In this way, time is manageable on both sides of the supplier-buyer link. The scenario goes somewhat like this: If something goes wrong, fix it fast. If a new product variant is needed, develop the ideas together. Cut through red tape and get it out fast.

We have to keep in mind the fact that the purchased value of goods is not included in the calculation of value-added. Time-stream management is, therefore, concerned with keeping the product moving through all of the plants in the system. This includes the supplier's plants as well as our own. We need to remember that our supplier is also value-adding upstream from us. Utilization of facilities is less pressing than achieving continuous throughput. It is critically important to avoid importing waste from the supplier, which includes poor quality and product carrying idle time burdens. It helps to be aware of the fact that our customer (who is downstream from us) feels precisely the same way about our value-adding abilities.

Internal Aspects of Fast Response

Production managers have always addressed the issue of moving product through the plant. However, the job shop tends to be messy in this regard. When there are many orders for a large variety of items, value-adding is badly done. If all of the competitors are equally bad, then you don't lose customers although you do give up profit. To improve the profit picture, production scheduling methods were developed to minimize throughput time, and to minimize job waiting time as well. The idea is that if you minimize job waiting time, then you also minimize customer waiting time. Such time-saving concepts to increase customer satisfaction have long been available, but management did not feel driven to use them. What is different now?

First, keen competition now exists. Any advantage will be used by those companies that have adopted the new technologies. They have confidence that comes from believing they have the competitive edge.

Second, the new manufacturing technology permits real advances to be made in cycle times, delivery dates, and so on. Flexibility and quality at an excellent price and rapid turnaround on new orders are hard to argue with as selling points.

Third, Japanese production scheduling methods, such as kanban, emphasize the importance of timeliness and balanced flows.[2] These methods brought creative insights to the management of the production process and gave competitive advantages to those firms that really worked at understanding how to use them—as opposed to those firms that were more casual in implementing the ideas.

Consequently, it is easy to differentiate between a fast response organization that can set up and deliver a new job in a day or two, from a slow response organization that requires two to three weeks. It is often said: go to someone who is busy to get a tough job done well, and fast. The underlying reason that this makes sense is that the busy firm has developed methods for dealing with fast response requests in a satisfactory manner. Global companies have been carrying these abilities to new levels of achievement. Entirely new products can be set up, run, and delivered with quickness never before available.

CONTINUITY OF PROJECT DEVELOPMENT SYSTEMS

Continuity of project development systems has been explained as a cascade of projects with on-going team management. Cascade was used to describe the way that the separate streams of ideas and experiences combine to form a succession of continually developing new products and process alterations. The on-going team management is needed to provide direction and purpose to the project planning system that operates continually. Almost everyone, no matter what their job, is part of at least one project team.

Projects are the means by which companies update themselves, carrying through their strategic plans. There are big projects, like designing a new auto and bringing it to production. There are little projects, like a design engineering change to modify a car door handle. Conventional approaches to project management have a start date and a targeted completion date. Progress is monitored for all scheduled activities between those dates.

There have been many concerted efforts to find ways to finish projects in a shorter time. One obvious approach is to employ additional people and equipment. This necessitates spending more money. But, using conventional project methods, there comes a point at which completion time cannot be further reduced. In fact, time to completion can start to increase when there are too many cooks. When additional resources, employed in traditional ways, actually start to increase the completion time for the project, then it is time to consider the new methods being developed by global companies. First, however, it will help to summarize the conventional project management methods known as PERT, CPM, and so on.

The Conventional PERT/CPM

Project Evaluation Review Technique/Critical Path Method and other variants of project management techniques were first developed around 1948.[3] Almost every organization involved in assignments (such as shipbuilding, mall construction, new product development, space vehicle launches) employed CPM and PERT-type models for managing the project's activities. These project techniques are so well known that everyone in business knows about them. They have been very effective in controlling the time (and cost) of the project, from beginning to end.

Until global companies began to flex their time-driven muscles, it was generally believed that project management methods could not get better. Enormous projects were successfully controlled in the old way. For example, NASA uses a gigantic PERT computer system for synchronizing the activities of their suppliers, and it has been very effective.

The conventional approach to project management can be summarized as follows:

- One project is done at a time
- Start time is set with a completion target
- Objectives are unambiguous
- Activities to achieve objectives are specified
- Resources required are listed
- The times required for each activity are assigned
- Quality standards are ambiguous

At this point, conventional time-based management is applied in the following ways:

- Critical path management is used to determine the longest chain of activities in the project network
- Resource leveling is used to bring activity times into balance
- Project activities are redesigned to help balance the network
- Time/cost trade-offs are used to move from normal time to crash time (normal time is the longest time with the least cost to do the job; crash time, which is the shortest time to do the job, usually has the highest cost)

Continuity with On-Going Project Development

The first major distinction between conventional PERT/CPM and the new project management approach is that the former has a starting point and a stopping point for a specific project. The project is started and stopped when completed. The project group is assembled to do the work, which goes through various stages. Different people are brought in, and rotated to other phases and stages, but when the project is completed the group is disbanded.

With the new project management approach, the project team is neither assembled nor disbanded. It is on-going so it can be rotated to other projects. For that matter, people are interchanged between various projects and project groups. The unique elements are as follows:

- The costs of assembling and disbanding project groups are not incurred. These costs include many intangible factors related to coming up to speed with project ideas and the appropriate orientation.

- Ideas are expected to cascade into other ideas. When any specific project assignment is completed, all ideas that were put on hold while driving for completion are opened up for further consideration.

- New projects are waiting in a queue for an opening with one of the on-going teams. This is quite similar to projects waiting their turn with an information systems development group. This analogy might turn one off because of the typical difficulty in dealing with overloaded information systems people. However, the project groups are not bureaucratized as are so many information systems development groups. To be forewarned, however, is to be forearmed.

- The continuity of the project groups is not entirely independent of their assignments, because learning is an important part of what drives the project systems continuity.

- Continuity means that, for all projects, the routine of starting-up, signing-off to permit next stages to continue, and stopping upon completion is abandoned.

- Continuity means that all the paperwork and the dedicated control systems, which cost so much to monitor milestones, checkpoints, and reviews for permission to continue, are eliminated.

There are major cost savings when project groups do not have to be created for each assignment. There are even greater advantages when the groups can augment project goals and formulate new objectives based on the previous experiences they have had. This is similar in concept to finding ways to reduce set-up costs each time a new product is to be produced on the same general-purpose equipment. In effect, we are talking about the production of projects, in a system where continuous improvement is rewarded.

Continuous project management has significant time to completion advantages in contrast to one-project-at-a-time, which we can also call single-product management (SPM). With SPM (e.g., launching one new car), there is a start-up time and an ending time. Frequently, needs arise for information, after the project group has been disbanded. Usually that is too late, because it is very difficult, even for the people who worked on the specific project, to go back to reconstruct what needs to be known. Often the files are stored in ways that make reopening them almost impossible.

On-going, or continuous, project management means managing a stream of multiple new products (such as a succession of new cars for the next ten years). Teams of people, often rotating, are assigned to various project development activities. The goals are basically of two different kinds: (1) projects are targeted to achieve successive incremental improvements; or (2) significant "breakthroughs" are sought by one or more of the project groups.

There has been growing awareness of the importance of the incremental aspect of continuous project development. But American firms tend to like the big breakthroughs. They gear up for these major projects from time to time, tending to ignore the important competitive advantages of continuous gains of small proportions.

An MIT report states that "technological progress rests on a foundation of both incremental improvements and radical breakthroughs, and finding the right balance between them is a constant challenge."[4] It has been noted that Japanese firms have been effective in combining the two approaches. Not unexpectedly, small and medium-sized firms are quite at ease with incremental improvement. Because of a lack of resources, they are constrained at managing major breakthroughs. Some of the large U.S. and European firms do manage to combine the two approaches, but these are the exceptions that prove the rule.

On-going project systems have the advantage of a memory for ideas with potential utility that had to be shelved. Deferral is used to capture good ideas that would otherwise have been killed the first time around because they did not fit the schedule or match the prior goals. This capacity to reexamine and learn from prior project steps has an inestimable value.

Time as a Surrogate for Measuring Opportunity Costs

Managing time has always been a prime directive of project management. The traditional goal is to achieve the minimum project duration using conventional project methods. On the face of it, achieving minimum cost seems to be of only secondary importance. However, below the surface is the fact that some major costs are not included in the traditional analysis. If all costs could be captured, then cost minimization would include the opportunity costs for not delivering the product as quickly as possible.

Conventional project management modeling rejected the use of speculative cost estimates. But because global companies compete on time, they accept weak estimates as being better than none at all. Only purists insist on robust cost measures. Thus, fuzzy estimates are deemed acceptable to represent the costs of sales lost from production delays, building rentals not realized, and penalties entailed by the need to reschedule the *Galileo* trip to Jupiter. The difficulty of specifying the opportunity costs for not being as fast as the competition tests the resolve of project managers. An alternative, which is being used by many companies, is to bypass the cost measures and substitute the goal of being fast and first.

The reason that time is so often the primary focus for projects is that time minimization is a reasonable surrogate for minimizing the opportunity costs of not being fast enough. Although these time-based costs are large, they are generally difficult to determine because they are composed of elusive opportunity costs involving customer satisfaction with product and process improvements and other competitive advantages gained from being operational first.

Traditional Versus Continuous Project Development Methods

PERT project systems can constrain creativity if they create an infrastructure that threatens to replace the old system with a new one. It is the natural response of the bureaucracy to defend itself in any way that it can. This also explains why so many projects do not succeed that had been touted as completely feasible.

What is needed is reorganization, often obtained by means of forging a new alliance, that will create an environment that enables something new to replace the older way of doing business. Those with major (vested) interests in the old system can be expected to resist disenfranchisement.

The use of incremental project methods also can work in a relatively inflexible environment. One of the best situations is to have a project system that "encourages" the introduction of small improvements on a regular basis. Some organizations, instead of "encouraging" incremental change, will "accept" or "tolerate" consistent small changes. Without encouragement, the typical organization will inadvertently conspire to resist constant change. So real receptivity of management is necessary to make such systems work well for the companies that are using it. It takes a complete modification of traditional organizational arrangements to actually achieve continuous project management systems.

Weaknesses with traditional PERT and CPM abound. One major flaw is that they cannot deal with problems resulting from the statistical variation so typical of real project developments. Another problem is that there is no provision for contingency planning. Also, while cost and time trade-offs can be analyzed realistically, the quality of the completed project remains ambiguous and intractable.

Also, the ability to complete projects quickly is assumed to be an engineering responsibility. Can the designers find ways to speed up completion? The new project methods encourage time-saving by having people work together in new ways. While crash-type resource allocation can be used to speed up project completion, it suffers from some severe drawbacks. The same can be said for resource leveling, which spread management attention all over the project system. When resources were equalized, many activities became "critical." This meant that if you slipped in meeting your deadline, it would make the entire project late.

The traditional PERT approach to speed up the delivery of a completed project is to crash the activities along the critical path. This means that all of the resources that can be brought to bear will be used in reducing activity times. The increase in budget entailed in crashing activities is supposed to produce a decrease in project time. It is wise to raise questions about whether these assumptions are correct. Crash methods can increase (rather than reduce) project time by creating a crisis orientation inducing error proneness. Shorter deadlines can produce personal anxieties, which deteriorate performance. Any one mistake can lead to a domino chain of other mistakes. Chain correction can require a great deal of time and cost to correct. That is what the maxim "A stitch in time . . ." is all about. Mounting pressures overpower the existing information system's ability to communicate with all of the project players.

Pursue Each Project Activity on a Three-Shift Basis

The use of three shifts is another aspect of reducing project time that deserves attention. Project work on any one activity is almost continuous when two or three shifts are used for each stage. A great deal of management coordination is required for teams that are working together 24 hours per day, 7 days per week. For example, engineers at General Electric-Fanuc (a U.S.-Japan joint venture) design devices that are used to control factory operations that function around the clock, using a telelink with Japan.[5] Each day's accomplishments are downloaded from GE in the United States to Fanuc in Japan in the afternoon, and uploaded from Japan the next morning.

Global companies are using round-the-clock shifts with CAD/CAM to design, test and then manufacture semiconductor chips.[6] An Italian motorbike manufacturer allows production workers and their families into the research and testing labs on evenings and weekends to explore new product and process ideas. As established companies are shutting down their older plants and consolidating their production in the newer ones, they are moving to three shifts. However, neither the managers nor the project teams adopt the three-shift basis. They continue on a one-shift timetable. This defeats the system that is striving to speed up project completion times. Ideally, project groups and management would work continuously on at least a two-shift basis and across weekends. This would result in a 180 percent increase in the amount of time being devoted to project developments.

Success with round-the-clock, or even two-shift, project management is dependent upon excellent information dissemination and coordination of activities. Information sharing is facilitated by computer networks that allow 24-hour, 7-day-per-week, real-time interactions. A variety of relational data bases can be combined by workstations that provide fast response technology for information sharing. For example, contingencies for team A activities are often anticipated by teams B and C. Members of these parallel teams have more flexibility to conjure up potential contingencies and to consider what to do about them.

INCREMENTAL IMPROVEMENT WITH MULTIPRODUCT PROJECTS

When continuous project management methods are used, the heavy burdens of start-up costs for new projects are partially bypassed, because teams are always occupied in improving, modifying and reformulating objectives based upon past accomplishments. Many individuals in the firm have on-going assignments to project teams, in addition to their routine line and staff assignments that are related to production. Project assignments are matrixed with production responsibilities. Project accounting charges are levied in accord with their share of labor costs. Instead of concentrating on one product from start-up to finish, the multiproduct emphasis is on producing a stream of innovative products and processes—often with short durations between releases.

This continuous form of project management is predicated on the ability to improve the product incrementally. At one extreme, the next car off the line is so slightly improved from the one that came off the line before it that the changes might not be immediately discernible to customers. The next change, or the one after that, might count with customers. The point is that a ladder of changes is being created that will eventually result in a discernibly better product. It may be as important that the line workers see continual improvement, as it is that the customer sees it. At the other extreme, the improvement can be large enough to warrant calling it a "breakthrough" because the changes in the product or process design are substantial. As previously noted, Japanese automobile manufacturers (e.g., Honda, Subaru, and Toyota), and electronic manufacturers (such as Mitsubishi, Sony, and Toshiba) have demonstrated the effectiveness of the continuous approach for both small and large design changes.

Incrementalism as a Strategic Approach

Incrementalism creates the perception of timeliness. The customer sees new product ideas coming to the marketplace all of the time. In fact, the project system can be moving slowly, thereby allowing ample time for consensus and testing. The view is that because ideas take a great deal of time to develop, you can't afford to start a new product idea going right after the last one is finished. This gives a linear model with long cycle times between new ideas reaching the market. Say it takes six months to work from start to finish. Then, every six months, consumers will see a new release.

The alternative model still keeps the six-month development time. However, a new idea is started in process every month. Then the consumer sees a new idea coming out every month. People make an assumption, which is that it takes this company only one month to develop a new idea. We call this the incremental improvement method because each of the six groups that is constantly working on a new version is making an adjustment rather than a major change that would disturb the concept we are developing.

The method of continuous incremental design changes is somewhat like a Ferris wheel. Each time the wheel turns to another stop, the ground car is emptied of its passengers, and then refilled with new passengers who will get to ride the entire cycle. The passengers disembarking are like the next new incremental design change. Thus, design changes appear to be occurring regularly, and often, as perceived by the customer. The system performs like a fast response system, when, in fact, each incremental change idea takes an entire cycle to mature and be ready for implementation. Meanwhile, the employees of the firm are encouraged to build up a backlog of ideas to be tried at a later point in time.

Software Release Model for Continuous Projects

Traditional project management discourages (or even prohibits) design engineering changes after some early stage of development. In contrast, continuous project management remembers and records potential changes for a later release version. Memory is one of the most important characteristics of the continuous, sequential product development process. To avoid disruption of the continuous flow of new releases, design changes are carried forward into the start-up planning stage for the next model. This release version approach, which emphasizes reusable modules, is commonly employed by software developers. Customers experience the results as a sequence of improved products associated with increasingly larger release numbers.

With traditional project management methods, quality goals are fixed at the start of the project. They do not change as the project proceeds. An alternative is to insist that quality goals be continuously upgraded. A Columbia University study of Japanese-owned companies located in Tennessee revealed that persistent raising of quality standards, within the framework of a specific project, is commonly accepted procedure.[7]

CONCURRENT PROJECT MANAGEMENT ACTIVITIES

Project managers have always tended to schedule groups of similar activities sequentially. While this isn't precisely the case, nevertheless the linear, sequential model dominates traditional project management thinking. To bring the description more in line with reality, let us modify the strictly linear configuration. We allow some of the activities to parallel each other, and others to overlap a bit, at the beginning and ends of the project stages. This is still not a completely accurate picture of a traditional project management configuration, but it captures the linear essence of putting one foot down after another.

Teams Can Complete Activities Linearly or in Parallel

Another way of viewing traditional project management is to liken the situation to a relay race where the first runner completes the circuit and hands the baton over to the next runner. This linear procedure continues until the race is finished. For projects, the equivalent is that each team must complete its assignment before the next team can begin its stage of the project. For example, a major U.S. computer manufacturer has a PERT chart with the following five stages:

1. Planning Cycle—Investigate problem areas, etc.

2. Design Cycle—Design (documentation) prototype

3. Model Cycle—Build and test prototype

4. Release Cycle—Enable and update manufacturing

5. Product Support Cycle—Factory service with cost and maintenance reduction

This milestone process of sign-off before start-up is pictured in Figure 7.3

Milestones are the points in an activity that trigger the beginning of the next activity. In Figure 7.3, these are shown by an x. For example, when the A team reaches x, then the B team is released to begin its activities (shown as z). The same pattern is repeated for the B and C teams. The linear character of the project is emphasized by the fact that the term "milestone" refers to the highway marker that lets the traveler know when the next mile has been reached.

Following the lead of others, we can compare the new method of concurrent or parallel management of successive project stages to rugby. In that game, all members of the team start at the same time and move the ball down the field together.[8] Teamwork of this kind requires practice. Excellent communication is the key to reducing the total time for completion. Each team has greater responsibility, in that all participants consult with each other about interactions that affect their primary concerns.

New methods have to be developed to account for situations where one team has to wait for results from another before proceeding with the actual project development. For example, say that certain activities of the B team must wait until other activities of the A team are completed. In order not to wait, the B team may simulate the expected result from the A team. Alternatively, the A team may change the sequence of its activities to fulfill the B team's needs as soon as possible. It is also true that the strictly parallel arrangement shown in Figure 7.4 cannot work out all of the time. To the extent that it does work out, the project can be completed in a shorter total time. This gives a significant competitive advantage to the company that uses project development methods depicted in Figure 7.4.

Various names are used for this kind of project development configuration. Simultaneous engineering is one of them, which has been used for many years. Concurrent engineering, which is of recent vintage, connotes a broader vision than simultaneous engineering. It takes the systems leap, putting engineering in touch with market requirements, the

Figure 7.3
Sign-Off at x Before Start-Up at z

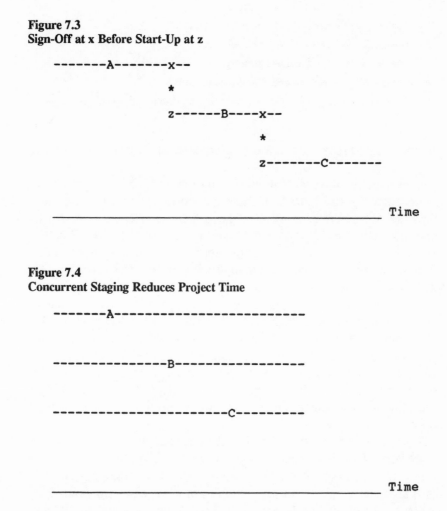

Figure 7.4
Concurrent Staging Reduces Project Time

status of competitors, the effect of project delays on overhead costs, quality improvement for the product, the servicing problems that are likely to be encountered, and the benefits of speeding the product to market.

There are several reasons why a cautious manager might prefer to design a linear project instead of using concurrent activities:

1. There is time to recognize mistakes and do something about them.
2. Control over the project seems too dispersed with the parallel configuration.
3. The compartmentalized functions of large companies do not lend themselves to the required degree of coordination.

4. The rapid pace is not supported by the customary procedures of the company.

The advantages of using the concurrent design can be summarized as faster to the market, better quality, and lower costs. But this is only realizable if the organization can handle the demands of a rugby-like project development plan.

There are various circumstances under which the rugby approach may not be applicable. Limited resources can cripple the ability to communicate. Project requirements can overtax abilities. Management's expectations can exceed the company's abilities to produce important breakthroughs. Project management can be dominated by a leader who is overpowering. Company culture and mind-sets do not change overnight. Also, high employee turnover is antithetical to success.

When circumstances are applicable, what is needed to make the rugby approach work? Foremost is a steadfast commitment from top management that is communicated unequivocally to all project participants. The management of rugby-type projects is based on a different mind-set than the traditional relay approach. Power sharing is evident in work assignments and cost allocations. Traditional project management organizations cannot function in this way, and therefore new organizational forms are required.

Concurrent Development Facilitates Coordination of Alliances

With concurrency, the partners of a new alliance can divide their responsibilities according to their areas of expertise. For example, A could be one partner and B,C could be another partner. The projects they share could be coordinated with an information system that allows them to communicate with each other at every step of the development.

Contrast this to the linear model for alliance partners. Each one waits for the other to finish its activities before starting to do anything. Delays lead to recriminations. There is little room for adaptation to meet problems as they arise. A finishes up its tasks and hands B a fait accompli (something done, which cannot be changed).

Many times it is easier to create the organizational cultures that are required to achieve successful concurrent project development with alliances than within any one company. This is especially true if the one company is what we have been calling a bureaucratic organization. For example, the emphasis on cross-functional communication may be farfetched unless all of the homework for successful alliances has been properly done.

Matrix management helps fracture compartmentalized functions. Many companies have been using the matrix concept to facilitate cross-functional communication. Usually, each individual is assigned responsibilities by both functions and products. Perhaps, instead of functions, we should have said specific jobs within such areas as sales, purchasing, inventory management, and quality assurance. As far as products are concerned, these depend on the specifics of the company, which can be as varied as shampoos and soaps, autos, airplanes, or industrial products.

The matrix form of organization lends itself to concurrent project development. A project matrix can be drawn up that connects people by functions and project stages to alliance partners, suppliers, and customers. Then a communications network must be activated that encourages regular transmissions of updated information. This is what is meant by the statement that fundamental competitive changes in the 1990s have forced organizations to redesign themselves with the goal of providing timely responses to competitive challenges.

THE SYNCHRONICITY OF TIME-BASED MANAGEMENT

The derivation of the word "synchronicity" comes from "chrono" meaning time, and "syn" meaning together. That which is timed to work, or to move together, is synchronous. For business applications, we might define this word as coordination between planning and controlling. At the same time, it is getting all the people and their functions to work together. How many parts must move together? Certainly, all of the main player parts, which means that the components of marketing, R&D and process/product development, production, finance, human resources, and accounting are all aware of what the others are doing.

One of the major elements for achieving synchronicity is an accounting (information) system that informs everyone who needs to know what is going on at all sensitive points. Computer integrated manufacturing captures the idea of what is sensitive. New accounting cannot ignore the problem of irrelevancy. A lot of data that are normally captured are misleading, so a first step for achievement is to throw out irrelevant information.

This accounting system must be on-line so that delays that can cause oscillations are near zero. The measures must be of the right things, and they must be the right measures that are timely. It is something like a strobe unit being pulsed at just the right rate to stop motion so you can see what is going on. Profit contributions are better than cost, and projections that permit short- and long-term profit contributions are ideal.

Timing

"A stitch in time saves nine" is a famous maxim that, we hope, every grade school still teaches. The message is clear: if you don't act soon enough, a small rip at the seam could quickly escalate and lead to an embarrassing situation. In the same book of maxims, however, there is the saying that "haste makes waste." There is an old Chinese story, credited to Chou Yung, which starts, "In the winter of 1650."[9] It tells about the delivery boy who met with catastrophe when he raced to get inside the village walls of Chiaochuan before the gate was shut. We prefer not to cite more recent events along similar lines.

It would be a mistake to think that these two maxims are contradictory. Both illustrate the importance of timing. An interesting term that is being used to signify control over timing is "synchronicity." We couldn't find this somewhat strange word in the big Webster's dictionary, but it has been appearing in various publications. Alternative nouns that are in the dictionary are synchrony or synchronousness. The dictionary suggests for the verb form: synchronizing marchers in a parade.

The essence of timing is reflected in an orchestra playing a symphony. All of the instruments are following the music written by a composer while watching the baton of the conductor in order to be properly synchronized. It is only in movie cartoons that the orchestra gets out of control with memorable cacophony resulting. In business, the lack of time sense and coordination in planning results in chaos, like the results of a composer gone berserk. If the orchestra, playing the music of the time-blind composer, does everything just right, it is still horrible to hear.

In business, the lack of time control produces results like an orchestra that is out of control, even though its music is perfectly good. However, with music you can hear the bad news immediately. In business, it may take too much time to get appropriate feedback. The delay in learning that what is happening is not the result of bad luck, but bad timing, may jeopardize recovery. Timeliness, which is a way of describing good timing, means going not too fast (haste), and not too slow (the stitch in time).

Management Achievement of Synchronicity

Synchronicity is the orchestration of all controllable factors by management to achieve optimal timing. The coordination required by an athlete to perform well is a model of sorts, but the analogy between the coordination of an individual, and that of an organization, does not really serve us well. The coordination of a team of athletes comes closest to the kind of systems coordination that the business manager must achieve.

Fast response organizations are systems of well-connected, interrelated functions. These functions are in communication with each other, transmitting only relevant information to provide decision support. It is proper to consider FROs as the organizational embodiment of effective synchronicity. All parts of the system have to function together in a balanced way to allow the organization to respond without delay to new challenges and opportunities.

There is a well-known story about how three blind people describe an elephant. One feels the tail, one the trunk, and one the leg. Even if someone had never been told this story, they could make a pretty good guess about how the descriptions would differ. It is obvious that an accurate picture of an elephant cannot be approximated unless a system's point of view is used. It is difficult to get all parties to sample the system properly. Then, it is difficult to get them to communicate fully, allowing ample time to synthesize the relevant information. Even with adroit coordination, the elephant would be likely to wobble quite a bit.

Many of the elements that allow management to achieve synchronization are inherent in this story. First, make sure that all of the important decision-makers in the system are connected by a user-friendly information network. Second, support relatively immediate, error-free communication between them. Provide a means for on-line analysis, discussion, and transmission of conclusions. Develop a fast way to reach accord, let alone consensus, and the know-how for rapid implementation.

Orchestration of strategies and tactics involves testing the tactical alternatives that are available for any given strategy. Then, if there are no tactics that can adequately deliver the hoped-for results with the strategies that have been chosen, reexamine the strategic alternatives. If a small group of planners is expected to do all of this, then the period for contemplation will probably exceed the relevance of the issue. However, when the information flow is disciplined, the contributions can be assembled quickly with judicious decisions resulting. Tactical and strategic aspects of time-based management have already been discussed. Both are feasible and attainable as separate functions, but the real effectiveness occurs when they occur together.

There is an analogy worth making. Air traffic control restricts the places where planes can fly, which brings them closer together. This increases the risk of collisions. However, because it is known where the planes are flying, proper control maintains spacing to assure safety. Similarly, letting everyone have a say in decision-making could produce pandemonium, unless the pattern of communication is orchestrated properly. The systems approach is needed to achieve optimal timing. When events move fast, competitive failure occurs from the inability to see the whole picture.[10] Some of the simple systems elements are based upon knowing the precise destination, the direction to the destination, alternative routes to be followed, possible pitfalls along the way, and optimal timing for the passage.

The sense of timing (knowing "when" as well as "what") is essential to conduct the players (as in a play) through the entire set of actions that must be taken to succeed. Working backwards on lead times, many actions require preparations that could only have been anticipated by accurate forecasts. Because forecasting is, at best, an imprecise combination of science and art, being "on target" necessitates preparations for more than one eventuality.

Contingency planning allows preparation for many possible outcomes, but it cannot control for the unanticipated. The best that can be done (ignoring the costs of being prepared) is to orchestrate the entire system in preparation for whatever can conceivably occur. The worst that can be done is to prepare only for the most likely events. The exposure to high-risk events, like natural catastrophes and competitive coups (a sudden, brilliant action, unexpected) cannot be tolerated by a fast response organization.

Orchestration is an appropriate word to use when the elements are reasonably predictable. By orchestration, we mean to connote the control of timing for a total set of factors (instruments). The conductor directs the instruments according to the score (plan). Success and failure are related to the harmonization of the systems components. Generals may not like the analogy of war games being fought by principles that apply to an orchestra. Business managers may also find the comparison unflattering, although possibly preferred to the role of the choreographer and dance master for the ballet. Both would say that the symphony and the ballet are not exposed to the kind of uncertainties that their spheres of interest are prone to experiencing. They would be absolutely right.

Nevertheless, there are some useful principles to be found in these analogies. By developing contingency plans, and on-line communication systems to avoid delays in taking action, the problems of business managers might be likened to those of a conductor, who at any moment has to be ready for a change of the musical score.

ANATOMY OF WELL-BALANCED FAST RESPONSE ORGANIZATIONS

The well-balanced FRO simultaneously orchestrates the *internal* and *external* components and their interactions. Emphasis on either one, to the exclusion of the other, fails to recognize the importance of doing the right thing, before doing the thing right. The operational cycle that integrates tactical and strategic planning is the

$$FIND_1 \rightarrow DESIGN \rightarrow MAKE \rightarrow SHIP \rightarrow FIND_2 \rightarrow ETC.$$

continuous project development feedback loop. It is shown in Figure 7.5 with annotations of functions added to the loop. To simplify reading and writing all of these words, let us call this the FDMS loop.

How fast should the steps in the FDMS loop be iterated? That is a question of synchronizing the multiple functions of the organization, including its dealings with suppliers. Market expectations play a major role, and they are conditioned by what the competition does. But, in turn, what can you make the market want? As we have previously said, invention has become the mother of necessity, rather than the much quoted other way around. How successful in making fast responses is the present configuration? How long can it stay ahead of the competition? Could the firm be more successful if it introduces incremental project management to perturb the existing situation continually?

Supplier Timing Systems

Suppliers are hooked into the timing system. They are an important part of the FDMS loop. Because they are crucial factors in the innovation, production, and assembly parts of the systems process, supplier alliances should be used effectively to increase the rate of innovations. There is no magic here. When you visit any of the manufacturing facilities or creative studios of the globally alerted companies, you find quite ordinary people working together in quite ordinary ways. But there are some simple differences in the way they communicate and coordinate. The

Figure 7.5
Continuous Project Development Wheel

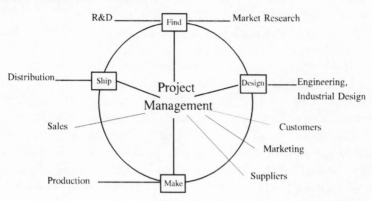

difference is spontaneous teamwork. It is not ordained or enforced from above. The opportunity for such teamwork springs naturally out of the creative potential of every situation, no matter how mundane it might seem.

Japanese manufacturers are well known for relying on their suppliers to produce a large part of each automobile. To a reasonable degree, it can be said that the highly efficient assembly plant is the starting point for value-added for companies like Toyota and Nissan. U.S. auto manufacturers do the same kind of thing. It has been standard practice in the auto industry to use suppliers' components and subassemblies for a major part of the value of each car made. In the United States, a continuing discussion is how much of the car should be domestic content. The kinds of percentages that we are dealing with range from 50 to 75, and even more. With these kinds of numbers in mind, it can be incredibly important to develop an FRO-type relationship with a few suppliers. The traditional approach, which is to purchase by price, hides the real costs and, more importantly, opportunity costs.

Yet we have noted that all of these car manufacturers use suppliers to an enormous extent. Both U.S. and Japanese companies could theoretically have access to the same suppliers. Why then is there such a difference between the results? Let's rephrase this question: Since suppliers' products constitute a major portion of every assembled automobile, why should there be a perceived difference between Japanese and American automobiles? The answer is that there would be no major difference if the U.S. companies could develop the same kind of synergistic relationships with their suppliers.

Various parts of this book have dealt with the issues of new management technology, and how it relates to suppliers. The Japanese firms have nonlegal, information-open trust relationships with their suppliers. These should be viewed as alliances that must insure mutual benefit to all participants. This kind of relationship encourages their suppliers to innovate. The suppliers receive rewards for coming up with new and better components on a fast response basis. And, because they do not hesitate to accept change and install it as quickly as they can in their own assembly lines, they are not disappointed by their suppliers. They have endowed their suppliers with high levels of autonomy to innovate. That makes the Japanese supplier network work.

Synchronization makes the production system run smoothly. It spells out the rhythm for cycle times and supplier deliveries. Time is the thread that connects all functions. Often these functions have adversarial positions. The time sense elevates the organizational objectives, above those of the separate constituencies, leading to cross-functional understanding of what creates well-being for the system. Timeliness dictates the rate of product and process innovations. The main objectives of process and project continuity are time-oriented. Concurrent project development is part of the timing issue.

For timeliness to be effective, the organization must have a systems perspective. This means that the parts of the system are seen for what they really are, which is parts of the whole. Alliances can help to provide the needed perspective when they are based on the realities of what is happening in a fast-changing world. The technology changes that are rapidly becoming the norm are time-driven. This is the next phase for the industrial revolution.

Fast Response Orchestration

Global winners are custodians of time. Orchestration is the best description of what fast response organizations do to take advantage of the crucial issue of timing-synchronicity. They are systems-oriented. Product design is driven by superfast market research, which communicates directly with the designers and the production department. Often, the best questions that market research asks come from suggestions of the production departments.

Responding to the fundamental competitive changes in the 1990s, organizations are being redesigned to provide faster responses. Alliance-making can provide a way around the inhibitions of traditional systems. Timeliness has become the major competitive objective, while low unit costs and high quality are crucial constraints. FROs understand the advantages of time-based tactics. They use them but do not abuse them—which means that they can provide only temporary advantage. Only strategic time-based advantages can provide long-term survival in a rapidly changing world.

Tactical-Internal Aspects of Fast Response

Fast response tactics relate to the time-efficient operation of the production process and coordination with suppliers. They are epitomized by production scheduling tactics that are designed to increase the percent of time that production activities are adding value rather than simply utilizing capacity. JIT, WIP reduction, and decreased defectives are all aimed at increasing value added. The focus is on minimizing waste, such as labor and materials expenditures resulting in rework and scrap. Waste is also caused by product failures covered by warranties. Unutilized space doesn't add value, nor does the waste of idle time of workers and equipment, or, worse, busywork to keep capacity utilization high, producing goods that inflate finished goods inventories. Staff support and other overhead functions are subjects of similar concern.

In many of these tactical instances, management science (MS) and operations research (OR) techniques are widely used to support waste reduction and improved timing. Since their military applications in World War II, MS and OR have provided mathematical and computer modeling of decision situations. They have been particularly successful in application to production scheduling and inventory management. With changing economic conditions, the emphasis upon cost reduction has shifted to quality improvement and timing effectiveness. In effect, this has elevated the scope of quantitative vision to include strategic insights such as production systems that can shift rapidly and inexpensively from one product to another. In general, mathematical and computer decision methods support the attainment of FRO objectives.

Among manufacturing companies frequently mentioned as being fast tactical responders are Brunswick, General Electric, Hewlett-Packard, and Motorola. Hewlett-Packard cut production time from four weeks to five days for electronic testing equipment; Motorola went from three weeks to two hours for pagers (and from thirteen weeks to five days to make a computer). Such tactical accomplishments send a signal to all potential competitors that the criteria for excellence in responding quickly to new technology and market opportunities are tougher than ever before. Figure 7.6 illustrates some of the tactical and strategic elements needed to support high performance with fast response through the FDMS loop.

Strategic-External Aspects of Fast Response

Cash flow and return on equity (ROE) are additional performance measures that cannot be ignored. The tactical side of fast response is easy to grasp; the strategic aspects are more complex. Continuity and concurrency of project management are vital to move ahead. But the integration of forward planning with the cash flow management of current activities is essential to maintain financial support for the firm. With U.S. financial markets, the ability to develop new products and manufacture them efficiently is not sufficient if that jeopardizes return on equity. Financial management input is essential.

Another strategic issue is marketability. The ability to sense and respond to market-driven forces is critical. Clever new products that can be marketed quickly will not suffice by themselves. As emerging technological changes are translated into market forces, each company must determine the appropriate timing for its product introductions. Fast forms of market research are being used by a number of companies to determine what to do (e.g., everyone in the company is asked to be a part-time market researcher by querying friends, taking observations, etc.). Marketing management input is essential to those responsible for projects and processes.

Design for manufacturability has to be factored into the FDMS loop. To obtain top quality from the production process without many missteps and wasted time, it is necessary to design the process so that it conforms to the idea, "do it right the first time." There is no time for backtracking. Fast response, given rapid technological change, anticipates the tech-effect on both product design and the processes used to produce and deliver the product. Company responses that are based on traditional project management methods may not be fast enough to accomplish what management agrees must be done. Engineering design must participate. Creative use of new-tech opportunities by production managers is essential.

Figure 7.6
Continuous Fast Response System

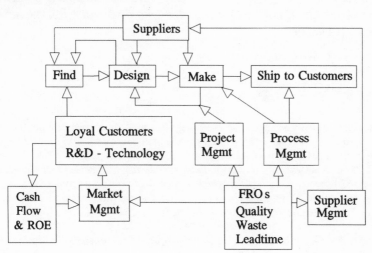

What companies are doing all of this? A number of them are talking about it. Among those often mentioned as going in the right direction are Ford Motor Company, Honda of America, AT&T, Nissan, Sony, Toyota, Xerox, and Hewlett-Packard. Honda reduced development time for new cars from five years to three years, while getting greater market share and improving their financial performance. AT&T decreased development time for new phones from two years to one year. Probably this increased its share of market and improved its financial performance in some minuscule way. For similar reasons, while Hewlett-Packard reduced computer printer development time from four and a half years to just under one year, it is not possible to cite market share growth, or the effect on cash flow and ROE. If the small successes are repeated over and over again, they will add up to what is observable winning perfor- mance.

The companies that are becoming global move through the FDMS loop as quickly and sure-footedly as possible. They are fast-track firms finding ways of making better products with suggestions from their loyal customers, creative R&D, and with smart factory know-how. They pursue the FRO condition with astute moves to new technologies of both kinds (manufacturing and management). They design and make better products with the help of their suppliers.

One thing is certain: those companies that master the FDMS loop so that their performance on all levels improves will be strong contenders for honors when it comes time to judge who among the fast movers are the global winners.

NOTES

1. Time-based management terminology has been developed and publicized by the Boston Consulting Group. For example, see George Stalk, Jr., "The Time Paradigm," in BCG's pamphlet series on Time-Based Competition, 1988.

2. "An important role of kanban is to provide the information that connects the earlier and later processes at every level. A kanban always accompanies the goods and thus is the essential communications tool for just-in-time production." Taiichi Ohno in *Toyota Production System: Beyond Large-Scale Production* (Cambridge, MA: Productivity Press, 1988 (Original work, 1978).

3. A description of the early project management developments is found in many texts. For example, see R. I. Levin, and C. A. Kirkpatrick, *Management Planning and Control with PERT/CPM* (New York: McGraw-Hill, 1966).

4. Michael L. Dertouzos, Richard K. Lester, and Robert M. Solow, *Made in America: Regaining the Productive Edge*, MIT Commission on Industrial Productivity. (Cambridge, MA: MIT Press, 1989).

5. Charles R. Morris, "The Coming Global Boom," *The Atlantic*, October, 1989, p. 56.

6. One of the most impressive examples of this use of computer-aided design and computer-aided manufacturing ability is in the textile industry. Companies from Italy and the Pacific Basin have been competing on their ability to discern what the market wants and getting the product to customers as quickly as possible.

7. Martin K. Starr, and Zhuang Yang, Principal Investigators, "Report on Japanese Managerial Skills and Practices: Based on the Study of Five Factories in Tennessee." Center for Operations, Graduate School of Business, Columbia University, July 1989.

8. Ikujiro Nonaka quotes a project manager of Honda: "Every one of us should run all the way from the start to the finish. Like a rugby game, all of us should run together, passing the ball left and right, and then reaching the goal as one united body." From a paper entitled "Speeding New Product Development Process" presented at CIS (Centro Studi d'Impresa) International Conference, Valmadrera, Italy, October 1987.

9. Chou Yung (1619-79), quoted in R.G.H. Siu, *The Man of Many Qualities—A Legacy of the I Ching* (Cambridge, MA: MIT Press, 1968), pp. 19–20.

10. For example, the U.S. semiconductor industry lost its start-up advantage because it did not create barriers to entry by continuing to lead in technological superiority. While Silicon Valley was coping with pressures for short-term profitability, global competitors invested heavily with subsidized support. The surprise was that competitive advantage could erode so quickly. This was not a case where the phoenix phenomenon was at work, but the transfer rates for semiconductor technology had accelerated beyond the point of providing reasonable return on investment.

APPENDIX A _____

Japanese Managerial Practices in the United States—Alliances for Quality

This represents a small part of a larger report conducted in 1989 at Columbia University.[1] The part that we have taken focuses on the use of alliances for quality. The costs of quality are clearly defined so that suppliers can deal as explicitly as possible with the costs and benefits of varying quality strategies.

Throughout the 1980s, while Japanese companies were investing in U.S.-based manufacturing facilities, U.S. firms were going offshore. The extent of the Japanese investment and its growth over time are both striking. According to the Keizai Koho Center of the Japan Institute for Social and Economic Affairs, as of March 31, 1989, Japan's direct overseas investment in the United States totaled $71.86 billion; as of March 31, 1990, it was $104.40 billion—a 45.3 percent increase.[2]

In the early 1980s, the managers of U.S. firms stated that they were going offshore because U.S. workers were too costly. In the late 1980s, the value of the dollar had fallen, so that wages in many world currencies made this claim less valid. At the same time, the proportion of labor in the cost of goods sold continued to diminish. Overall, this implied that factors other than labor costs were driving decisions by U.S. firms to go overseas. Some of these firms stated that the performance of American workers was inferior in quality and productivity to that of workers in Pacific Basin countries. If this were true, we wondered, why would companies from Japan be making such major investments in the United States, where they would be using American employees?

The research methodology that was used for this report included initial written surveys followed by on-site visits with the managers of five factories in Tennessee. There was a follow-up mailing for critiquing the final report. In addition to written survey questions, we used partly structured, open-ended interviews with senior and junior Japanese and American managers. Our questions focused on corporate culture, organizational structures, product quality, production methods, manufacturing technology, and human resource management.

Tennessee is an excellent state for direct Japanese investment. The state government has dedicated itself to attract Japanese investors by sending their authorities to help the companies set up their operations in Tennessee. There are initial tax incentives and a policy of spending heavily for training programs aimed at improving the quality of the work force.[3]

There were 71 major Japanese firms located in Tennessee during the time of our study. The criterion we used to choose from this group was based on our desire to visit firms that have at least 100 employees, locally hired, regardless of the type of products they produce or the time their plants began operation in Tennessee. By the process of elimination, and the acceptance of the visit at the proposed time, five Japanese plants offered to be our hosts. Confidentiality was respected, and all were sent copies of the final report. The five Japanese factories included:

1. An electronic components plant, 50–50 owned by two Japanese companies. The reason that the parent companies built a plant in Tennessee was to produce high-quality automobile speakers and electronic capacitors for both the Japanese and U.S. markets. The company began operation in September 1982 and was established as an independent company in 1985, with over $2 million monthly sales since 1987. The products are very competitive in quality and price by industry standards. Honda of America uses about 85 percent of the speakers produced in the plant. The plant has 300 employees—55 percent are female workers, 45 percent are high school graduates or higher. Plant management emphasizes efficiency and high quality to satisfy customer needs.

2. A heavy industrial equipment plant, which is one of the leading construction equipment producers in the world. The Japanese parent company set up a plant in Tennessee in 1986 that produces four major products for the U.S. and Japanese markets: wheel loaders, dump trucks, hydraulic excavators, and bulldozers. In early 1988 the Japanese parent company successfully formed a 50–50 joint venture with a leading U.S. construction equipment company to expand its product sales base and further penetrate the American market. The Americans entered into the

joint venture after the Japanese company culture had already been installed. The combined facility upgraded the company as the uncontested No. 2 supplier of construction equipment in the Western Hemisphere. The joint venture became fully operational in September 1988, with an estimated first-year sales of over $1 billion. The joint venture increased U.S.-based production, improved economies of scale in purchasing and manufacturing, and expanded the distribution base. The Tennessee plant is the only facility of the joint venture's seven plants in the United States that is being managed with a strong Japanese management philosophy. The plant visited has about 180 employees.

3. A car and truck tire plant is owned by one of the largest tire manufacturers in Japan. It is one of the world's three leading manufacturers of tires and related rubber products. The Japanese tire company acquired 100 percent of an American tire factory in early 1983, with the goal of penetrating the North American market and expanding its marketing and distribution base in the United States. The Japanese company has 14 plants in Japan and manufacturing facilities in five other countries. The Tennessee plant, after being technologically upgraded by the Japanese firm, has been producing radial tires for trucks and passenger automobiles. With a daily production capacity exceeding 6,000 passenger radials, the plant now employs over 1,500 employees and is unionized by the United Rubber Workers.

4. An auto component company moved from Japan to Tennessee in the early 1980s, following Nissan's move to the U.S. It was established to supply Nissan with auto air conditioning systems, exhaust systems, and radiators. The firm began operations in May 1983. It employs about 500 workers at a location with 230,000 square feet of facilities. The company has increased its production and sales goals over time by expanding its customer base to include the Ford Motor Company, Mazda, Delco (GM), and the Harrison Radiator Division of General Motors. While it continues to expand its base, the company remains one of Nissan's major suppliers.

5. A TV assembly facility is the oldest plant of the five factories. Highly labor intensive with a total of 650 employees, the plant was set up in 1978 at least partly in response to antidumping threats from the U.S. government. It is an entirely owned transplant of a large Japanese consumer and electronics company. The company's goals were to expand its U.S. market share of television sets and microwave ovens, its two major products, and enlarge its distribution base in North America. The company became unionized in 1979, after losing narrowly in the unionization certification election over the issue of a second work shift. This

occurred a year after its operations began in Tennessee. For the past several years the firm has been able to keep about 5 percent of the TV market share in the United States.

PRODUCT QUALITY IS CRITICAL

Product quality is extremely important to all of these companies. The most striking impression from our interviews with Japanese and American managers is management's strong and deep commitment to high product quality and as near-zero product defects as possible. Uniformly, the most important corporate mission is to produce the highest quality product for customers.[4] Superior product quality is viewed as a major strategic objective in all five factories. It is given top priority in defining the companies' long-term goals in the United States and the world market.

Quality consciousness begins with top management and is built into the whole factory system that links corporate strategy, human resource policies, job structure, hiring, training, product design, product engineering, process technology, sales, and marketing. In some firms, this is known as total quality control, in others as quality function deployment or companywide total quality control The key concept with all of these approaches is complete dissemination of information relevant to quality enhancement, and responsibility for quality attainment, throughout the company and its suppliers. In one way or another, customers are also included.

When senior managers and production engineers at the five firms were asked about their strategies in competing with other firms in the U.S. market, they all emphasized "product quality." Few managers perceived product price and product quantity as the most important factors on which they compete with others. Speed was considered to be less important than persistence. Incremental improvement was part of what was meant by persistence.

Framework to Discuss Quality

A logical framework existed for discussing quality in terms of costs and benefits. The categories used to go by many names, but they can be summarized as the costs of prevention, appraisal, and failure.

Costs of Prevention

It is believed that building in superior product quality through good design of product and process, which is called designing for manufacturability, pays off. Thus, spending more time on prevention of quality problems, before going into production, is preferred to putting out fires, after the fact. This approach lowers the costs of both quality appraisals and quality failures, as described below.

Costs of Appraisal

Being able to spend less on the inspection of suppliers' shipments, work-in-process, and finished goods is a powerful savings advantage. There is also a hidden cost of appraisal that is related to the way in which defectives are found. If the workers are not responsible for their own quality, then a police-type system is required, whereby an organizational morale problem can be encountered. We refer to all of these as the costs of detection (of defectives).

Costs of Failures

When defective rates are decreased, the costs of rework, repair, scrap, or salvage are lowered. The cost of warranty fulfillment is also reduced. Furthermore, if the production system does not have to be stopped, or slowed down, there are tangible and intangible savings. It is often difficult to establish the intangible savings that are gained when the production system runs smoothly. Although these production cost savings are hidden, they can be, and usually are, quite substantial. We call these the costs of correction.

In addition, customer dissatisfaction can be diminished by increasing product reliability, durability, and such. These quality improvements result in increased customer loyalty. The costs of customers' defection, which produces lower market shares, are also related to the losses of revenues associated with the lifetime-value of customers. Thus, market share does not properly reflect the savings that can be achieved by holding on to present customers by means of superior quality products.

Alliances for Quality with Suppliers

There are some statements about quality that are repeated over and over by the people who work in the five companies. One of these is the fact that alliances with suppliers (by whatever name they are called) are crucial to the success of quality planning and quality control. Whatever name is used, it means a special trust relationship that is developed for the mutual benefit of all partners. Quality is considered to follow the rule that a chain is as strong as its weakest link. Therefore, suppliers to suppliers are included in quality considerations.

Alliances for Quality with Employees

A second quality alliance is forged between groups of workers and the company. Sometimes these alliances are called quality circles. Whatever name is used, successful groups are viewed as alliances for quality that allow all members of the group to contribute to the success of the company.[5] Quality discussions with suppliers and with employees often address the following issues.

Cleanliness of the Shop Floor. Plant workshops are extremely clean. Vendors with sloppy housekeeping are unlikely to become suppliers. Marriages that start out cleanly are likely to end in divorce when sloppy habits return. It is a sine qua non that everything should be kept in first-rate condition. There is an alliance with all workers to achieve cleanliness.[6]

Responsibility for Process Quality Control Is Equally Shared. Contrary to common American management practice that has put a greater percentage of the responsibility for quality control on managers and engineering staff, Japanese management has been developing a work environment and organizational structure under which everyone—from shop floor workers and foremen, to supervisors, middle and top managers—is involved and charged to share responsibility for quality control during the whole production process. Vendors whose employees are not empowered to contribute to quality improvement are unlikely to become certified suppliers of these companies.

The Next Person Is the Customer. This is a recurrent theme, which stresses internal quality for white-collar, blue-collar, and gold-collar workers.[7] Other topics encountered: teams are the engines for quality improvement, cross-training is vital, jobs are not constrained by work standards, constant improvement is continuous (called Kaizen), everyone knows how their job contributes to the final product, total quality control training emphasizes an understanding of production technology and statistical quality control,[8] there is company commitment to the value of people.[9]

Importance of Production Technology

Group-oriented quality control programs stress the importance of production technologies. The Japanese modify existing machines and bring in new technologies. They do this selectively, choosing the best investments to improve quality and to increase production efficiency. After the Japanese took over the tire plant, they continuously modified machines and equipment to Japanese standards and specifications. Many of the modifications resulted in productivity increases. For example, in 1982 one of the tire machines turned out 17 tires a day; in 1989 it manufactured 44 tires a day. Forty Japanese engineers work as advisors to help production workers deal with production problems. American managers expressed admiration for Japanese knowledge of producing tires and their contribution to the new technology.

The Japanese construction equipment plant uses advanced production techniques in every phase of the manufacturing process. Computer-controlled scheduling, ordering, and inventory control programs keep the construction facility running smoothly. Welding robots and sophisticated machine tools are supplemented with vigorous training programs. The television plant actively engages in R&D and technological innovations. The plant, equipped with the newest forms of high technology, is prepared to enter the high-density television market in the near future.

NOTES

1. Martin K. Starr and Zhuang Yang, Principal Investigators, "Report on Japanese Managerial Skills and Practices: Based on the Study of Five Factories in Tennessee" (New York: Center for Operations, Graduate School of Business, Columbia University, July 1989). Used with permission.

2. In Canada, the figure grew from $3.23 to $4.59 billion (a 42 percent increase), increasing the sum for North America from $75.09 billion to $108.99 billion. Because the North American direct investment is dominated by the U.S. investment, the North American increase was 45.1 percent, which is just a bit lower than for the United States taken alone. Japanese direct overseas investment in Europe was $30.164 billion as of March 31, 1989, and $44.972 billion as of March 31, 1990—a 49 percent increase, which is even larger than the growth of investment in the United States. Total worldwide Japanese direct overseas investment was $186.356 billion as of March 31, 1989, and $253.896 billion as of March 31, 1990, which represents an increase of 36 percent.

3. Many tens of millions have been spent on training programs. *U.S. News and World Report,* (May 9, 1988, p. 50) stated that Nissan had received $20 million for training new workers.

4. In the tire factory, defect rates are found through regular and random checks of the durability of tires. The quality standards for all the Japanese plants we visited are set by Japan. Standards always change in response to new market demands.

5. At the car parts plant, 75 quality circle teams were in operation. Each circle planned to achieve three major goals in 1989. Full-time facilitators on each team represented and sustained the company's value system within the plant. Facilitators hold periodic training seminars. One of their functions is to provide the groups with guidance about the company's value system.

6. In one factory, janitors were not hired. A senior manager explained that management thought it was the responsibility of every person in the factory—from managers to line workers—to keep the factory clean, rather than relying on janitors. This same strategy of relying on all employees to achieve certain company goals is used to obtain excellence in product quality as well.

7. "Gold collar" is a term that has been coined for workers who work with computer technology. These include programmers for office systems as well as CAD/CAM and FMS of all varieties.

8. A Japanese production engineer in the tire plant said: "When we first came here, we found that many American employees had back problems by making tires . . . . They had many problems with their shoulders as well. . . . The first task of the Japanese takeover was to [use technology] to . . . eliminate hard jobs."

9. This includes a stable employment policy, well-designed recruiting policies, emphasis on job training, competitive wage rates and benefits, egalitarian-based company policies, non-police-type supervisory style, first-line managers work with their hands, and labor-management relations based on trust.

APPENDIX B _____

Performance of Foreign-Affiliated Firms in America

What follows is a modification, dated August 1990, of the original survey report. In particular, figures have been added to replace most of the tables of data. This has been done to make the report easier to read—visual rather than analytic. However, numbers are occasionally shown on the figures. Otherwise, approximate numbers can be estimated from the figures, and numbers from the tables are often cited in the text. Also, comments and observations have been updated.

SUMMARY

The Center for Operations at the Graduate School of Business, Columbia University, has been doing tracking studies of foreign-affiliated firms (FAFs), and companies with strategic alliances in the United States, since 1982. Appendix B reports on a follow-up study to the January 1989 survey report on the Performance of Foreign-Affiliated Firms in America (FAFIA).

The study emphasizes comparisons between the performance of Japanese, European, and U.S. firms in America. The results show significant differences between these three groups of companies, many of which are forming new global alliances. As shown in Figure B.1, the geographic patterns of these alliances are distinct. FAFIA are forming more new alliances with U.S. firms (42%), than with European and Pacific Basin nations (each has 26%). (The figures and tables will appear later in the text.)

Referring to Figure B.2, the key strength gained from the new alliances was cited as "closer ties to the marketplace." There was general agreement about this. From Figure B.3 we see that "improvements in production processes" was considered to be more important by the U.S. and Japanese firms than by the European firms. The same applies to "faster implementation of improvements."

Still referring to Figure B.3, European firms were more concerned with deriving "greater innovative results from R&D" and "faster development of new products" than the Japanese or U.S. firms. A possible explanation for the Japanese is that they have already mastered this capability. It isn't that easy to explain the results for the United States. We also note that Japanese firms are more concerned about "faster development of new services" and "better performance from suppliers" than the European and U.S. firms. Japanese firms tend to eschew the goal of faster decision-making.

As displayed in Figure B.4, personal computers lead the pack for new technology. Workstation use is pretty high, and so is the use of teamwork. In Figure B.5 we observe that Japanese and U.S. firms do not accent novel methods (such as new accounting approaches) and innovative technology (such as workstations), whereas the Europeans do. Merit pay is commonly used by many of the European firms. It is not much used by the United States and, surprisingly, more so by the Japanese firms.

As shown in Figure B.6, European firms report greater use of new project management methods than the Japanese and U.S. firms. Across the board, few firms are experimenting with the new project methods. With marginal differences, the United States is doing the most experimenting and Japanese firms the least.

Examining Figure B.7, we note that over 90 percent of the European firms consider themselves as MNCs. Among the Japanese foreign affiliates, only 52 percent see themselves that way. The U.S. firms fall in between with about 70 percent. In Table B.2, the data show that the Japanese alone indicate efforts to move toward MNC status.

Figure B.8 shows that all respondents stated that Europe 1992 will be important, but the European firms feel more strongly about this than the Japanese or U.S. firms.

From Figures B.9, B.10, and B.11 it is clear that the Europeans have a clear preference for European alliances. However, for production know-how (Figure B.9) and joint marketing efforts (Figure B.10), there is some interest in the Pacific Basin for new alliances. There is no interest for improving strategic planning (Figure B.11).

Again, referring to the same figures, the Japanese are not polarized in either direction. Still, they do show some preference for European alliances when it comes to strategic planning. Also, there is a clear split for joint marketing efforts, and a small preference for the Pacific Basin for production know-how. U.S. firms prefer European alliances. The one exception is for production know-how, and that is split.

Figure B.13 presents the average percentage of women working in the three categories of line, staff, and management. For European firms, 29.4 percent of line workers are women; for Japanese FAFs, 19.5 percent; and for U.S. firms, 17.1 percent. All respondents have the highest percentage of women working at the staff level. Women managers are the smallest percentage for all three country categories: 11.1 percent for U.S. firms, 10 percent for European firms, and 6.9 percent for Japanese firms.

From open-ended questions, we found that Japanese firms are less comfortable with changing leadership styles than European or U.S. firms, but no one is too comfortable with change. There is general agreement that centralized organization should be used for global planning. Local decision-making requires decentralized organization.

In joint ventures, Japanese management seldom sees itself in a secondary role, whereas, U.S., U.K., and West German managements often sees themselves in secondary roles. The data show that foreign affiliated firms in the United States are actively engaged in forming new alliances with other firms in the United States, Europe, and the Pacific Basin.

INTRODUCTION, SAMPLE, AND METHODOLOGY

This follow-up study to our January 1989 survey report on FAFIAs concentrates on some specific topics: the extent to which companies are forming global alliances, the geographical patterns of these alliances, the degree to which fast response is considered to be an important factor for global competitiveness, and the extent to which new methods and technology are considered to be competitive factors.

One year after the first study, we requested follow-up information from the companies that had responded to the original 1989 FAF study. Of the original 121 companies, 55 (45.5 percent) agreed to continue with the second phase of this study. While this would not be considered a sufficient sample size for beginning a study from scratch, it is reasonable for a tracking study such as this one. Questions 1A and 1B provide information about the sample.

Question 1A: What is your company's primary country affiliation?

Table B.1 shows a percentage comparison of the Respondents by Countries for the two studies. The percentages are derived for the 55 respondents to the 1990 study.

Table B.1
Primary Country Affiliation

Sample Size		Percentage of Respondents	
		1989 Study	1990 Study
22	Japan	41	40.0
23	Europe	36	41.8
10	U.S.	23	18.2

The percentages for Japan, Europe, and the U.S. are nearly the same in the 1989 study as in the 1990 study. The differences that exist are minor. Because of the percentage similarities, it is reasonable to surmise that many of the statistics that describe the characteristics of firms reported in the 1989 survey study can be attributed to the sample of companies surveyed in 1990. For the original data base, see The Performance of Foreign-Affiliated Firms in America (Survey Report, January 1989).

Of the 22 Japanese foreign-affiliated firms, 20 are manufacturers ranging in size from small to large. Two banks are the only service firms in the sample. The 23 European foreign-affiliated firms are all manufacturers of varying size, and composed as follows: one each from Belgium, Denmark, Finland, Italy, Norway; two each from France and Switzerland; three each from the United Kingdom and Sweden; eight from West

Germany. There are ten manufacturing firms, of various sizes, in the U.S. category. Seven are U.S. firms with international involvements; the remaining three companies are Canadian.

Question 1B: What secondary country affiliations exist?

No secondary affiliations were reported by 35 percent of the companies, and those companies that had any secondary affiliations averaged almost two (actually 1.83) such associations. A number of less developed countries (LDCs) and smaller countries that did not appear in the primary list were mentioned as secondary affiliations.

The United States, the United Kingdom, and West Germany account for 42 percent of secondary affiliations. These same three countries accounted for 33 percent of the primary country affiliations. While Japan leads in the primary country category with 40 percent of the sample, it is one of the least mentioned secondary countries, cited by only 6 percent of the companies. Other secondary nations are Australia (2), Austria, Belgium, Brazil, Canada (2), Finland (2), France (4), Indonesia, Italy, Korea, Mexico, Netherlands, Philippines, Portugal, Singapore, Spain, Switzerland, and Thailand.

SURVEY RESULTS

Throughout this report, there were cases where there were no answers, or the data were not available or not applicable (N/A). These have been removed from the data so that percentages sum to 100 percent. Also, for simplicity, we use the following abbreviations: EF = European firms, JF = Japanese firms, USF = U.S. firms.

Question 2: Is your company making any new alliances with companies in Europe__, Pacific Basin__, U.S.__, Other places__?

The point of Question 2 was to probe the issue of where new alliances are being made. Since all of the respondents are at present located in the United States it is not surprising that new U.S. alliances were the clear first choice (42%). At the same time, European and Pacific Basin alliances were a common occurrence (26% each). Figure B.1 shows the percentages of companies saying that *many* new alliances are being formed in the specified regions. The data show that foreign-affiliated USF are actively engaged in forming new alliances with other firms in the United States, Europe, and the Pacific Basin.

Figure B.1
Regions of Many New Alliances
(As stated by respondents)

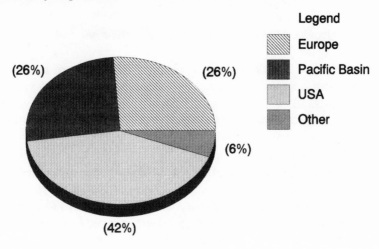

Question 3: What strengths can be gained from new alliances?

Question 3 asked respondents to categorize the relative importance of the eight factors shown in Figures B.2 and B.3. It is easy to see that the single most important factor is closer ties to the marketplace, with a value of .64. The second most important factor was improvements in production processes, with .42. Four of the remaining factors show some interest in fast response, but response rate doesn't take on any significance until comparisons are made by foreign affiliations in Figure B.3.

Reference to Figure B.3 allows a comparison between national groupings. With respect to improvements in production processes, the USF rating of .68 is greater than the JF rating of .55, which, in turn, is significantly greater than the EF rating of .31. JF and USF appear to be considerably more concerned with improving production process technologies than EF.

There is a similar relationship for faster implementation of improvements with ratings of: USF .45, JF .34, and EF .20. Thus, here too, JF and USF appear to be more concerned with faster implementation of improvements than EF. EF seem to be more interested in deriving greater innovative results from R&D than JF.

For faster development of new products, EF consider this to be very important, whereas JF do not and USF appear to consider it

Figure B.2
Strength Gained from New Alliances: Relative Importance of Factors by All Respondents

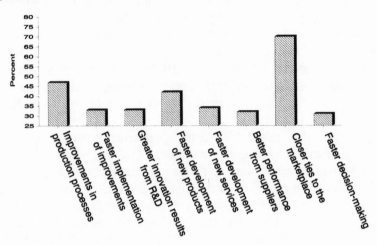

Figure B.3
Strength Gained from New Alliances, by Foreign Affiliation

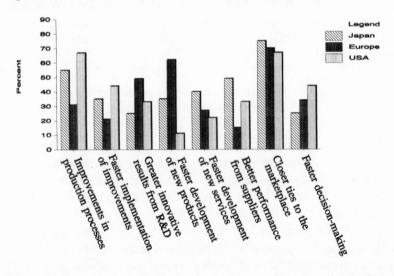

unimportant. A previous explanation is that the Japanese have already mastered this ability and therefore do not consider it to be essential. Another explanation, which requires understanding some of the material presented in Chapter 7 of this book, is that incremental improvement methods do not have to be fast to give the customers the impression that they are fast. The low rating accorded by USF is surprising. It might be attributed to the small sample size of this group. A less flattering interpretation is that USF continue to believe that the status quo is the best possible situation.

We note that faster development of new services is considered more important by JF than by EF, which have an only slightly greater rating than USF. There are indications that JF do not believe they have taken full advantage of the competitive benefits of better service. Meanwhile, the service edge is still considered only somewhat important by EF and USF.

The factor that deals with better performance from suppliers is revealing in the difference of perceptions between JF and EF. JF seem to consider supplier relations to be far more important than EF do, and USF results put these firms in the middle. Several respondents pointed out that JF like to consider suppliers as part of the family. In the United States, there have been increasing efforts to emulate the Japanese successes in this regard. Perhaps the foreign-affiliated EF still have the same attitudes toward suppliers that previously predominated in the United States.

Everyone seems to agree with the importance of having closer ties to the market. On the other hand, JF follow their tradition of consensus, which makes the goal of faster decision-making unrealizable. Similarly, USF pride themselves on their ability to make decisions quickly.

Question 4: To what extent do your production systems use new methods and technologies?

This question was designed to assess the degree to which new methods and technologies were being employed by the foreign-affiliated firms for their production systems. Figure B.4 illustrates the relative importance for all countries taken together. Figure B.5 breaks the results down by foreign affiliations.

Personal computers and workstations are much used, at least for the whole sample. However, when the sample is broken into JF, EF and USF, it can be seen that USF and JF tend to use less of the new technology and new methods than EF. Workstation usage is notably less than for both EF and USF.

It seems fair to say that these EF are (on the face of it) stronger advocates of new technology and new methods than either JF or USF. But this probably is misleading. The response may measure caution as

Figure B.4
New Methods and Technology: Relative Importance

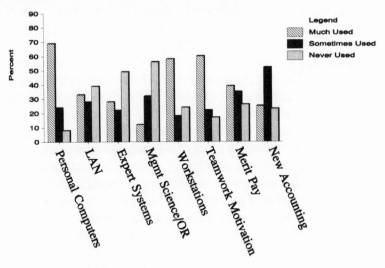

Figure B.5
New Methods and Technology: Importance Rated by Foreign Affiliates

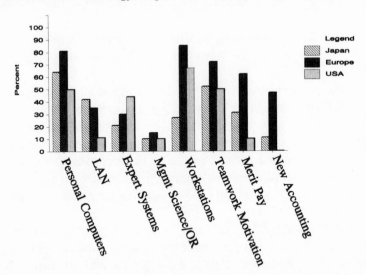

well as enthusiasm. We know that JF are cautious about using technology if training will do. Apparently, USF tend to be even more cautious about adopting new technology than the already cautious Japanese.

There are some specific points worth mentioning. EF use personal computers and workstations for their production systems far more than

JF. USF employment of personal computers seems inexplicably low. Both JF and EF appear to use local area networks (LAN) more than USF. Expert systems are used more by USF than EF; and EF use them more than JF. Management science and operations research (OR) are sometimes used, but not much used by all respondents.

An unexpected finding is that teamwork motivation is employed more by the foreign-affiliated EF than by the foreign-affiliated JF, even though the Japanese (in Japan) are renowned for its use. USF employ teamwork at about the same rate as the Japanese.

Merit pay for performance is used much more by EF than by JF. This is not surprising in view of the traditional Japanese management methods that eschew such individual rewards. Teamwork motivation and merit pay for individuals are not consistent. Thus we assume that merit pay was interpreted to apply to group performance. In a question and answer that isn't shown here, USF were quite high in saying that sometimes they use merit pay, which is consistent with its application to only certain functions in U.S. production systems.

JF were very low users of new accounting methods. USF had a zero response. EF are really interested in changing, which seems to be in accord with European accounting practice today.

Question 5: Is your company using new project management methods such as continuous, on-going project management?

In answer to query 5, we found that 24 percent of all respondents said yes while 65 percent said no. Only 5.5 percent indicated that they were experimenting with new project methods, and 5.5 percent did not answer the question. Because awareness of the competitive advantage of on-going project management methods is recent, it is interesting to find that as many as 24 percent said they were already using such an approach. In the same vein, finding that only 5.5 percent of the firms were experimenting seems quite low.

The breakdown by JF, EF, and USF reveals some unexpected findings. It turns out that EF are responsible for the big percentage of respondents saying yes, they are using new project management methods. Figure B.6 shows a similarity between JF and USF, and a major difference with EF.

To sum up, a surprising number of EF are using the new project management approaches. This ties in with the previous results indicating that EF rate faster development of new products as being very important. In contrast, JF and USF rate this very low. There appears to be a striking

Figure B.6
Using New Project Methods

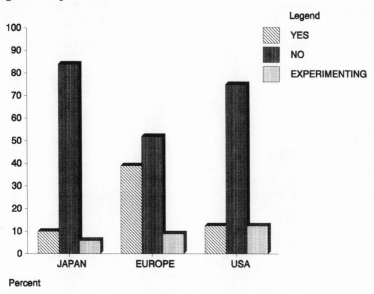

difference between EF, JF, and USF in this regard. There is some basis for presuming that the European foreign affiliates are emulating their parent companies, at home in Europe. Also, it is worth noting that, across the board, fewer companies are experimenting with new project methods than one might have supposed.

Question 6A: Is your firm a multinational corporation?

We wanted to know how many of the respondent companies considered themselves to be multinational corporations. Figure B.7 presents the results, which indicate that almost all (.91) of EF are multinationals. The comparison is striking with the others. Only .52 of JF are multinationals, while USF are halfway between EF and JF with .70.

Question 6B: If you are not at present an MNC, is your corporation moving toward becoming one?

Of the JF, 14 percent said yes and 32 percent said no. For the EF, none answered yes and 9 percent said no. Table B.2 presents the complete set of figures.

Figure B.7
Multinational Corporation?
(ratings of respondents)

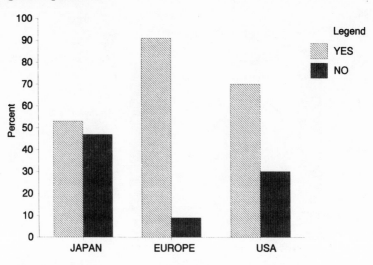

Table B.2
Becoming an MNC?

	Yes	No	N/A
JF	.14	.32	.55
EF	.00	.09	.91
USF	.00	.20	.80

This appears to confirm the observation that EF have a history and tradition of being multinational corporations, JF do not and USF fall in between.

Question 7: Are the changes expected from Europe 1992
important to your company?

The overall answer to this question showed that the frequency of yes was 67 percent. This two-thirds result was pretty high, but not as high as we had expected. USF and JF were lower than EF, but they were all in the same range, as shown in Figure B.8. Not surprisingly, EF expect the largest effect. However, many of the foreign affiliates pointed out

Figure B.8
Will Europe 1992 Affect Your Firm?
(percentage of yes answers)

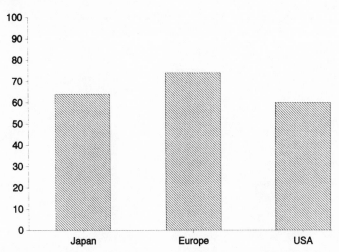

that it was their parent company that would feel the major effect and not them. USF were the least responsive to the question, while JF had very positive feelings one way or the other, i.e., yes or no.

Question 8: Do you prefer an alliance with a company in Europe or in the Pacific Basin for the following three activities: (A) For sharing production know-how? (B) For joint marketing efforts? (C) For improving strategic planning?

The three activities considered in Question 8 are shown in Figures B.9, B.10, and B.11. We found a note on six surveys saying "Whoever speaks English." Only one U.S. company specifically stated this condition. However, it was implied by the answers of a number of other firms that stated that ease of communication was a critical factor in choosing a new partner.

The Europeans have a clear preference for European alliances for all three categories. Because of recognition of Pacific Basin know-how in production, there is a surprisingly low interest shown by EF in Figure B.9. With respect to joint marketing efforts, Figure B.10 shows JF split in their choice for alliance preferences. The same applies to alliance preferences for strategic planning, as shown in Figure B.11. In the latter case, JF do show a small preference for European alliances when it comes to strategic planning. USF have a distinct preference for European alliances. The one exception is for production know-how, and that is split.

Figure B.9
New Alliance Preferences for Sharing Production Know-How

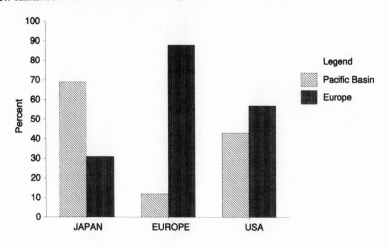

Figure B.10
New Alliance Preferences for Joint Marketing Efforts

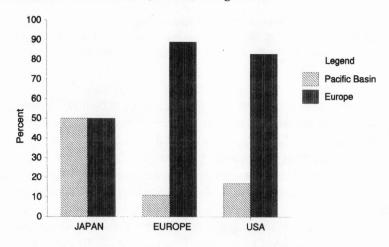

Figure B.11
New Alliance Preferences for Improving Strategic Planning

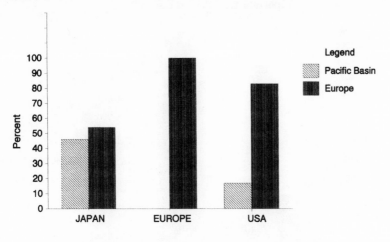

**Question 9: Do you see your company's role in exporting
as more or less important than domestic sales?**

There is remarkable similarity between each of the respondent groups—"less important" is the majority vote. Explaining why they have selected less, three companies cited their multinational corporate status. One USF and two JF selected "equally important," which is an option not pictured in Figure B.12 The fact that "less important" dominated the result is not surprising. Most of these FAFs are in the United States to deal with the American markets. In a sense, they are already on foreign territory.

**Question 10: Will the Europe 1992 changes be as
important as the media indicate?**

EF are not certain; USF are also divided about 50–50. However, among JF, the yes answer was favored over no in the ratio of 2.6 to 1.0 (see Table B.3). Perhaps the reason for the difference is that EF and USF have been doing business in Europe for many years, whereas the Japanese are just recently moving their business interests to Europe. Two European respondents said they were uncertain because the answer was dependent on developments in Eastern Europe.

Figure B.12
Export Versus Domestic Sales?
(Export more or less important than domestic sales?)

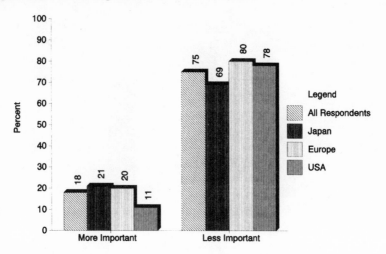

Table B.3
Will Europe 1992 Be Very Important?

	JF	EF	USF
Yes	.59	.43	.40
No	.23	.39	.40
Uncertain	.14	.13	.10
N/A	.05	.04	.10

**Question 11: Women comprise what percentage of: line
workers___?, staff workers___?, managers___?**

JF and USF have about the same percentage of women line workers—
19.5 percent and 17.1 percent, respectively. On the other hand, EF have
a substantially larger number—29.4 percent. The results for USF might
be questioned because of its small sample.

All three categories have their highest percentages of women operating
at the staff level. As will be seen from Figure B.13, the order of these
percentages is USF most with 43.3, EF in the middle with 37.9; and JF
least with 27.4. The same order applies to women managers, with USF

Figure B.13
Average Percentage of Women in Each Category

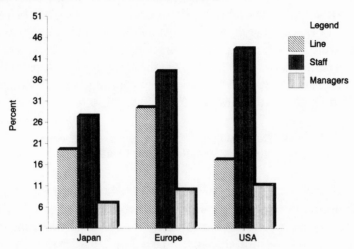

having 11.1 percent; EF with 10 percent; and JF having 6.9 percent. Because of the sample sizes, these numbers are not likely to have statistical significance, but they do indicate general tendencies.

Table B.4 presents the ranges for each of the categories. For example, three JF reported 0 percent women working on the line and one JF reported 80 percent of the line workers were women—the smallest and the largest percentages that were cited. Consequently, the range for this category is shown as 0—80. Table B.4 also lists the number of N/As for each respondent class

Table B.4
The Percentage Range for Women in Each Category, and the Number of N/As

	JF	EF	USF
Line	0–80	0–95	0–50
Number of N/As	14	1	2
Staff	0–50	5–80	25–95
Number of N/As	8	1	2
Managers	0–25	0–35	0–30
Number of N/As	14	1	2

Because JF had such a large number of N/As, it is evident that it was more difficult for them to answer Question 11 than for the other firms. This is particularly noticeable for line workers. On the other hand, EF and USF all appeared to know the exact numbers. In fact, many of their answers were the kinds of precise numbers, such as 24.3 percent, that are required for Equal Employment Opportunity reports. A particularly noticeable characteristic of all firms' percentages was the high variability, which is reflected by the ranges listed in Table B.4.

Question 12: What kind of organization and leadership style is emerging in your firm?

For JF, there were 9 N/As, whereas for EF and USF there were none. This seems to indicate that the JF were less comfortable with the notion of a changing style of leadership. In fact, about half of the respondents indicated that there is little change from the traditional Japanese management methods for organization. For example, there were specific statements: HQ determines major capital expenditures; the standard hierarchical ladder is used; consensus operates (2); participatory style of leadership prevails (3). The other half of the respondents indicated that efforts at change were in process. Several indicated that there was no established style. One stated that the firm was totally unorganized (which was interpreted by us to be quite different from being disorganized).

About half of EF seemed to be at ease with changes that were increasing teamwork (5); flat organizations and short decision lines; consensus management (2); and employee participation (4). Other respondents emphasized autocratic and top-down leadership. Several said they were now using a matrix organization with significant effectiveness. There was one mention of the use of Management by Objectives. A few emphasized that their firms were project-goal-oriented, and others spoke about enhancing entrepreneurial responsibilities. Overall, there was a difference between JF and EF. This can be characterized as the difference between the group (JF) and the individual (EF).

This same type of distinction applies to USF, which were more like EF but still uniquely different. This point prevails despite the same kind of attention to the importance of team management methods as in JF. But such references were also paired with contrasts to traditional Japanese management style. Specifically, there were a number of firms preferring top-down leadership, fast action, and the reward of entrepreneurial pursuits. What was uniquely different from either JF or EF were the references to customer-driven and mission-driven strategic management styles, and the marketing and sales orientation of the organizations.

The above discussion should not be construed to mean that EF and USF were at ease with anything other than small kinds of changes and experiments of various kinds. There were numerous references to preferences for keeping things (more or less) the way they are (satisfactory).

Question 13: Is your company characterized by a number of decentralized business units or by a large centralized structure?

As in Question 12, JF had nine N/As, whereas EF and USF had none, so the same interpretation applies. JF split their responses with half being centralized and the other half being decentralized. The notes that accompanied these answers were quite explicit in stating that the firms were decentralized units participating in a centralized system with the parent company to the mutual benefit of all participants. Some start-ups begin with a decentralized point of view and as they develop tend to move into the centralized system for benefits of inventory and production planning. Others seem to start-up with centralized decision-making and financial control. Then as they develop, they gain greater autonomy with respect to local issues.

EF were remarkably similar in their views of the benefits of centralized and decentralized management systems that operate simultaneously to take advantage of both organizational communication styles. However, one-third of EF said they were centralized systems and two-thirds said they were decentralized. Three firms mentioned their orientation as profit centers, whereas, the JF never used these or similar terms.

As a final note, it should be mentioned that since 1985, employees of various FAFs have experienced increasing difficulty in identifying the nationality of the company for which they are working. It was noted in this book that all kinds of mixed ownerships occur when multiple alliances begin to be made. In such companies, for the 1989 tracking report, the percent of employees who are not certain about the firm's primary nationality has risen to about 25 percent of the total number of employees we surveyed.

Bibliography

Deming, W. Edwards. *Out of the Crisis*. Cambridge, MA: MIT Center for Advanced Engineering Study, 1986.

Dertouzos, Michael L., Richard K. Lester, and Robert M. Solow. *Made in America: Regaining the Productive Edge*, MIT Commission on Industrial Productivity. Cambridge, MA: MIT Press, 1989.

Drucker, Peter F. *The Age of Discontinuity: Guidelines to Our Changing Society*. New York: Harper & Row, 1969.

_____. *Innovation and Entrepreneurship: Practices and Principles*. New York: Harper & Row, 1985.

Harrigan, Kathryn R. *Managing for Joint Venture Success*. Lexington, MA: Lexington Books, 1986.

_____. *Strategies for Joint Ventures*. Lexington, MA: Lexington Books, 1985.

Imae, Ken'ichi. "The Legitimacy of Japan's Corporate Groups." *Economic Eye*, 11, no. 3 (Autumn 1990). Tokyo: Keizai Koho Center, Japan Institute for Social and Economic Affairs.

Klein, Philip A., ed, *Analyzing Modern Business Cycles*, Essays Honoring Geoffrey H. Moore. London: M. E. Sharpe, 1990.

Kondratieff, Nikolai Dmitrievich. *The Long Wave Cycle*. Translated by Guy Daniels, introduction by Julian M. Snyder. New York: Richardson & Snyder, 1984.

Lewis, Jordan D. *Partnerships for Profit: Structuring and Managing Strategic Alliances*. New York: The Free Press, 1990.

Monden, Yasuhiro, and Michiharu Sakurai, eds. *Japanese Management Accounting: A World Class Approach to Profit Management*. Cambridge, MA: Productivity Press, 1989.

Murray, Alan I., and Caren Siehl. *Joint Ventures and Other Alliances: Creating a Successful Cooperative Linkage*. Morristown, New Jersey: Financial Executives Research Foundation, 1989.

Ohmae, Kenichi. *The Borderless World: Power and Strategy in the Interlinked Economy*. New York: Harper Business, 1990.

Ohno, Taiichi. *Toyota Production System: Beyond Large-Scale Production.* Cambridge, MA: Productivity Press, 1988. (Japanese edition: *Toyota seisan hoshiki.* Tokyo: Diamond, 1978.)

Stoken, Dick A. *Cycles: What They Are, What They Mean, How to Profit by Them.* New York: McGraw-Hill, 1978.

Young, John A. *Global Competition: The New Reality*, Report of the President's Commission on Industrial Competitiveness. Washington, DC: U.S. Government Printing Office, January 1985.

Zuboff, Shoshana. *In the Age of the Smart Machine: The Future of Work and Power.* New York: Basic Books, 1988.

Index

About the Author

MARTIN K. STARR is a Professor at the Columbia Business School as well as Director of the Center for Operations based there. He has authored, co-authored, or edited nearly 100 books and articles on such topics as production systems and interactive marketing distribution.